Welcoming the Word in Year A
Building on Rock

Verna A. Holyhead, S.G.S.

Ad multos annos
Fr. Earl

LITURGICAL PRESS
Collegeville, Minnesota

www.litpress.org

Cover design by Ann Blattner.

Year A: ISBN 978-0-8146-1832-5

1	2	3	4	5	6	7	8	9

Library of Congress Cataloging-in-Publication Data

Welcoming the word in Year C : with burning hearts.
   p. cm.
  ISBN-13: 978-0-8146-1835-6 (set)
  ISBN-13: 978-0-8146-1834-9 (alk. paper)
  ISBN-10: 0-8146-1834-0 (alk. paper)
  1. Church year meditations.   I. Holyhead, Verna.

BX2170.C55W58 2006
242'.3—dc22   2006005796

Contents

Acknowledgments

Extracts from poems "In and Out of Time," "Christmas Suite in Five Movements," and "Dust" from *Elizabeth Jennings: New Collected Poems* by Elizabeth Jennings, ed. Michael Schmidt (2002). By permission of Carcanet Press Limited.

Excerpts from "The Dry Salvages" in FOUR QUARTETS, copyright 1941 by T. S. Eliot and renewed 1969 by Esme Valerie Eliot, reprinted by permission of Harcourt, Inc. (English language rights in the United States, its territories and possessions, and the Philippine Republic.)

Excerpts from "The Dry Salvages" in FOUR QUARTETS are from *Collected Poems 1909–1962* by T. S. Eliot, reprinted by permission of Faber and Faber, Ltd. (Non-exclusive English language permission throughout the world excluding the U.S.)

Extract from "The Victory" by Thomas Merton, from THE COLLECTED POEMS OF THOMAS MERTON, copyright © 1946 by New Directions Publishing Corp. (U.S., Canadian, and open market rights only.)

Extract from "The Victory" by Thomas Merton, from THE COLLECTED POEMS OF THOMAS MERTON, copyright © 1946 by New Directions Publishing Corp. Reproduced by permission of Pollinger Limited and the proprietor. (Non-exclusive English Language rights throughout Australia and New Zealand.)

Extract from "Five Days Old" in *Cap and Bells: The Poetry of Francis Webb* (1991). By permission of HarperCollins Publishers.

Extract from "The Coming" by R. S. Thomas, from *Collected Poems: 1945–1990* (2002). Permission from J. M. Dent, a division of The Orion Publishing Group.

Extract from "To the Holy Spirit" by James McAuley, from *Collected Poems 1936–1970* (1971). Permission from HarperCollins Publishers.

Extracts from "The Wreck of Deutschland" and "God's Grandeur," from *Poems and Prose of Gerard Manley Hopkins* by Gerard Manley Hopkins, eds. W. H. Gardner and N. H. MacKenzie (1970). By permission of Oxford University Press for the works in copyright on behalf of the British Province of the Society of Jesus.

Extract from "The Kingdom of God" by Francis Thompson, quoted in *Sound of Heaven: A Treasury of Catholic Verse*, ed. Russell Sparkes (2001). By permission of St. Paul (formerly St. Paul Publications), U.K.

Extract from "Grace" by Judith Wright, from *Collected Poems 1942–1985* (1994). By permission of Tom Thompson Publisher (*A Human Pattern: Selected Poems*, ETT imprint, Sydney 1996).

Introduction

One thrust of the human endeavor that has emerged in our times arises from a fascination with the conquest of space. We have made extraordinary advances in space exploration, but half a century ago when Sputnik's odyssey was only two years old, Abraham Heschel, the American Jewish philosopher, commented:

> To gain control of the world of space is certainly one of our tasks. The danger begins when in gaining power in the realm of space we forfeit all aspirations in the realm of time. There is a realm of time where the goal is not to have but to be, not to own but to give, not to control but to share, not to subdue but to be in accord.[1]

For observant Jews, the celebration of the Sabbath is an expression of their fidelity to such time: a weekly welcome to "bride Sabbath" who is the sign of God's eternal covenant fidelity to them, a constant security in their repeated insecurity of exile and return. The "seventh day" is the culmination of the Genesis timeline, for it is on the Sabbath that God finds a place of rest, of mutual creative presence in the depths of humanity and in all that God has made.

For the early church, building on its Jewish heritage, Sunday evolved as the "eighth" day—or the "first" day of the new creation on which we celebrate the recurring memorial of the marriage in Christ of God and humanity, the paschal mystery that is the hub of human history. Each week Christ calls us to gather for a time, either at the Sunday Eucharist or at Sunday worship in the absence of a priest, to affirm our identity, our being as a member of his body. We come to surrender thankfully to God a short time of our week: without competition, without what can often be the show business of everyday life, without the insular companionship of only those whom we like or associate with at other times.

In an article on the meaning of Sunday, written when he was Cardinal Joseph Ratzinger, Benedict XVI quoted an incident from the year 304 in

North Africa. Some Christians had gathered one Sunday as church at the home of a local Christian leader named Emeritus. The Roman proconsul interrupted their gathering to ask Emeritus why he had allowed these people into his house. Emeritus replied that they were his sisters and brothers. The proconsul insisted that this was a dangerous gathering that should have been forbidden. Emeritus then replied, "Without the day of the Lord we cannot live."[2] How many of us today could answer with the same commitment, with the same conviction that it would be dangerous *not* to gather on Sunday?

The life of the Sunday assembly flows from the two tables of Word and Sacrament. When the Lectionary readings are proclaimed, the Word of God becomes audible, visible, and present at the heart of the local gathered church. When in faith we welcome the Scriptures, Christ speaks to us as a community of disciples—to challenge and to comfort us in our own global, ecclesial, and personal "now."

> The Great Christ has done this
> Not "done" but "does" for past is always missing
> When Jesus comes in all his mysteries.[3]

But it is not just a matter of listening to the Word. At the end of the Sermon on the Mount, Jesus tells the parable of the "Two Builders" in order to move the emphasis from *hearing* to *acting* upon "these words of mine" (Matt 7:24). The wise builder expended time and energy in order to dig deep to rock foundations, and so his house withstood the onslaught of the furious storms. He is an image of us when we are disciples who energetically and persistently build our lives on the rock of Jesus' word as an unshakable foundation. This enables us to stand firm and meet the demands of gospel living when life batters us and when even the church itself may sometimes feel like shifting sand beneath our feet. The foolish builder is the inattentive "quick fix" person who builds without concern for the foundation: sand is good enough and easier to dig. When we just listen but do not act on his words, says Jesus, we are like this foolish builder. When our lives are hit by storms and the flash floods of unexpected tension or tragedy, our discipleship collapses and is washed away, or it gradually erodes because of our small but repeated infidelities.

It is in the weekly Liturgy of the Word that most Christians hear the Scriptures, but it is beyond the liturgy, in our families and communities, our workplaces and leisure time, that we are called continuously to act on the Word. The reflections that follow will, I hope, be of some small help in our continuous and deep digging into the Word of God—in both the Old and New Testaments—that will enable us to build our lives on the firm foundation, this rock. We build houses so that we can live in them and welcome others into a shared space. When we enter into the Word as preachers, teachers, lovers of sacred reading (*lectio divina*), and as Christ's faithful united in the diversity of our ways of life, we find shelter in the Word for both our stormy and calm days. Isaiah calls his people to "enlarge the site of your tent" (Isa 54:2) so that they may welcome new descendants into a joyful and safe dwelling. We are called to make room in our lives for new insights and greater hospitality to the Word of God, so that building on this rock of the Word may be a continuous joy and challenge, not only for ourselves but also for those with whom we share it—by both word and example.

Aspects of my life have also been built on other words that are an echo of the Bible and a commentary on it: the words of St. Benedict in what he called "this modest Rule for beginners" (*Rule of Benedict*, 73.1). Many people find in this fifth century spiritual master's text a wisdom that endures as a help in their seeking God today in very different contexts from the original monastic context for which it was written. At the beginning of his Rule, Benedict says that the search for God was always to have "the Gospel as our guide" (*Rule of Benedict*, Prologue 21). In his last chapter, he repeats his conviction (with a significant emphasis on *humanity,* characteristic of the man and his Rule) that the Old and New Testaments are "the truest of guides for human life" (RB 73.3). Therefore, as in the first book of this series, *Welcoming the Word in Year C: With Burning Hearts*, I have added for those who may be interested, and as the sixth chapter, a brief weekly reflection from the Rule that can be mixed with the biblical Word as an additional leaven to help us rise in our commitment to the Word proclaimed each Sunday. The continuing personal challenge for me is to test for myself, at least from Sunday to Sunday, the belief that the monastic life, and indeed the Christian life, would be stillborn without the Scriptures—read, prayed, and lived. That Benedict continues to pass this test has been acclaimed by numerous authoritative judges. This is my small contribution towards encouraging a conversation between the Word of God and the Rule.

Verna A. Holyhead, S.G.S.
Melbourne
September 2006

Notes

1. Abraham Heschel, "The Sabbath: Holiness in Time," *Between Man and God: An Interpretation of Judaism* (New York: The Free Press, 1959) 214.

2. Joseph Ratzinger, "The Meaning of Sunday," *Communio* 21, no. 1 (1994) 7.

3. Elizabeth Jennings, "In and Out of Time," *Elizabeth Jennings: New Collected Poems*, ed. Michael Schmidt (Manchester: Carcanet Press Limited, 2002) 313.

1

The Season of Advent

In many ways, Advent is a season of contradictions. Chronologically, we are between two calendars: celebrating the beginning of the new church year while turning to the last month of our civil calendars. Socially, we are caught up in the surge of gift finding and gift giving for family and friends, yet as we make our often impatient way through the shopping crowds, we may be tempted to dislike rather than love the rest of elbowing humanity around us!

Even in the flow of the readings for the Sundays of Advent there seems to be a liturgical riptide that, on the First Sunday, drags us out of a logical time sequence to proclaim the second and as yet unrealized coming of Christ at the end of human history, and then tosses us back on a wave of remembrance of the first coming of Emmanuel in our human flesh on the last Sunday of Advent.

The presence of John the Baptist in the Advent liturgy also seems to be contradictory. Quite confident of his messianic proclamation of Jesus at the Jordan on the Second Sunday, by the Third Sunday the Baptist is imprisoned not only by Herod, but also by his own doubts about the identity of "the one who is to come."

Yet this tension is not meant to pull us apart, but rather to urge us forward, out of the slackness and tiredness of the old church year, toward an eager understanding of the gospel reversals in our lives and the fidelity to us of a God who "reversed" his divinity to share our humanity:

> A child so terrified he asks for us.
> God is the cry we thought came from our own
> Perpetual sense of loss.[1]

1

First Sunday of Advent

• Isa 2:1-5 • Ps 122:1-2, 4-5, 6-9 • Rom 13:11-14 • Matt 24:37-44

T. S. Eliot wrote:

> But to apprehend
> The point of intersection of the timeless
> With time, is an occupation of the saint . . .
> For most of us, there is only the unattended
> Moment . . . .[2]

At the beginning of the liturgical year the church tries to make us more attentive to, hopeful about, and prepared for the moment of the great advent of God: the Second Coming of Christ when human and cosmic history will have run its course and the timeless, eternal kingdom is fully established. God will come to us, but we also must make our pilgrimage to God.

The first reading dreams of the time when all nations and peoples, regardless of nationality, gender, age, or culture, will answer God's invitation to come to him. Obedient to the word of the Lord, the nations will stream to God's dwelling place, symbolized by the city of Jerusalem. The highest point of that city is Mount Zion, the site of the temple, but it is not to attain a strategic advantage over any security threats that the mountain of the temple of the Lord will be significant. What will be won from there is the peace that comes from dwelling with God and obedience to his word, and so in the responsorial Psalm 122, a pilgrim song, we express a longing for our homecoming to God in peace and justice and love.

Outside the United Nations building in New York is a bronze statue entitled "Let Us Beat Swords Into Plowshares," by the Russian sculptor Evgeniy Vuchetich, and presented to the UN by the former Soviet Union. The strong, muscular male figure holds a sword in one hand, and in the other he wields a hammer with which he is beating the sword into a plowshare. At the base of the statue is inscribed the words of Isaiah which we hear today in the first reading: "They shall beat their swords into plowshares."

Our world may seem to be so far from realizing this hope as nations converge in advances of military might or "coalitions against terrorism." To avoid the temptation of again taking up arms that have been laid down after successful peace treaties, these weapons of war must be melted down and beaten into instruments of peace that will enhance, not destroy life, and cultivate, not rape the earth. Isaiah's vision is not one of passive nostalgia. Transplanted into our liturgical assembly, it becomes a call to our active, spiritually "muscular," and social efforts to be peacemakers in a world where poverty oppresses two-thirds of the world's population, where social inequalities lead to hate and envy and the bitterness that provokes violence against the affluent and arrogant, and where the consequent desperation leads to desperate acts. Our world still waits for radical transformation: for fields that grow crops, not land mines; for the transfiguring light of Christ, not a disfiguring atomic wasteland; for poverty to truly become past history.

Vatican II reminded us that:

> The expectation of a new earth must not weaken but rather stimulate our concern for cultivating this one. For here grows the body of a new human family, a body which even now is able to give some shadowing of the new age.[3]

In his letter to the Romans, Paul is explicit about the "arms" that Christians should take up. They are the weapons that help us to walk as people of the day, in the light of Christ, as we struggle against the darkness of sin. This was symbolized at our baptism by the presentation of the lighted candle and the accompanying prayer: that the one being baptized may always walk as a child of the light because the flame of Christ's love burns in his or her heart. Translated into contemporary concepts, Paul emphasizes that the "armor" with which we clothe ourselves is a balanced lifestyle, reverent expression of our sexuality, and peaceful relationships with one another.

In the gospel Jesus warns his disciples that they are not to be like the people of Noah's generation who were so immersed in the ordinary and everyday that they were unaware of the flood of evil that was gradually encroaching on their lives. But this does not mean that we go into a pious retreat from life's everyday demands. As the gospel tells us by its own imagery, the fields still have to be plowed, the flour still ground at the mill, but work or leisure or human relationships cannot be so all consuming that we are not alert and committed to the coming of God into our lives. One of the problems of the early church was that, because of the expectation that Jesus' Second Coming (or *parousía*, "appearance") at the end of human history was just around the corner, Christians might as well do nothing except wait for it—or try to calculate its arrival—a temptation that continues to surface in our own time despite repeated failures! Such passivity is the opposite of the active, discerning vigilance that makes us alert and committed to the daily possibilities of establishing the rule of God in our own life and the lives of others. John XXIII once remarked that if he knew the world was about to end, he would tell the citizens of Vatican City to look busy!—busy with God's work for the kingdom.

In the two mini-parables that Jesus tells, the men working in the field or the women at the mill are outwardly no different, but one is ready for the kingdom, the other is not. For Matthew, readiness consists in nothing "rapturous," but in doing the work of God in the spirit of the Beatitudes (Matt 5:1-12) and the Parable of the Last Judgment (Matt 25:31-46). In another daring image, Jesus compares his coming as Son of Man to a burglary. Any prudent householder who expects to be burgled is on the alert to frustrate the robbery. We are to be alert for the day when Jesus will break into our lives—not to frustrate him, but to allow ourselves to be "stolen" for heaven.

Jesus will come definitively to each one of us at our individual end-time, our death. For the whole of creation, it will be the *eschaton*, the "end time" not so much *of* the world but *for* the world. Individually and cosmically, this will be a new birth, as unimaginable and yet so much more hugely real than the world that awaited us when we were born from our mother's womb.

During Advent 1968, on December 10, Thomas Merton was accidentally electrocuted in his room while attending a meeting of Asian Benedictines and Cistercians in Bangkok. Twenty years earlier in the poem, "The Victory," he had written of the sudden coming of the Son of Man as an event of joy, not fear:

> . . . make ready for the Face that speaks like lightning,
> Uttering the name of your exultation
> Deep in the vitals of your soul.
> Make ready for the Christ
> Whose smile, like lightning,
> Sets free the song of everlasting glory
> That now sleeps in your paper flesh, like dynamite.[4]

During Advent, our "paper flesh" can often be torn as we plow our way through Christmas shopping or grind through the pressures that the end of the work year demands. But can we find a few moments each Advent week when we "make ready for Christ," the Son of Man whom the gospel reminds us "is coming at an unexpected hour"? A few minutes daily for the reading of Scripture, a short prayer of gratitude to God for the greatest gift of his Son as we see the enticements of Christmas gifts in shops or on TV, the practiced mindfulness that Jesus comes in our flesh in our sisters and brothers, especially those most in need—these will help us to be ready for his advent. Advent is our reminder that Jesus is coming: daily by grace, liturgically at Christmas, at the unknown time of our own death, and at final birth of the new heaven and earth that will be delivered to God by Christ at the time of his Second Coming.

Second Sunday of Advent

• Isa 11:1-10 • Ps 72:1-2, 7-8, 12-13, 17 • Rom 15:4-9 • Matt 3:1-12

During Advent, one strong voice that tries to rouse us to the demands of our discipleship is that of John the Baptist. He comes from the wilderness, eager to share what he has learned there in the privileged place of covenant making and the dangerous environment of temptation to covenant breaking.

In "those days" of new beginnings, the Spirit thrusts John the Baptist onto the banks of the Jordan River to be Israel's awakener to what God will do in and through Jesus. Sharpened in wisdom and words by his desert experience, John cuts his way through hypocrisy and sinfulness, and offers to the Jordan crowd his baptism of repentance.

Matthew has no infancy introduction to the Baptist. We might be eager for "dear little baby Jesus," but the Lectionary demands that we first go through "Checkpoint John" to be examined for our integrity, our repentance, our fruits of justice, before we approach the adult Christ. John is not an elegant preacher, not a person of the establishment, not one who would make the most acceptable parishioner. He is disturbing. He had found his voice in the desert's eloquent silence. Shaggy in dress, he is clothed like a new Elijah (see 2 Kgs 1:8), and eats the ritually pure food of the poor (see Lev 11:22). John's sudden appearance may be the evangelist's way of reminding us of one emphasis of last Sunday's Liturgy of the Word: that God's action in history is often unexpected. Matthew applies to John the words of consolation of Second Isaiah, originally addressed to the returning Babylonian exiles in the sixth century B.C.E. But whereas Isaiah dreamed of God cutting a smooth way home through the wilderness for his people, in today's gospel it is the Baptist's strident and fiery words that blaze a trail for the coming of God-with-us in Christ. The wilderness is not just the physical place in which the Baptist preaches; it is also the barren places of our hearts in which a trail of repentance needs to be cut.

It was at the Jordan River that the Hebrews came out of their wilderness wandering and crossed through the waters into the Promised Land. Over twelve hundred years later, the Baptist calls their descendants into the waters for another transition, another entry into the promises of God. If, in retrospect, the calendar year which is almost finished seems to have been something of a desert wandering—personally, politically, socially and ecclesially—Advent is a call to new hope and conversion to Christ. The biblical meaning of "repentance" to which John summons us is much more than just "being sorry." It implies a radical change in our attitudes and matters of the heart, a total transformation of our priorities, the beginning and end of all in us that is not God.

The Pharisees and Sadducees slither around the fringes of the crowd like a brood of dangerous vipers, sizing up John, ready to inject some of their poison into those who accept the Baptist—who certainly does not fit their establishment profile. The same judgmental attitudes can always assail Christian leaders (see Matt 7:15-20). With sharp and ironic word play, John deflates the attitudes of the religious leaders about what they consider their privileged religious status, proclaiming that God can, with inexhaustible creativity, turn stones (Hebrew *ebenim*) into children (*benim*) of Abraham! We cannot put our trust in our own achievements, our own virtues, our own culture, and exclude others from God's love. To be true to the Advent mystery, which John announces, the axe of conversion has to be laid to the roots of any arrogant superiority or intolerance in our hearts.

St. Augustine reminded us that John was a voice for a time, but Christ is the Word for all eternity. John has no illusions about his own status. He considers himself to be the servant of the coming Messiah, a person not even worthy to perform the menial job of a slave who carries his master's smelly and dusty sandals. Although Jesus' ministry begins after John's, he precedes the Baptist in importance. Jesus' baptism, says John, will be with the Holy Spirit and with fire, a symbolic way of speaking of purification and refinement. Jesus will be the Harvester of the end time who will winnow humanity. The redeemed will be like the substantial kernels of wheat that, when tossed into the air by the farmer's fork, fall to the ground for harvesting, while those who are not repentant will be blown away like useless chaff.

In the first reading, Isaiah proclaims that the axe has been laid to the tree of Jesse. In the divine plan, a king was to be a "sacrament" of justice, as the responsorial Psalm 72 sings of him. He was charged by God to be the servant of his people, the one who "delivers the poor when they call, the poor and those who have no helper." For the most part, however, the Davidic kingship descended from David, son of Jesse, had been neither healthy nor vigorous in its growth and commitment to the disadvantaged. Yet the prophet believes that, like the charred and ravaged trees swept by bushfires, there persists in its root a tiny sprig of hope and life. When watered and tended by the Spirit, this will one day bud forth a king who will inaugurate a reign of holy, human, and ecological harmony. Advent is the season for our pondering on what this peaceable kingdom could be like, and also for our striving, first of all, to make our own hearts a place where lion and lamb can lie down together. This demands that we try to live as welcoming, forgiving people toward those who are "beastly" enemies, and take care ourselves to do no harm to those who are as vulnerable as little children.

It is to such a program of practical, everyday action that Paul calls us in his Letter to the Romans. We are encouraged to hold fast to hope by the stories of how our ancestors endured, stories which we encounter in our prayerful reading of Scripture. To be tolerant of others is a great challenge that, when met with love, gives glory to God. It is regrettable that the Lectionary reading does not start three verses earlier with Paul's plea that his Roman Christians, who do consider themselves strong in faith, need to be accepting of the failings of those who are weaker in their commitment.

Perhaps all the talk about peace, about the light of Christ, and the joy of his coming may seem irrelevant when we experience darkness and fear, especially the darkness of a loss of faith in God, ourselves, or other people. But Sunday after Sunday during the four weeks of Advent we light a candle on the Advent wreath—a fragile flame that reminds us that in these weeks we are preparing to renew the welcome into our lives of the vulnerable One who was announced by a star rising in the darkness and a song echoing through the night. Jesus still comes when we seem to be starved of stars and can find little to sing about. Then, in faith, we can rejoice.

A woman who is both a mother and a theologian made this timely comment:

> The readings of the Second Sunday of Advent remind me of a sense of concern which pervaded pregnancy for me. It was a concern about the world into which my child would be born. It was a peace wish and a justice wish that made me think (and I still think) that if we mothers . . . black, white, yellow . . . if all of us would unite and tell the makers of war that we resent and will not tolerate any force that tries to undo what we have knitted together so patiently in the womb for nine months—if we did that, I believe that we would ensure peace from generation to generation. By extension, if we as members of a pregnant mystical body of Christ did this, made known our concerns by our seeds of justice and deeds of peacemaking, the promise of the Second Sunday of Advent would come true . . . . Advent is the only future worth waiting for.[5]

Third Sunday of Advent

• Isa 35:1-6a, 10 • Ps 146:6-10 • James 5:7-10 • Matt 11:2-11

It is the experience of many prison chaplains that when prisoners are on death row they frequently—and understandably—ask life and death questions that would never have occurred to them before. Almost two thousand years ago, Matthew describes the poignant questions that John asks of Jesus through the messengers he has sent to him from Herod's prison. Doubts breed in loneliness and darkness, and they take John a long way from his confident self whom we met in last Sunday's gospel on Jordan's banks. With desperate hope, John sends his disciples with the question: "Are you the one who is to come, or are we to wait for another?"

Jesus' response echoes the Baptist's own convictions that we heard him voice last week: it is by their fruits that the man or woman of the kingdom is recognized. Jesus reminds John's messengers about the fruits of his own ministry. Jesus has harvested the blind who see again, the lame who now dance for joy, the lepers who can again kiss their loved ones, the deaf who are startled by a bird song, the dead who are raised to life. Take this good news to John, says Jesus.

As the Baptist's disciples depart, Jesus turns to the crowd to praise John in terms that would make an excellent Advent review of life for us. John was not a vacillating crowd pleaser, not a reed that bends in the wind of public opinion. He was not a compromiser, not a well-dressed and powerful "in-group" person, not a political entrepreneur or someone welcome at prestigious places like Herod's palace. Where John did end up was in Herod's prison, and there he would lose his head, but never his heart, to that king's lack of integrity and fear of losing face. John's heart had been lost long ago to Jesus, and no doubt the message sent back to him in prison confirmed John in his love and offered him the truth that the way to deep faith so often goes through deep doubt. At least, to some degree, do we measure up to such praise—or blame?

The prophets had strong faith in the transformation that God could work in the barren physical and spiritual wilderness, and throughout the weeks of Advent in Year A, Isaiah sings and dreams of the transformation that God's coming will work. Just as Israel came through the long wilderness wandering to enter into the Promised Land, so God will again lead his people out of the desert of apathy and despair. Creation will be healed, and the wasteland of human disabilities, fears, disappointments and oppression will blossom into joy when watered by God's grace. Isaiah is speaking from experience; he has been through humiliation, slavery, and exile, but he assures us that we must keep on dreaming—not as people of the night who wake to find their dreams are fleeting and insubstantial, but as dangerous daytime dreamers who act with open eyes, unsealed ears, and embodied resolve to make their dreams of the reign of God a reality. John the Baptist was such a dangerous, practical dreamer.

With the responsorial psalm, verses from Psalm 146, we sing our faith in God who brings justice to those in greatest need. Isaiah never saw this

God take flesh in Jesus, but he believed in his spirit-filled dream. The antiphon that is our response repeats the words of Isaiah as again and again we insist: "Lord, come and save us."

James tells us in his letter that growth and harvest do not happen overnight. Just as a farmer works hard to prepare his fields for sowing and then must wait patiently for rains over which he has no control, so Christians have to work at their discipleship, knowing that it is God who gives the increase. We must endure as nonjudgmental people of hope and love who wait for the advent of the only just Judge. The longer the Harvester's delay, the more enduring our patience must be. We need the season of Advent to sow again in the field of our hearts the sure hope of our salvation in the face of helplessness and distress.

Fourth Sunday of Advent

• Isa 7:10-14 • Ps 24:1-6 • Rom 1:1-7 • Matt 1:18-24

> Sawing the wood,
> the splinters hacked at his heart.
> Hammering the nails,
> her revelation pounded at his peace.
> Carting the timber,
> he was loaded still with love.
> Splicing the joints,
> he put together a private plan.
> Dreaming in the night,
> he awoke to fearless fatherhood.
> . . . And he named him Jesus.[6]

This is Matthew's Joseph who comes to center stage as the Advent drama moves into the final act. Matthew gives us no account of an annunciation to Mary, but recounts the angel's dream revelation to the agonizing Joseph: that the child Mary has conceived is "from the Holy Spirit." How Joseph had learned of Mary's pregnancy we are not told. We may speculate whether it was from Mary herself, or through sharp-eyed village gossip about "women's business." However it happened, Joseph is torn between his loyalty to the Jewish Torah and his love for his young wife.

Mary is truly his wife, not a pregnant, unwed teenager as some homilists preach with zeal for the "religion" of contemporary cultural relevance but with ignorance of biblical interpretation or first century Jewish culture. The confusion is heightened by the translation of "betrothed" as "engaged" in some versions. Betrothal was, by Jewish law, the first stage of marriage, a legal agreement that bestowed on the couple the status of man and wife. Since Jewish girls were legally and frequently married at an early age, as young as twelve, they continued to live at their parental home for about a year. After this time of adjustment to their new status, a husband would take his wife to his own home to cohabit with him. Further proof that the betrothed were married are the facts that betrothal could be terminated only by death, after which the remaining spouse was considered widowed, or by the man divorcing his wife. Any infidelity on the woman's part during betrothal was regarded as adultery. The strong honor code of the Middle Eastern world demanded that no man could take possession of what belonged to another, including a child in the womb who had been conceived by another man. Joseph had his dreams of married life, but then comes the nightmare, and the painful, human agony of a just man torn between his loyalty to the Jewish Torah (law) and his love for Mary—pregnant, but not by him—and therefore considered an adulteress who could possibly be stoned, or at least subjected to public humiliation (Deut 22:23-24).

But Matthew describes Joseph as a just man, who plans to make some attempt to reconcile steadfast love and law. With deep unease in his soul, perhaps remembering the prophets had proclaimed "mercy, not sacrifice" (Hos 6:6), Joseph decides to divorce Mary quietly to spare her as much public shame as possible. Such an attitude is an overture to the mercy that Jesus will show in his interpretation of the Law (see Matt 9:13, 23:23), and surely a reminder to the church of all ages to listen to the echo of the prophetic words.

In a dream, a messenger of God tells Joseph not to be afraid of what he cannot understand, not to disown the mystery but enter into it. Joseph wakes up and succeeds where we often fail: he does something about his dream. Obedient to God's word, he responds for the first of many times "as it was commanded" (Matt 2:14, 21, 22). This biblical dreamer is also a person of action. Joseph offers the hospitality of his love and lineage to Mary and to the Stranger Child whom she carries in her womb. He is the radically blessed poor man, ready to surrender the right to choose a name for the child, and generously offering to Jesus, "he who saves," a paternity not of his own flesh. What onlookers might consider a scandal, Joseph and Mary believe is the action of the Holy Spirit, who continues to do "scandalous" things in our midst.

Joseph is cast by Matthew along the lines of another Joseph, the patriarch of Genesis, who was also a man of dreams (Gen 37, 40) and a man of God's providence (Gen 45:1-15). Out of the granaries of Egypt over which he was the Pharaoh's chief steward, Joseph cared for his family in time of famine, despite their treatment of him as a young man (Gen 37:15-36). The Joseph of the gospel also cares unobtrusively for his family, stewarding the Grain and the Bread which continues to feed our hunger at every eucharistic assembly.

In the thirteenth-century cathedral of Chartres are four stained-glass windows known as the Evangelists' Windows. In each one, an evangelist is depicted as sitting on the shoulders of an Old Testament prophet. Matthew sits on Isaiah's shoulders. If we sit on someone's shoulders we can see more than the one who carries us. It was impossible for Isaiah in the eighth century B.C.E. to see Jesus as Emmanuel, God-with-us. On the other hand, without Isaiah, Matthew would not have been able to search the Hebrew Scriptures for the Spirit-filled words which would be a fitting vehicle with which to carry the good news of the long-awaited Messiah's advent to his predominantly Jewish-Christian community. Matthew's purpose in the use of such texts is to share with his community his conviction that Jesus is the fulfillment of Israel's messianic hopes. As Eugene Boring comments, "What Matthew's use of Scripture reflects is not apologetics addressed to outsiders, but confession directed to insiders."[7] Every generation uses contemporary approaches to biblical interpretation, and Matthew uses a subtle and sophisticated Jewish method that accepted an adaptation of an earlier text to fit more closely with its fulfillment. Matthew looks back to the messianic hopes of the Old Testament and forward to the consequences of their fulfillment in Christ for the Christian community. In today's first reading we hear the Isaian verse that is the first of many such Old Testament references.

In contrast to Joseph, King Ahaz is far from being a "just" man; he is, rather, a reflection of the political expediency and spurious virtue that can still be found too often in society and church, as well as in ourselves. Challenged by Isaiah to rely on the providence and covenant fidelity of God to the royal house of David to which Ahaz belongs, and not an alliance of convenience with Assyria, Ahaz parades false piety and lame excuses before the prophet. Isaiah realizes that the king does not want any sign from God that might demand change and conversion. Life is more comfortable (many politicians still seem to agree!) if he stays with his own preconceived ideas. With just anger at Ahaz's stubbornness, Isaiah does offer him a God-given sign: not a sign of military might, but the frail sign of a young pregnant woman, probably a princess in Ahaz's own house, whose child will be "Emmanuel," enfleshing God's continuing promise and presence to the royal and messianic line of Judah. As parents know, every child is a sign of hope, announcing that God is still with us.

To this reading we respond with some verses of Psalm 24, a psalm probably recited at the entrance to the Temple as a reminder of what should characterize those who come to worship before God, the Lord of glory. What is required are the clean hands of the peaceful and nonviolent and the purity of heart that is an unreserved commitment to God. Such worshippers seek to have their priorities right with regard to God and other people. Joseph is surely such a person; Ahaz is not. What about each one of us at worship this Sunday? In these terms, are we fit to enter into the house of God?

The promise of the Emmanuel who is born of Mary is now an abiding promise with us "always, to the end of the age." These are the last words of Matthew's Good News, spoken by the Risen Jesus (Matt 28:20).

The beginning of Paul's Letter to the Romans gathers together many of the themes of the first reading and the gospel. In Christ Jesus, God has been faithful to his promises to the house of David; in human powerlessness, God reveals the divine power and wisdom; and Paul, both a proud Hebrew and a citizen of Rome, has no hesitation in glorying in his role of "slave" of Jesus because it is his apostolic mission to proclaim that Jesus is not only his Lord but the Lord of all peoples and nations. All this is the work of the "scandalous" Spirit. Through baptism into Christ, every Christian is called by the Spirit to be Christ's slave, not in cowering subservience, but with wholehearted freedom and integrity. From this identity flows our mission to proclaim the gospel and serve our sisters and brothers in the grace and peace of Christ.

Notes

1. Elizabeth Jennings, "Christmas Suite in Five Movements," *New Collected Poems* (London: Carcanet Press Limited, 2002) 143.

2. T. S. Eliot, *The Complete Poems and Plays* (London: Faber and Faber, 2004) 190.

3. Vatican II, *Pastoral Constitution on the Church in the Modern World*, art. 39.

4. Thomas Merton, "The Victory," *A Man in the Divided Sea* (Norfolk, CT: New Directions, 1946) 88.

5. Doris Donnelly, "Advent, The Most Difficult Season," *Origins* (September 10, 1987): 209.

6. Author's own words.

7. Eugene Boring, "Matthew," *The New Interpreter's Bible*, Vol. VIII (Nashville: Abingdon Press, 1995) 153.

2

The Season of Christmas

In his first encyclical, Benedict XVI describes the Incarnation as the "dramatic form" of God's unpredictable activity.[1] The Liturgy of the Word during the weeks of the Christmas season invites us to be committed players in—not just an audience at—this drama of God who, in becoming flesh of our flesh and bone of our bone, has proclaimed the divine love for our humanity and our world in the most personal way possible. In the Christ Child we cannot say that God is hidden, detached, distant, or even "dead."

In the Old Testament prophets, to whom we listen in this season, we hear their passionate hope: that the light would shine out in the darkness, that the tent of Israel would be pitched wide enough to be a welcome place for all peoples, that God's blessing would be as wide as the inheritance of all the nations and, at the same time, would be as intimate a world as the love of parents and children. And readings from the letters of the early church emphasize that the fulfillment of these hopes in Christ calls us to new responsibilities in our daily lives.

The Word is pronounced over us to tell us that we, too, are newborn, vulnerable, and wonderful because of Emmanuel, God-with-us. Yet this birth is not a one-time event that happened in a certain time and place "back there." It is a celebration of every Christian's birth and ongoing growth to the maturity of faith in Christ, whose wooden feeding-trough cradle became the wood that raised up his body to nourish us with salvation, whose whimpers became the adult voice inviting disciples to follow him to death and resurrection, and whose food would be not only the milk of his mother's breast, but the will of his Father. As the poet says, this mystery is given into our hands:

> Christmas is in the air.
> You are given into my hands

Out of the quietest, loneliest lands.
My trembling is all my prayer.
To blown straw was given
All the fullness of Heaven . . .

In the sleeping, weeping weather
We shall all kneel down together.[2]

Christmas Day

Dawn Mass

(As the texts for Christmas Day are the same in Years A, B, and C, the reflection for Midnight Mass is found in *With Burning Hearts: Welcoming the Word in Year C*.)

• Isa 62:11-12 • Ps 97:1, 6, 11-12 • Titus 3:4-7 • Luke 2:15-20

The angels have gone back to heaven, and the shepherds go back to Bethlehem—perhaps a very appropriate gospel for the Church to choose for the Dawn Mass, for the Christmas mystery is not just about listening to angelic voices; it is also about doing something in response to what we have heard from messengers of God, however these may manifest themselves to us.

The shepherds are an unlikely lot to be in communication with angels, but Luke's message is clear: those first invited to approach the Child are considered unrighteous, unpopular people on the margins of first century Palestine. Socially, they were materially poor, often suspected of conniving in theft, and often recipients of the wrath of other shepherds or landowners when their sheep strayed onto a neighboring property. Religiously, their handling of animals rendered them ritually unclean. From the beginning of his gospel, Luke emphasizes that it is for the poor and disregarded that the Messiah would come as Redeemer. Like the shepherds who had to watch and keep awake on their hillside, it is also the poor who are often better and more grateful "watchers," more attentive listeners than the self-sufficient and powerful. They need to be—because their life depends on it. And our life as Christians depends on our watching and listening for the presence of Jesus in unexpected places and people—and then hastening to meet him there.

One of the most moving of the many artistic depictions of the Nativity is one by an unknown sixteenth century Flemish artist, entitled *The Adoration of the Christ Child*, now in the New York Metropolitan Museum of Art. Behind Mary, Joseph and the Christ Child kneel two angels who are easily recognizable as having what we now call Down syndrome, a condition defined by John Langdon Down in 1866. They are perfectly at home and accepted there; they belong at the manger, just as do the shepherds and all the poor.

The shepherds hasten to Bethlehem to join the other poor people at the center of this mystery: a young woman who has just given birth, the husband who hovers protectively over her and the child—the child about whom the shepherds repeat what the angels had told them, that he is the Savior, the Messiah, the Lord. It is a poignant scene: the poor affirming for the poor their faith in the word of God that had come to them in different annunciations. And Mary treasures and "ponders" these words. The Greek word that Luke uses here for "ponders" has the sense of "throwing/getting things together." Mary has surely to try to throw together the paradoxes of joy at the present moment and the dread of the unknown future, of revelation and concealment, of a poor baby lying before her in a manger and the promised inheritor of the throne of David.

The shepherds go back to their hillside and their daily work, and now it is their human voices, not an angelic choir, that glorify and praise God for what they have heard and seen. What we have heard and seen this Christmas dawn with the eyes and ears of faith, we too are called to announce in our own places of the ordinary everyday; we are challenged to try to put together the paradoxes of living in the church at the heart of the world, and to keep watch for what the poor can tell us about faith and hope and love.

There is a feeling of quickening excitement in the first reading from Isaiah. The prophet underlines the significance of these words by making them the Lord's personal proclamation to the whole world that salvation is coming to Zion. It is as though God is announcing the birth of a new daughter. No longer exiled, the "daughter of Zion," the people of Israel, will be given a new identity. Despite their sins they will be reborn to salvation as "the Lord's Redeemed" and "the Holy People," who are saved from their sinfulness by their God. When this happens, others will hasten to join them, to seek the presence of God in the holy city whose people are not forsaken by God. Our humanity is given a new identity when Jesus is born in our flesh. As a vulnerable child, God is not distant, not hidden, but the sought out and found one, especially for those exiled from the centers of power and wealth.

Jesus is given to us as God's most wonderful gift, which we have done nothing to earn. Today we will unwrap the presents that are mysterious, colorful packages at the foot of our Christmas trees, in our Christmas stockings, or hidden around the house or garden. What God gives us in Jesus we will continue to "unwrap" throughout our lives. For the faithful disciple, his mystery will never be discarded, only explored, even in eternity. All this, says Paul to Titus, is because of God's compassionate loving kindness that makes us his newborn children in Christ through the waters of baptism and the outpouring of the Holy Spirit. Those who love a child hold out great hopes for his or her future. So the great hope for every child of God is the inheritance of eternal life at our second birth—by which we are delivered from the womb of this world into eternal life in the kingdom of God. This may seem a dark mystery, but as we proclaim with faith in the antiphonal response to Psalm 97, "A light will shine on us this day: the Lord is born for us." We are to tend that light of Christ and keep it burning throughout our lives, as the baptismal rite reminds us when the candle is presented to the newly baptized: "You have been enlightened by Christ. Walk always as a child of the light and keep the flame of faith alive in your heart. When the Lord comes, may you go out to meet him with all the saints in the heavenly kingdom."

Sunday in the Octave of Christmas

Feast of the Holy Family of Jesus, Mary, and Joseph

• Sir 3:2-6, 12-14 • Ps 128:1-5 • Col 3:12-21 • Matt 2:13-15, 19-23

Like all the great feasts and seasons of the liturgical year, Christmas also celebrates something of the paschal mystery of life and death: the scandal of the Word becoming flesh in a human family, the Christ who empties himself into the frailties of our humanity and so into the limitations of a particular historical moment, culture, and religion. Normand Bonneau comments that: "To express this sublime mystery, the Christmas season manifests a predilection for the language of darkness and light, the same symbolic threads that embroider the rich tapestry of the Easter Vigil."[3] On the Sunday after Christmas Day (or on December 30 if there is no Sunday between December 25 and January 1), the church unrolls the tapestry that is embroidered with Old and New Testament reflections on the significance of the family. This is the most recent of the feasts in the Christmas cycle and, given the situation of many families today, one of the most challenging to integrate spiritually and practically into the Christian significance of the season. The feast of the Holy Family has wandered through the liturgical calendar for just over a century since Leo XIII established it in 1893 as an optional celebration for what was then the Third Sunday after Epiphany. Originally it was a call to remember the sanctity of family life and morality in the face of the social changes of the nineteenth century that threatened it. Made a feast of the universal church by Benedict XV in the early twentieth century, and further emphasized after the reform of the Roman calendar by Vatican II, the feast has settled in its present position.

The family is "the beginning and basis of human society,"[4] an image of the relationship between Christ and his Church, and a foreshadowing of the hope that through the preaching of the gospel "the human race might become the Family of God, in which the fullness of the Law would be love."[5] In the twenty-first century, "family" has many cultural and moral connotations and challenges for Christians. We are all aware of those who belong to separated, divorced, blended, or single parent families. Discussion of same sex family and civil partnership rights takes place in government bodies, churches, and gay and lesbian groups. The public, and above all parents, are horrified by child abuse and pornography that reaches its tentacles into home, school, church, tourism, and the Internet to strangle relationships in the family and with those in whom families have put their trust. What then, does the Liturgy of the Word proclaim and affirm about family life that does not seem light years away from our contemporary realities, hopes and fears?

The author of the book of Sirach (or Ecclesiasticus) is named as Ben Sira. This second century reading reflects the wisdom that Ben Sira has gleaned from personal experience and his Spirit-filled discernment of God's action in everyday life. Sometime after 135 B.C.E., Ben Sira's grandson translated his grandfather's Hebrew text into Greek to make it more accessible to the wider audience of those living outside Israel but still committed to the Jewish tradition and law (see Prologue). We might say, therefore, that this book is a "family" effort. Although the family structure of that time was patriarchal, it still proclaims values that are important for our very differently structured families: reverence for parents, both father and mother—the equivalent honor for the latter being very significant, given the patriarchal dominance—and the obedience that children owe to their parents. Not only the father, but also the mother, is mentioned in this context. The "children" of this text are adults, as is obvious from the closing exhortation to sons to take care of their fathers in their old age, for no matter what the age, their love and respect is enduring and mutual. Probably the mother is not mentioned here because it was presumed that women would be cared for by the male members of their family. In the typical extended family of Ben Sira's experience, there were undoubtedly tensions to resolve as well as wisdom and love to be shared. In the verse following today's reading there is this beautiful encouragement to the adult children who show kindness to a father (and we can well add mother): ". . . in the day of your distress it will be remembered in your favor; like frost in fair weather, your sins will melt away." We are now much more skilled in diagnosing and treating dementia and Alzheimer's disease in the elderly, but are we any more skilled in matters of the heart regarding our frail aged parents? For those many faithful daughters and sons making the hard decisions to support a mother or father at home, or who visit them day after day, week after week in a care facility, the answer is obviously "yes." But there are also the nursing home rooms of the frail aged that are decorated at Christmas with paper and tinsel, but where no one comes. Is it to them that the Word is in deeper, more silent conversation than ever before in their lives, a conversation in their sacred depths where physical disability is no barrier? "Happy is everyone who fears the Lord, who walks in his ways" (Ps 128:1) is our response to this reading.

Like Mary, Joseph, and Jesus, families may endure situations of hardship and distress. In today's reading from Matthew's Gospel, this meant flight into Egypt because of Herod's fear of royal competition from the child born to be king of the Jews. The infancy narrative is an overture to Matthew's Gospel, and like a musical overture it will introduce themes that recur throughout the rest of the work. Matthew's description of the wise men's questing and questioning, of Herod's wish to seek and kill the child competitor, and of the religious cohorts that gather around him in Jerusalem (Matt 2:1-4), looks forward to the arrest, trial, and crucifixion of Jesus in that same city (Matt 26:57, 59). As happened at his annunciation, (Matt 1:20-21) the just and obedient Joseph again dreams and then wakes up to do something about his dream. Guided by divine providence, he leads his family on another exodus, down into Egypt. Moving between the two testaments, Matthew awakens in his community the memory of Moses, saved by the family shrewdness of his sister and mother and taken by Pharaoh's daughter into safety in Egypt. From there Moses will one day lead his people in their exodus out of slavery into freedom in their own land.

Like the displaced and desperate refugee families of our present times, the Holy Family knows hardship and distress in their search for a safe place. When Herod dies, God calls his son out of Egypt in another of Joseph's dreams, but hostility and fear still threaten the family in the person of Archelaus, Herod's son. Again Matthew emphasizes the divine initiative that comes in the dream warning to Joseph and causes him to respond by withdrawing into the town of Nazareth in the region of Galilee. So "He will be called a Nazorean," (Matt 2:23) a title that is sometimes connected with the Hebrew *nezer* or "branch," perhaps recalling the branch that Isaiah promised would spring from the genealogical root of David (Isa 11:1). Although Jesus' life style of holiness was so different from theirs (Matt 11:19), another opinion links "Nazorean" with similar wordplay but with the Hebrew *nazir*, a name for a member of the ascetic sect of Nazarites, regarded as particularly "holy ones" who, according to the vows they made, were set apart (Judg 13:5, 16:7). Theologically, Matthew is making the point that Jesus begins his Jewish childhood in the city of David, goes into exile, and then returns to the humbler town of Nazareth in Galilee, a region where the Gentiles will have a more ready access to him. Royalty and humility, withdrawal and manifestation, rejection and acceptance, will be the rhythm of the Messiah's life. We who share his life by baptism into a royal, priestly, and prophetic people (see 1 Pet 2:9) can expect no more or less.

In the second reading, the author of the Letter to the Colossians echoes this conviction when he calls Christians "God's chosen ones." But such choice brings with it responsibilities, and it is appropriate that we who are graced by a new humanity in Christ should reflect on these at the beginning of a new year. To know ourselves as loved and forgiven by God demands that we relate to others in the same way. We all have experienced how difficult this can be at times, especially if we have been unjustly treated. Perhaps all that we can do is to thank God for what he loves in that person, while we humbly take the path of avoidance or escape from confrontations when attempts at reconciliation have failed. Even the holy John Henry Newman had to go to the Birmingham Oratory while Francis Faber remained in London, so that the peace of Christ could dwell in the space between them!

Mutuality is important in community relationships. We hear in the Letter to the Colossians that Christians will be transformed by the sharing of the word and the singing of psalms and hymns in what seems to suggest both a liturgical context and a practice of everyday Christian life. The concluding verses of the reading situate love, forgiveness, and peacemaking within the intimate context of the family. Given the patriarchal structure of first century families, the practice of the virtues to which this Letter calls Christian families does not underline patriarchal privilege, but rather the mutual obligations of love, gentleness, and obedience which will transform the social customs of the time—and not only those of the first century, but also of our own twenty-first century where, in vastly different social contexts, the same relationships are a challenge for parents and their children. There is a challenge, too, for the church: to take imaginative, practical initiatives to support families, and to advocate with governments for their appropriate responsibility for the quality of the family life of their citizens. And what of families who are exiled through divorce or separation? Surely the search must continue for ways in which they can be called back from contemporary "Egypts." Nor can we, the church which calls itself the family of God, ignore those who are suffering because of the absence of any human family bonds. How do we show them respect and love and invite them into the Christian family?

Octave of Christmas

Solemnity of the Blessed Virgin Mary, the Mother of God

• Num 6:22-27 • Ps 67:2-3, 5-6, 8 • Gal 4:4-7 • Luke 2:16-21

The gospel for this feast is the same as that for the Dawn Mass of Christmas Day, except for the first verse which describes the departure of the heavenly angels and the obedience of the very human shepherds, and the last verse. This last verse is significant, as it proclaims the circumcision and naming of the child Jesus. That Mary and Joseph are obedient to the Jewish Torah is part of Luke's good news. The rite of circumcision, celebrated eight days after birth, is called the "covenant of circumcision," and marks the male child's formal entry into the covenantal Jewish community (Gen 17:10-11). Every circumcision is a call to Abraham's seed to renew the covenant but, in Jesus, the rite cuts the deepest: the covenant that is made in his flesh will one day be poured out not only in a drop of foreskin blood, but in the tortured flesh of the Son of Man and of God, crucified for the world's salvation.

At circumcision the child is also named, and Jesus is given the name that was announced to Mary before his conception (Luke 1:31): "Jesus," (or Joshua) meaning "savior." It is not just an external ritual but a matter of identity, a marking of the heart (see Jer 4:4). For present day parents, what they call their child is important: will it be a family name, one discovered by pouring over the baby name reference book, or perhaps that of the latest celebrity? The naming of the Jewish child within the circumcision rite is a significant life-cycle event, for the name links the child to past generations and expresses hope for the future. After the *Shoah*, many European Jews gave their child the name of a parent or dear relative who had perished in the Holocaust, for in such naming the memory of the dead person is symbolically "born again into the world." Jesus, Savior, is a name for all generations, for the salvation of all. Although we do not know the words of the first century rite, the prayer that accompanies the Jewish child's naming today asks: "May his heart be wide open to comprehend Thy holy will, that he may learn and teach, keep and fulfill Thy laws." Jesus would do this most faithfully. We who are named Christians are given our deepest identity by our baptism into Christ. After his resurrection, the early church repeatedly preached and worked miracles "in the name of Jesus," that is, in the power of his personal presence in the Spirit (e.g., Acts 3:6, 4:7-12).

January 1 has also been designated as the day on which the Church prays for world peace, and the Solemnity of Mary focuses our gaze on her silent wonder as she contemplates her child, trying to put together the significance of what had happened in the past nine months, dreaming about what the future might hold. In all the gospels, Mary remains a woman wrapped in silence throughout Jesus' preaching, death, and resurrection. After the resurrection, Luke will place Mary at the heart of the community of disciples, still the silent mother, drawing around her the new family of Jesus. It is the peace of Christ that we hope and pray for at the beginning of a New Year: peace in our own hearts and in our families, in our church and in our world.

The reading from the Book of Numbers is one of the oldest liturgical and poetic blessings in the Bible. It was pronounced by the priests but, as is emphasized by the triple repetition of "The Lord . . . ," it is God who blesses. God "puts his name on" his people as a sign of loving ownership that protects and graces them with an intimate relationship. All of this culminates in the gift of God's peace—peace whose opposite is not just military war, but personal and communal chaos. Does "familiarity breed contempt," especially with regard to the liturgical blessing that sends us forth from every Eucharist with the name of God and the mission and peace of Christ upon us?

The response to the first reading is from Psalm 67, a harvest song of thanksgiving for the yield of the earth. God's blessings are not only spiritual but also material. Our planet is a blessed gift from God that we can too easily and thoughtlessly destroy.

The greatest blessing of our earth came, of course, in the Incarnation, in the "fullness of time" of which Paul writes to the Galatians. This is the privileged moment when the messianic hopes of Israel take flesh in Jesus. "Born of a woman" designates Jesus as belonging to the human family; his sending as God's Son declares his divinity. The family metaphor is appropriate to this feast, and Paul also draws on the social customs of his day. If a child was too young to claim an inheritance legally, a legal guardian would be appointed until the child reached the appropriate age. The Jewish law was like such a trustworthy guardian but, with the coming of Christ, Christians are no longer minors; they have been adopted as heirs, as sons and daughters in the Son, with a new identity, a new maturity, and a liberating share in the Spirit of Jesus. The ecstatic family cry of "Abba, Father," is a profession of faith, freedom, and gratitude for this empowering gift of God offered us in Christ. It is a cry that can be not only a profoundly simple mantra for us, but also an urgent summons to live as heirs of the kingdom with respect for the humanity of our sisters and brothers and the holiness of God in whose image all of us "born of a woman," are made.

The Epiphany of the Lord

• Isa 60:1-6 • Ps 72:1-2, 7-8, 10-13 • Eph 3:2-3a, 5-6 • Matt 2:1-12

Stargazers, seekers, risk takers, outsiders who come from afar lead a procession of those who down the ages will be drawn from all the nations and guided by God to the mystery that is revealed in Christ. Each reading is radiant with the light of God's intention of salvation for all creation: for the heavens above and the earth and its peoples below. Today is a feast of manifestation (*epipháneia*), of the showing forth of Emmanuel to the nations represented by the Magi. It is another movement of the infancy overture which Matthew plays to the story of Jesus' future destiny: the religious and political intrigues of Herod who gathers the chief priests and scribes as an expedient support group, the disturbance among his lackeys in Jerusalem at the rumor about a "king of the Jews," their plotting to dispose of this "upstart" king, and the fulfillment of prophetic dreams when the risen Christ sends the eleven to make disciples of all nations with the promise that he will be Emmanuel, "God-with-us" to the end of the ages.

In T. S. Eliot's "Journey of the Magi," the three travelers reflect after their long and hard journey on where they had been led and what they had experienced. They agree that it was certainly a birth that they witnessed, but their intuition tells them that there was also death lurking in the shadows: death of their old certainties and gods, and death that would be hard and bitter for the child before whom they had knelt to worship and offer their gifts. In the symbolism of these gifts Matthew hints at the paschal mystery: the myrrh is for embalming, the frankincense for fragrancing sacrifices to be burnt before the Holy of Holies, and the gold is a fitting gift for a king.

Today is a feast of gospel reversals. Herod had taken the title of king of the Jews to himself and perverted it by his ambitious grasp for power. In contrast, Jesus was born a powerless king of the Jews, the title that will be ironically nailed to the humble throne of his cross. Historical controversies aside, the Magi thrill our imagination and bring wonder and excitement to the faith-filled search for Jesus that is the focus of every disciple's journey through life. The Magi are the surprising seeing ones, guided to Jerusalem by their own drive to seek wisdom and by nature's partial revelation in the star that rises in the east. In that city they learn where they will find the child from the special revelation of God's word and wisdom to Israel. They see through the hypocritical protestations of Herod's wish to go to pay homage himself to the newborn child. Herod and his coterie are blind; they have access to the wisdom of the Scriptures but they refuse to see the meaning of what the prophets wrote, and choose to be and to serve a corrupt earthly king. Herod is frantic at the possible risk to his power, while the Magi, aristocratic scholars from abroad, are almost naively willing to take risks and add to their scholarly wisdom the wisdom of the Hebrew Scriptures in their search for the royal child. In the wolfish company of Herod and his cohorts, Matthew sees the Magi as witnesses to the later call for all disciples to be "wise as serpents and innocent as doves" (Matt 10:16).

The beauty of this imaginative narrative encourages us to what poetry encourages us: to keen listening, to silent reflection, to transcendence of the ordinary by giving it our full attention. A star, a baby with its mother, human and holy words, can lead us with the Magi into and beyond the mystery of Christ in silent homage. In our Christmas cribs the Magi may seem "odd men out" in the humble company of Mary, Joseph, and the child. But with their traditionally turbaned heads, opulent robes, black and yellow and brown faces, they do belong there, for they are symbolic of every nation on earth that, in the words of the responsorial Psalm 72, we pray will come to adore God and participate in a kingdom of justice and peace that only God can establish, especially for the poor and needy of the earth.

As we gaze on the Magi and hear their story, are we mindful of strangers that come to our own place, not in rich robes but usually in the poverty of contemporary seekers and stargazers: the refugees and asylum seekers from many nations, those tired of hypocrisy and disillusioned about political power mongering, the young who want a star to rise in their lives that is worth following even though the journey may be difficult, the old and middle aged who still dream of something more to enlighten them? And do we not all, at some time, feel ourselves to be strangers and foreigners seeking to belong to a true home (see Eph 2:19) that will be the new Jerusalem? Genevieve Glen challenges us to see in the Christmas Child of the Epiphany and the hard journey of the Magi:

> . . . a gauntlet thrown down before the potential possessiveness of our personal and devotional spiritualities, unwilling to relinquish the pleasantly undemanding images of childishness to which we have grown accustomed for the demanding journey across desert and mountain and river to reach the place where the true Child is born. In the vulnerability of Christmas, the Child forever offers us Herod's choice. We can still our fear of the threat to our

comfort by smothering the proclamation in the tight swaddling clothes of sentimental spiritualities. Or we can lay the gift of all our inadequate images beside the gold, frankincense and myrrh, and bow the knee in worship. Then will the Child in whose image we are being made become our end . . . and our Beginning.[6]

In Isaiah's prophetic vision, the heart of sixth century B.C.E. Jerusalem expands and throbs with joy as not only abused and exiled sons and daughters stream home into her, but other nations also are drawn to Jerusalem and the new future that will be found there. Grateful for this, the nations come to despoiled Jerusalem bearing gifts of gold, frankincense, and myrrh—an obvious reason for the Lectionary's choice of this first reading as a companion to the gospel. As with the Magi many centuries later, their gifts are not only about economic prosperity but also about the worship of God. The prophet's words are full of hope and promise for a people who have been shrouded in the darkness and despair of captivity, because now the city is radiant with the glory of God who returns with and in his people. Jerusalem is not only restored; it is also given a mission to witness to this glory of God and be a light for the nations that are still shrouded in darkness. Isaiah never had our privilege of recognizing the glory of God on the face of the Christmas Child, but his hope was large and passionate.

The author of the Letter to the Ephesians also proclaims God's love and glory revealed in Jesus Christ. Regardless of where people come from or what their social or ethnic origins, all may become heirs to the same divine promises, all be part of the same body of Christ Jesus, all become one new humanity through the free workings of the Spirit. Do we really accept, do we really want such a revelation of this mystery of Christ?

The Christmas season will soon be over, but the *epipháneia* of its mystery must lead us to make more than a "courtesy call" to a crib. It must draw us into a lifelong and hard but joyous journey toward the vision of a new and reconciled humanity united in Christ; to a personal experience of a birth, a death, and a resurrection.

The Baptism of the Lord

• Isa 42:1-4, 6-7 • Ps 29:1-4, 9-10 • Acts 10:34-38 • Matt 3:13-17

Today we witness Jesus' first adult appearance and hear his first words in Matthew's Gospel. When Jesus insists that he needs to be baptized by John, John at first protests that it should be he, the Baptist, who is baptized by Jesus. The lamp speaks to the Sun, the voice to the Word, the friend to the Bridegroom, but this is how it is to be for now, says Jesus. He will be baptized not for repentance, but for solidarity with the sinful, burdened humanity of which he has taken flesh. The Incarnation is God's most radical way of fulfilling "all righteousness," that is, of bringing everyone and everything into right personal and cosmic relationship with God through obedience to what God desires.

As destructive as a tsunami, as welcome as drought-breaking rain, water is an ambivalent symbol for both life and death through the whole Bible, from its first chapter in Genesis (Gen 1:2) to its last chapter in Revelation (Rev 22:1-2). Jesus is the humble servant who will be engulfed in the flood of passion and death, yet from this he will rise to the new life that transforms the whole of creation. Matthew, post-Pentecostal evangelist, cannot look at either the water-drenched Jesus on the Jordan banks or his baptized community from any perspective other than that of the paschal mystery. This is the perspective that is expressed in the inscription on the ancient baptistery of the Roman Basilica of St. John Lateran, the "mother church" of the world:

> . . . This is the fountain of life,
> which purges the whole world,
> taking its course
> from the wound of Christ.
> Hope for the Kingdom of heaven,
> you who are born in this font.

Here on the banks of the Jordan there is a new epiphany of the adult Jesus' identity and mission already revealed at his conception and birth (Matt 1:18-25; 2:1-12). Isaiah's cry for the heavens to be rent open so that God might come to his people (Isa 64:1) is quietly answered; the Spirit hovers gently over Jesus as it brooded over the face of the deep (Gen 1:2), and the voice from heaven acclaims not only to Jesus but to the onlookers, that in him there is a new creation: "This is my Son, the Beloved, with whom I am well pleased."

We who are baptized into Christ have the same assurance; we are beloved sons and daughters of God, not because of any good works we have done or may do in the future, but simply because of God's gift of union with his Son. Nowhere is God's generous graciousness more obvious than in infant baptism (and especially when this is by immersion). The small, vulnerable child who is plunged into the font has offered God no obedience—except that of being born. The assembly claps and smiles, and wonders what this naked and dripping child will be, what joy will flood her or his life, what chaos may threaten. . . . Yet we believe that in the water the child has been reborn as a descendant of Jesus, a survivor of death, a lover of life. To live as such, to say "yes" to this identity in the years ahead, is the baptismal challenge.

By juxtaposing what God speaks through the prophet Isaiah and Matthew's gospel, the Lectionary asks us to reflect on the servanthood of "my chosen, in whom my soul delights." For Isaiah, the coming of this elusive, mysterious individual or communal Servant remained a hope that he would never see realized. Six centuries later, God will empower Jesus, the Beloved, to carry out the Servant's mission, and it is not hard to imagine that, as he tried to discern the implications of his own mission, Jesus would have searched his Hebrew Scriptures, especially the prophets such as Isaiah. Endowed with God's spirit, the Isaian Servant is called three times in four verses to establish true justice among the nations. This justice will not be judgmental, but consoling; it will not crush those already bruised by suffering, nor extinguish their flickering hope. In Matthew's theology, the Beloved Son of God is servant of the marginalized, the disregarded, the disadvantaged, the broken. Later in his gospel, in the context of Jesus' healing ministry, Matthew will quote explicitly from this first Suffering Servant Song (Matt 12:17-21). For the servant, God will have an intimate, sustaining covenant love that will also lead him beyond Israel to heal, enlighten, and deliver the nations from darkness.

In the responsorial Psalm 29, the psalmist hears God's voice resounding through the cosmos, thundering on the waters, awesome in the mighty storm. But this strong and glorious God will bless his people with peace. At the Jordan waters, the voice of the Father is gentler, as will be the Son's, but in the Son the ultimate power over the chaos of death will be realized, and the blessing of peace bestowed.

In his speech to the Gentile God-seeking centurion, Cornelius, this is how Peter describes Jesus. Anointed by God with the Holy Spirit and with power, Jesus went around "doing good and healing all who were oppressed," creating *shalom*, peace, out of the chaos of human suffering. Now Peter has entered into what, for a law-abiding Jew, was the turbulence of the Gentile world; he risks the condemnation of the law as "unclean" because he enters into a Gentile house. But Peter has been enlightened by the Spirit (Acts 10:1-33), and now understands that not only is there no food that should be ritually unacceptable but, also and more important, there is no human being who is unacceptable to God. "God shows no partiality" for any nation, gender, status. It is regrettable that the Lectionary did not continue for a few more verses so that we might hear of the descent of the Spirit in a Gentile Pentecost before Peter finishes speaking. The confirming choice is

God's, not Peter's. The apostle simply affirms this election by baptizing Cornelius and his household.

In the liturgical calendar, this Sunday is both the last Sunday of the Season of Christmas and the first of Ordinary Time. The Church does not want us to forget our joy at the birth of Jesus, but reminds us that to be true to this we need to be reborn and renewed every day in the Spirit of Jesus, that we need to go forward through the weeks of the year as women and men on whom the baptismal water is never dry, as those who will work for justice, for right relationships with God and with one another, as people who will be impartial in our love, and gently generous in our service.

Notes

1. *Deus Caritas Est*, par. 12.

2. Francis Webb, "Five Days Old," *Cap and Bells: The Poetry of Francis Webb* (North Ryde, NSW: HarperRow Publishers, An Angus and Robertson Book, 1991) 156–57.

3. Normand Bonneau, o.m.i., *The Sunday Lectionary: Ritual Word, Paschal Shape* (Collegeville: Liturgical Press, 1998) 111.

4. Vatican II, *Decree on the Apostolate of the Laity*, art. 11.

5. Vatican II, *Pastoral Constitution on the Church in the Modern World*, art. 32.

6. Genevieve Glen, "What Child Is This?," *Assembly* 11, no. 2 (November 1984): 269.

3

The Season of Lent

We are dust from our birth
But in that dust is wrought

A place for visions, a hope
That reaches beyond the stars . . . .[1]

So reflected the poet Elizabeth Jennings. And so, too, does the church reflect as we enter every year into Lent, touched with dust. That this dust is "wrought" in the sign of our salvation on our foreheads on Ash Wednesday reminds us that we are entering the season that leads "beyond the stars" to the great hope and vision of Easter. At no other time in our adult life is our Christian identity so visibly marked on our skin. We were first marked with the cross at baptism, proudly made royal, priestly, and prophetic, but through the years this identity has been damaged, although never completely destroyed, by our sinfulness. The Lenten anointing is a rougher, grittier, dirtier marking, and is accompanied by the stark words: "Remember that you are dust, and unto dust you will return" or the demanding words: "Repent and believe in the Gospel."

Ideally, the ashes with which we are anointed at the beginning of Lent should not come from a screw top jar in the sacristy cupboard, but from the burning of last Passion Sunday's palms (or other branches) which we have brought to Mass three days before and watched being burned. We held those palm branches in our hands when we cried out or sang our "Hosannas" a year ago. When we came home that day we may have put the palms on our wall, behind a crucifix where they became dusty and brittle, or just thrown them out. Our discipleship can be like that: sometimes discarded, often crumbling. Through prayer, fasting, and almsgiving during the weeks of Lent, we are preparing for Christ to again cast his holy Easter fire upon our forgetful discipleship, the dryness of our faith, the brittleness of our patience and peace. Mixed with the waters of baptism, the promises of which we will renew at the Easter Vigil, our dust and ashes become a rich and fertile soil for the gospel seed to grow within our hearts and transform us.

The liturgical reforms of Vatican II restored the baptismal orientation of Lent, and this is most consciously celebrated if the parish community has catechumens who are following the Rite of Christian Initiation of Adults (RCIA) and have been received as the elect just before or at the beginning of Lent. Gathered around and with these elect at the scrutinies of the third, fourth, and fifth Sundays of Lent, the members of the parish community will scrutinize their own hearts and commit themselves to ongoing conversion from sin and witness of their fidelity to the elect. This is a pilgrimage on which we are led by the crucified and risen Christ, through all that has turned to dust and ashes in our lives, toward the new life of Easter.

First Sunday of Lent

• Gen 2:7-9; 3:1-7 • Ps 51:3-4, 5-6, 12-13, 14, 17 • Rom 5:12-19 • Matt 4:1-11

On this First Sunday of Lent, we are invited to enter into two privileged biblical places, the garden and the desert, and reflect on the testing of our fidelity to God in these symbolic contexts.

On Ash Wednesday we were reminded that, as in the initial story we hear in the Genesis reading, each of us has been scooped from the soil, that the dust or clay (Hebrew *adamah*) of our humanity (*adam*) is always fresh upon us. Our potter God has lovingly, painstakingly shaped us, and the spirit of our creating God is breathed into the clay to imprint every human being as the masterpiece of God's hands. The dust of the ground and breath are both good, both gifts of God, both realities of our existence as "living beings," but both need to be kept in balance if we are to live in harmony with God, with ourselves, with other people, and with the whole of creation.[2] Too often we flirt with the temptation to disharmony, to smothering the Spirit/Breath and living more as women and men of dust, despite the gifts with which God surrounds us. This is the situation of humankind in the Genesis story. God has created man and woman, placed them in a garden where not only their needs for bodily nourishment can be satisfied but where they can also nourish themselves from the tree of life. The tree of the knowledge of good and evil is mentioned in today's reading, but not God's command to refrain from eating it (Gen 2:17) under pain of death. The garden is God's gift, but God puts limitations on the use of its gifts, for the sake of the man's and woman's wellbeing. God's creatures are to live according to the Creator's will, and human life will always involve permission and prohibition.

Into this paradise of Eden enters the crafty Serpent. A creature that appears "naked," it slithers into a conversation with the woman. It is not the "talking snake" that is the focus of the narrative, but the content of the conversation which exposes the woman's temptation that we can all recognize: the temptation to deny who and what we are, to refuse our creaturehood, and want to be "like God," to overreach and take what is not ours. There are subtle shifts, small deliberate distortions of the word of God on the part of both the Serpent and the woman, and so the choice is made; God does not create human beings to be programmed puppets controlled by divine strings. As Shakespeare would later write with his insight into our humanity: "Things sweet to taste prove in digestion sour."[3] Although the dialogue has concentrated on the woman, the man is with her; their sin is social. There is no suggestion of the man being seduced by the woman; they sin as a pair, in solidarity that distorts their togetherness. Their relationship is now less like what God intended, and more like the Serpent: a naked exposure that causes them to gaze on each other with an unrestrained desire and shame that acknowledges their separateness from God, from one another, and from the primeval unity of creation.

This is the timeless human predicament that the Church confronts us with at the beginning of Lent. We are greedy for life and blessings, arrogant in our refusals to admit that we do not know everything, that the God who created us is entitled to ask us to trust our greatest good to him. We can deny who we are and what God wants us to be: baptized sons and daughters of a loving Father. We can forget that every sin has a social dimension, is not just "between me and God" but has implications for the human community and the cosmos. Vatican II restored the social perspective to the sacraments, especially in the reformation of the rites of the Sacrament of Penance. *The Constitution on the Sacred Liturgy* reminds us of the baptismal roots of our identity, and puts this into the context of our Lenten penance which "should not be only internal and individual, but also external and social" (arts. 109-110). That is what sin is, that is what our Lenten discipline should be. How can we fast that others may be fed? Is our prayer self-centered or does it reach out in praise and lamentation and intercession for our world? And is our almsgiving comfortable or costly?

Immediately after his baptism, the Beloved Son is led by the Spirit into the wilderness for his testing. Whether we choose to see this forty-day temptation as telescoped into a single event or stretching through his whole life, in his own personal history Jesus recapitulates the history of his people, God's people, in their forty-year wilderness experience—and he proves to be the most faithful Israelite. Like the man and woman in Eden, like ourselves, Jesus will spend his life making choices. At his baptism he was named as God's Son, the Beloved, and in the wilderness he will be tested in his fidelity to this identity and in obedience to his Father. Fasting from physical food, feasting on the Spirit, Jesus is famished, and at this low point in his resistance the Tempter or Devil slithers in to put him to the test three times in a verbal battle where the word of God is misused by Satan and used correctly and faithfully by Jesus. By putting nothing but the words of the Hebrew Scriptures (from the Book of Deuteronomy) on Jesus' lips, Matthew witnesses to his readers and listeners, including our eucharistic assembly, the significance of the Word of God as a "sword of the Spirit" (Eph 6:17) in the fight against temptation. Matthew is not concerned with how Jesus thought of himself, but with how the Christians of his and future Christian communities would think about Jesus.

Jesus is the trusting Son of God who will not overreach his humanity and ask for miraculous exceptions to an authentic human life. Hunger and vulnerability go together, and the first temptation is for Jesus to work a miracle and command the stones to become bread. Imagine the social ramifications of this! But for Jesus there is a time for miracles and a time for refraining from miracles. The Hebrews in the desert grumbled and tried to manipulate God's will, demanding food from heaven and then becoming dissatisfied with the manna, so Jesus' response to this first temptation is the reminder that "one does not live by bread alone, but by every word that comes from the mouth of God" (see Deut 8:3). Is this word our sustaining nourishment, or are we more addicted to overeating, to junk food, to keeping a full food and drink cupboard while millions of our sisters and brothers go hungry? The "miracle" that will turn stones into bread for the hungry will happen when, as individuals and local communities, we share our wealth with the poor and hungry, and when we responsibly vote for politicians who, through global and national action, will really "Make Poverty History."

The devil then takes Jesus up to a high part of the Jerusalem Temple, and tempts him to another miracle: the suspension of what we would call the laws of gravity. Let Jesus toss himself off this pinnacle and force God's hand so that angels will catch him. But Jesus has other "wings" that will save him: his trust in God's loving protection (Ps 91:4), and again he refuses to put God to the test (see Deut 6:16). We may wish for, pray for the miraculous intervention of God in our lives, but often this has much to do with our self-centeredness and little to do with faith in God's care for us.

Finally, the devil takes Jesus up a high mountain, and there presents himself as the one with dominion over the powers of the world. In Matthew's Gospel, the mountain is a privileged place of God's revelation, not the devil's (Matt 5–7; 17:1-9). Jesus will have nothing to do with the seductions of political power and wealth. He will be the powerless servant, but the one who has the authority to command, "Away with you, Satan!" because homage is due to God alone (Deut 6:13). At the end of Matthew's Gospel, after Jesus has passed through the wilderness of suffering and death and has been exalted in his resurrection, he will stand on another mountain with his disciples, and there they will worship him with a very human mixture of faith and doubt. Jesus, the Son of God, then gives them a share in his authority so that they may go to make disciples of all nations, baptizing them, and teaching them to obey all that Jesus has taught them (Matt 28:16-20).

In his Letter to the Romans, Paul sees sin and death as tyrannical powers that were unleashed by Adam's sin. Adam is representative of humankind, of all men and women, and a dark foil to Jesus Christ, the Second Adam, who personifies and effects God's grace that overcomes sin. This grace is offered to humanity and claimed by those who accept the gift of faith. What Adam did, Christ undid; where Adam failed, Christ succeeded; where death reigned in Eden through disobedience, so much more will life reign through the obedience of Christ. Like Matthew, Paul focuses our gaze on Jesus, on his obedience and mercy. With this focus, human frailty and sinfulness fade into the background.

In all our deserts—in our personal and communal illusions, in our failures to trust God, in our acceptance of the superficial glitter of appearances, in our lust for small and greater power, we turn to God, and in the words of Psalm 51, we pray: "Have mercy on me, O God, according to your steadfast love."

Second Sunday of Lent

• Gen 12:1-4a • Ps 33:4-5, 18-20, 22 • 2 Tim 1:8b-10 • Matt 17:1-9

The Jewish rabbis maintain that to understand the meaning of a passage of Scripture, one should read what comes immediately before and after. This is important for the gospel that we have come to call the "transfiguration" of Jesus, although a better description might be "transformation." In the preceding verses (Matt 16:21-28) Jesus has told his disciples that he is to be a suffering Messiah, handed over to his enemies, put to death, and then raised on the third day. Peter is the spokesman for the bemused disciples, determined to "exorcise" (the meaning of "rebuke") Jesus of the possession of such a crazy idea! But it is Peter who must be exorcised of his misunderstanding. To be a disciple of Jesus means taking up the cross and following him; there is no other way into glory. So, "six days later," Jesus takes the privileged inner circle of disciples, Peter, James, and John, up a high mountain to give them a glimpse of this glory. Just as Moses had glimpsed the glory of God after six days on Mount Sinai (Exod 24:15-18), and Daniel had seen the vision of the radiant Ancient of Days (Dan 7:9), Jesus will allow these disciples a glimpse of divine glory erupting through his humanity. Clay and dust and suffering are not the whole story—neither for Jesus nor for us.

The face and garments of Jesus become transformed. The glory of God shines on the face of Jesus and the dazzling white of his clothes radiates his holy identity. Two of his ancestors, Moses and Elijah, appear in conversation with him. Both of these were men of the mountains who had experienced both suffering and glory in their leadership of God's people; both had gone to the mountain of Sinai to seek the wisdom that they needed on the plains (Exod 19:3-9; 1 Kgs 19:8-13). They talk with Jesus who is both in continuity *with* and the fulfillment *of* the law and the prophets. Then Peter makes what he thinks is his own brilliant suggestion: that Jesus, Moses, and Elijah be settled down here in three tents (or booths), which Peter will build in order to celebrate a kind of extended Feast of Booths/Tabernacles. Since childhood, Jesus and the disciples had celebrated this feast, so Peter grasps at an action that will restore some familiarity to this unfamiliar event. But the Transfiguration is not about slipping back into the security of the past, not about settling down, and what seems to Peter to be his dazzling contribution to the scenario is immediately overshadowed as the Father takes the initiative and tents over the mountain with a bright cloud. Peter's words are silenced by the voice from the cloud: "This is my Son, the Beloved; with him I am well pleased; listen to him." The identity of the Son was proclaimed at his baptism, but now the command to "listen to him" is added. To understand Jesus, the disciples must listen and listen and listen about what Jesus says about suffering and death and resurrection; they must hear his good news that is announced in his transfiguration of crippled bodies and minds into whole and healed humanity, in the transfiguration of sinners through forgiveness, in the transfiguration of bread and wine into his body and blood. And after they have seen Jesus on another hill, raised up and broken on a cross, they will learn to believe in the transfiguration that brings him from the tomb to the mountain of their great commissioning by Jesus, the risen and glorified One.

As a sign of this transfiguration that is to come, Jesus touches and raises the disciples from their fear—fear of what might be the implications of this mountain revelation for themselves. Then they see "no one except Jesus" on the mountain. For all disciples in every age, he is the one whom we must trust to grasp us, raise us up from our fears, and lead us into the new. As Jesus tells Peter, James, and John, they are to say nothing about him until they have understood that both suffering and glory belong in his mystery.

Immediately after the mountain transfiguration, down on the plain, Jesus will heal and transfigure the lives of an epileptic boy and his father. This is where transfiguration belongs: not only in the privileged peak experiences of our lives, but also in the trudge across the flat plains of the everyday. In Lent, our prayer, fasting, and almsgiving are the practices that will help transform us into the likeness of Jesus as we journey toward the celebration of his Easter glory.

Peter may have wanted to settle down on the mountain, but in the first reading we hear how Abram (Abraham) was ready to move on when God called him to leave the three realities that defined a person in the ancient world—country, kindred, and home—and set out for a land that God would show him. Abram leaves his past origins, his present place in society, and his future inheritance, and trusts in God's promise to bless him and make him a blessing to a new family of the nations. God speaks; Abram obeys. He is, as the first Eucharistic Prayer describes him, "our father in the faith," modeling the ready obedience that would be most perfectly lived by "Jesus the Messiah, the son of David, the son of Abraham" (Matt 1:1). Our response to this reading, in the words of Psalm 33, is praise for God's loving kindness (ḥesed) for those who trust and hope in God. The psalmist names God as "our shield," and images on ancient monuments and carvings throw light on this naming. In ancient warfare, shields were carried by shield bearers who went ahead of those needing protection, putting themselves in danger. God, our shield, goes ahead of us, accompanying us in danger and, in Christ, dying for our salvation.

A disciple of Paul, or someone close to him who was a sympathetic commentator on Paul's life and mission, may have written the Second Letter to Timothy. Whether authored by such a commentator or by Paul himself, it reflects Paul's loneliness and suffering in prison as his death approaches. There is no self-pity, no regret over the hardships Paul has to endure. He knows himself to be called to holiness and blessed by a gracious God, so that whatever he suffers is a suffering with Christ for the sake of the Gospel. Timothy is encouraged to follow Paul's example, not because of any pride Paul takes in his own faithfulness, but because God's grace will enable Timothy, as it does Paul, to endure the weakness that is a necessary complement to an experience of God's power. In a culture where the "honor-shame" ethic was so significant, Paul charges Timothy not to be ashamed of his discipleship to one whom many would regard as put to a shameful death. By enduring such a death, Jesus destroyed its power. No longer death's prisoner, Christ rose to new life. Such is the freedom which Paul, a prisoner now, will one day attain through his enduring faithfulness to "our Savior Jesus Christ."

Two weeks into our Lenten journey, today's readings offer us, as support for our faith, the example of those who are our ancestors in the faith. Abraham goes forth supported by God's word and promises; despite his suffering, Paul reaches out to offer support to Timothy; Jesus needed the support of Moses and Elijah (especially when his disciples were offering little), but he himself is the ultimate support who will touch us and lift us up from fear and misunderstanding. To "chew" and devour these scriptures (see Jer 15:16; Ezek 3:1-3; Rev 10:8-11), to try to savor their sweetness during the coming week, will help us continue to be transfigured into the mystery of Christ and be a blessing to our sisters and brothers whom we serve on the daily "plain."

Third Sunday of Lent

• Exod 17:3-7 • Ps 95:1-2, 6-9 • Rom 5:1-2, 5-8 • John 4:5-42

In the gospels of this and the next two Sundays we see how several individuals become aware of who Jesus is and what faith in him will demand. Jesus' encounter with the Samaritan woman reads in some ways like poetry as it plays with images: pairing, contrasting, moving between double meanings. This is especially true of the central image of water. Water is an ambivalent symbol of both life and death; in today's readings it is the former. Water is contained literally in the thirst-quenching well of Jacob in Sychar, yet it will also, figuratively, become a spring that gushes up to eternal life; from being water drawn from the well in the woman's water jar, it becomes a reality in her personal depths from which she draws life and gives testimony to the Messiah.

This gospel has an added significance for the worshipping communities in which there are candidates preparing to enter the waters of Easter baptism, for on this and the next two Sundays the scrutinies are celebrated after the homily. Those now called "the elect" stand with their godparents and sponsors before the parish community to pray together the intercessory prayers that are to help them scrutinize their hearts in these last weeks of their journey to baptism. And the elect also call us, the already baptized, to scrutinize our own fidelity to the mystery of living water into which we have been plunged and for which, like the Samaritan woman, we must continually thirst.

Jesus has turned his back on Judea where, in the three verses immediately preceding the Lectionary text, we hear that there was a debate among some of his opponents about who was winning more disciples—Jesus or John. Compiling comparative statistics of successful religious affiliation seems to disgust Jesus, so he goes back to Galilee by way of Samaria, "enemy territory," and comes to Sychar, the place of Jacob's well. What is one of the longest and most Spirit-filled conversations in all the gospels, begins not with "God-talk," but with the shared and elemental human experiences of weariness, hunger, and thirst; not with discussion with other faithful Jews, and male Jews at that, but with a woman belonging to the Samaritans with whom orthodox Jewish believers had relationships of national, religious, and political enmity. Samaritans were the reviled remnant of the ancient northern kingdom, regarded and despised as hybrid Jews who, having excluded themselves from Jewish orthodoxy, were regarded as worse than the Gentiles.

None of this extraordinary encounter could have happened if Jesus had not been the most radical liberator who breaks taboos and crosses boundaries. He asks the Samaritan woman for a drink, crossing gender, national, religious, and moral boundaries. He is free to be fully human, humbly admitting his exhaustion, and asking a despised woman for a drink. For people in barren lands, the well is a source of life-giving water; in the biblical world it was also the place of covenant making and betrothal. For example, Isaac and Rebekah (Gen 24:45-48), Jacob and Rachel (Gen 29:1-13), Moses and Zipporah (Exod 2:16-21) all meet and pledge themselves to one another at wells. When John wrote his gospel he was well aware that Samaria had been the first region beyond Jerusalem to receive the good news (Acts 8:2-9; 9:31), and so it had moved from being a despised people with "no husband" to being "betrothed" to Christ. So in his chapter 4, John combines the characteristic attitudes and actions of the Johannine Christ with the symbolism of encounters at the well and the strong belief of the evangelist's community in the validity of the acceptance of Jesus. John is writing after the fact of the historical acceptance of the Gospel, but sees it as what it truly is: an encounter with Jesus through the preaching of the early church. An intelligent, daring *woman* is at the center of the shocking inclusiveness for which our contemporary church is still striving.

Then, as now, Jesus makes those who respond to him into sharers in his freedom. The despised woman, who comes to the well at high noon to avoid the judgmental eyes and tongues of the other women at the usual drawing time of morning and evening, hurries back to her own town. She is no longer ashamed of the story of her life because she has a more urgent story to tell about the man who lowered a bucket into the well of her soul and drew up the deep living water within her. Now she can leave behind her usual water jar. She has been helped to see what she was looking for, what her own inner reality and truth are, and that she must worship the God in this spirit and truth. John presents us with a "litany" of names for Jesus. First the woman speaks to him as "Jew," then "prophet"; as she hesitates to call him "Messiah," or "Christ," Jesus reveals himself as the one anointed with the Holy Name, the "I AM," "YHWH," in his human presence; and after Jesus has stayed in the woman's Samaritan city, its inhabitants name him as "Savior of the world."

When the disciples return with food, they are shocked, not so much because Jesus has been talking with a Samaritan, but because he has been relating to a woman! What Jesus tells them is that he has food that they know nothing about: the woman's questions, her insights, her energy and acceptance have nourished Jesus, for in such an encounter he is doing the will of the One who sent him and sowing in Samaria the grain that will be harvested for eternal life.

The woman announces to her Samaritan village what she experienced with Jesus, but until they have experienced him personally they cannot truly believe. Only then can he be named "Savior of the world." This is the faith that calls us, with the elect of our parish communities, to a scrutiny of what quenches our deepest "thirsts," what nourishes our spirits as well as our bodies. Do pleasure, power, exclusiveness satisfy us? With what "enemy" are we unwilling to sit and talk, to eat and drink? How tolerant are we of those who belong to other religious or cultural traditions? Do we believe in the value of creative conversation, even when exhausted, even with our own young people who may have questions—sometimes abrasive, often welling up from deep longings within them? Can we move out of our comfort zones, leave our old "water jars" behind and welcome the gifts of God that are being offered to us, especially in this privileged season of Lent?

The Exodus reading chosen for today proclaims God's faithfulness to his people, even when they show how shallow is their faith in the divine promises. At Massah ("testing") and Meriba ("dissatisfaction") the Israelites grumble: "Is the Lord with us or not?" But once again God answers their complaints with an abundantly gracious response. Not acting alone, but with some of the significant leaders, Moses obeys God's command. He takes up the rod, that symbol of the saving authority of God that Moses had stretched out over the Sea of Reeds to enable a safe Passover for the people (see Exod 14:16). With it, he strikes the rock, and life-giving water flows from what was hard and dry. Lent is the season when the church calls us to strike the rock of our hard hearts with the rods of fasting, prayer, and alms-giving, assuring us, as Jesus assured the Samaritan woman, that God will increase in our personal depths the flow of the life-giving spring of grace. For us, this source is our baptism; for the elect, this is their thirst. In the "today" of our liturgical assembly, we respond by praying Psalm 95 and ad-mitting that we are the hard-hearted grumblers who so often fail to trust our provident God. Yet we are also God's "flock" who struggle along to the pastures of word and sacrament, praising God and hoping in salvation.

Such a hope is not deceptive, Paul tells us in his Letter to the Romans, because the faithful love of God shown us in Christ is poured into our hearts by the Holy Spirit. We are loved not because we are perfect, but be-cause we are weak. What really proves that God loves us is that Christ died for us as sinners. Through our sins we are flawed and wounded men and women, but the Easter mystery toward which Lent is leading us reminds us that the body of the risen Christ still shines with wounds. Through him and in him, our flaws have been glorified.

Fourth Sunday of Lent

• 1 Sam 16:1b, 6-7, 10-13a • Ps 23:1-6 • Eph 5:8-14 • John 9:1-41

Sometimes a personal or historical event opens our eyes to a truth to which we have been blind. It might be the revelation of extraordinary human dignity and endurance of the victims in the face of natural disasters or accidents, and the compassion of volunteers who flock to help them. Or it might be the shocking images of the unconcern and blind indifference of those who see no reason to be involved, to interrupt a pleasant holiday, or who indulge in "politic-speak" without action.

In a well-known and much loved hymn, there is a line taken directly from today's gospel. It was written by a man who had experienced such a revelation that he could write: "I once was blind, but now I see." The mo-ment of "Amazing Grace" came for John Newton on March 21, 1748. Caught in a raging storm, he had tied himself to the helm of his battered ship. A sailor from the age of eleven, he had been involved in slave-trading, and his coarseness had earned for him the nickname of "the Great Blas-phemer." From his childhood memory of his mother's Christian faith, a prayer for deliverance was sucked out of Newton by the storm, and: "On that day the Lord sent from on high and delivered me out of deep water." He subsequently left slave trading and, in 1764, at the age of thirty-nine, became a minister, beginning a forty-three year ministry of preaching and hymn writing. In 1805, aged 82, he was still writing in his diary on the anniversary of the day of "amazing grace": "Not well able to write; but I endeavor to observe the return of this day with humiliation, prayer, and praise."[4]

John's dramatic ninth chapter that describes the healing of the blind man, and the range of responses to it, is played out against the background of the Jewish Feast of Sukkoth or Booths mentioned in John 7:2. For this feast, the people build small portable booths as a reminder of the fragile existence their ancestors experienced in the wilderness. Sukkoth is not a celebration of the Passover event, but of the daily challenges of existence after the Passover: the maturation of the Israelites as they walked the long road to freedom. As one Jewish commentator has written, Passover celebrates with a festive meal; Sukkoth marks the hasty lunches, the cleanups during the wanderings, the moving on. It is a celebration of faithful endurance. Part of the ancient liturgy of the feast was the daytime water-drawing ceremony when, amid much singing and dancing, the priests drew the "first water" (of the autumn rains) from the Pool of Siloam (meaning "sent") into which flowed Jerusalem's chief spring. They then carried it to the Temple and poured it out as a libation, with prayer for a plentiful rainfall in the coming months and the memory of the scarcity of water in the wilderness. The other aspect of the feast was the lighting of huge menorahs (branched candlesticks) that illumined the Temple area during the seven-day festival. Against this backdrop of water and light, John situates the healing of the man born blind.

Nobody brings the blind man to Jesus; the man himself makes no approach to Jesus. What seems to be the catalyst for the miracle is the distorted vision of his disciples who see the man's blindness as caused either by his own sins or those of his parents. Jesus refutes this cause-and-effect. What is to be revealed is not the cause of sin but the manifestation of God's grace by the Sent One who is the light of the world. And Jesus' disciples are to be associated in this: "We must work the works of him who sent me," says Jesus. The Light of the world is to be carried through the world by his disciples.

For those seeking Easter baptism and today celebrating the second scrutiny, and for all the baptized, the good news of John 9 is that sin has nothing to do with physical or mental sickness, or with intellectual disability, but everything to do with one's blindness to the revelation of God in Jesus. To believe is to come to the light; to disbelieve is to be spiritually blind and walk in darkness.

The stuff of the miracle is spittle, mud, and the fingers of Jesus—the first two the images of messiness and the stuff of folkloric healing—but both transformed by the humanity of Jesus and the power of his outstretched hand which reveals the creative work of God (e.g., Deut 26:8) as incarnate and continuing in him. The blind man, however, must also do his part, must obey Jesus, the Sent One (John 7:28-29; 10:36; 12:44-45), and go to the Pool of Siloam to wash his eyes. Then the blind man will see and himself become a sent one, a witness to what has happened to him not merely physically, but also because the eyes of his spirit have been opened to the truth of Jesus.

The healed man immediately becomes the center of attention and controversy, yet he remains steadfast in his witness to Jesus as the one who healed him, and secure in his identity as the "born blind" but now re-created and seeing one. A cast of players appears on stage: neighbors, Pharisees, parents. The man's witness to Jesus is the cause of division among the religious leaders, those supposed to be insightful but blind to the truth about Jesus. Like the Pharisees with their Sabbath myopia, we can misjudge others because of our ingrained religious prejudices; like the man's parents, we can be too frightened to get involved in any controversy, especially with a powerful yet unjust authority. There is so much finger pointing in this gospel, so much accusation of sinfulness. The man born blind, his parents, and Jesus himself are all accused by Jesus' opponents. Abandoned by his neighbors, rejected by his parents, driven away by the Pharisees, the once-blind man is found again by Jesus in the last few verses. In the absence of Jesus, he has clung to the strange new experience of light. Just as the Samaritan woman progressively named Jesus with greater insight as her faith in him grew, so with this man. From simply knowing him as called Jesus (v. 11), he calls him a prophet (v. 17), and proclaims he comes from God (v. 33). As always, Jesus seeks out the abandoned one, and finds him in the Temple. When Jesus reveals his identity, the man makes his profession of faith: "Lord, I believe." And he worships this Son of Man.

As individuals and communities, this gospel challenges us to examine how we see with the eyes of faith and how we are willfully blind to the Sent One, turning away from the Light of the world. What are our contemporary blindnesses? Sin sells newspapers, so the media says. Are we more interested in sin than in grace? Are we brave enough to accept being sometimes ostracized by others when we choose to walk in the light of Christ rather than stumble away from him along our complacent, selfish, and socially pressurized paths of darkness. The second reading from the Letter to the Ephesians reminds us that when we are committed to Christ in baptism we become children of the light. Much earlier in this Letter the author had prayed that his community might have "the eyes of your heart enlightened" (Eph 1:18), and today we hear that this enlightenment is to be made public and visible as the Ephesians live their new identity with moral excellence, in right relationship with God, and in the truthfulness that opposes hypocrisy. The light of Christ that shines through such lives will expose the darkness of shameful living. The reading closes with what was almost certainly part of an ancient baptismal hymn that sings its promise of life and light in Christ into the hearts and hopes of those about to be baptized and already baptized.

In the first reading, the prophet Samuel is told by God to take no notice of outward appearances when searching for a king among the sons of Jesse, for God looks at people's hearts. The one chosen to shepherd is the last son, the youngest, the one, humanly speaking, who is hardly considered a viable choice. As eighth son, he is at the bottom of the familial pecking order, and seems a considerable political risk. But he is God's chosen one. The blind man was anointed with mud, David is anointed with oil, we are anointed by baptism. And most of us, apparently very ordinary people with not much potential, not much claim to social greatness, have been seized by the transforming power of God's spirit which comes mightily upon us from that day of baptism throughout our lives. As Christians, we have a royal and messianic identity more real than David's.

We find the biblical images of darkness and light and water not only in the gospel, but also in the responsorial Psalm 23. Together we sing our faith that, led by our shepherding God, we will come through the dark valleys, find the restful waters, and dwell in the house of the Lord for ever and ever.

Fifth Sunday of Lent

• Ezek 37:12-14 • Ps 130:1-8 • Rom 8:8-11 • John 11:1-45

In *Crime and Punishment*, Fyodor Dostoyevsky describes the brilliant but crazed Rodion Raskolnikov who, tortured and on the brink of mad despair by his self-doubt and self-hatred of himself as a murderer, is living a life that is more like death. When he meets Sonya, a prostitute who works the streets to support her family, he considers that there are only three future options open to her: she will accommodate herself to what he considers her disgusting trade, or she will go mad because of the pressure and tensions in her life, or she will commit suicide to escape from prostitution. But Sonya does not agree that these are the only choices possible for her. Rodion forces her to reveal what is her saving secret, and eventually Sonya reads to him the story of the raising of Lazarus. And she reads it from the

Bible given her by the woman whom he has murdered. To her, it is a precious story that gives her hope that one day she will "come out" of her life of degradation. For the skeptic Rodion, it is symbolic of the death of his soul. Yet in the epilogue, Rodion, now in a Siberian prison camp and loved by Sonya, reaches for the same book of the gospels and rereads the story of Lazarus. He reads with hope . . . hope of a return to his humanity, hope in someone who loves him, hope in his chance to be "resurrected."

This is what today's gospel proclaims: that no one is so far gone into death that Jesus cannot call him or her back to life, for he *is* the resurrection and the life which is more than just physical life, in the present as well as on the other side of death. John 11 is both a touching human narrative and a profound theological statement. The gospel shows us Jesus unbinding his disciples and his friends from their partial faith and calling them to unbind Lazarus. Now as then, Jesus knows our struggles, will stand by the grave of our dead hopes, will weep with us in our pain and loss, and will reveal to us the glory of God that frees us from death if we believe in him as the resurrection and life in all those events when something in us seems to have died. Like Sonya, the option of this saving faith is always open to us.

When Jesus receives from Martha and Mary the news that his friend, Lazarus, is sick, he delays for several days to come out of the safe place across the Jordan to which he had withdrawn to escape arrest (John 10:39-40) and go to Bethany. The disciples misunderstand Jesus' reference to Lazarus as "asleep," responding that sleeping is a good sign that Lazarus will recover. Jesus then tells them bluntly that "Lazarus is dead," and that what he is about to do is not just a private favor for Martha and Mary but a public, culminating revelation of his own personal truth, for the sake of God's glory. Soon will come the darkness of Jesus' passion, death, and tomb dwelling; the time of his mission in this world is limited, just as the hours of daylight are limited. Thomas expresses what must have been each disciple's reaction to what seems Jesus' foolhardy stupidity: "Let us also go, that we may die with him." This is Johannine irony that expresses a Christian paradox, for to journey with Jesus the Light, especially into dark and dangerous places, will mean life—not death.

Martha and Mary are models for our journey—never a direct, straight line event—to profound faith. Martha takes the initiative in welcoming Jesus, and professes a typical Jewish faith (held by the Pharisee party) in the resurrection "on the last day," the day of judgment and resurrection at the end of time. But in the Fourth Gospel it is important that faith is not just focused on a distant event but is a death-defying affirmation of the "now" reality of God's presence and power in Jesus. That reality calls us to come forth trustingly into life from the narrow confines of our daily anxieties, from the fears of our mortality, and from what seems to wither and die in us from day to day. So to Martha, Jesus proclaims that: "I AM the resurrection and the life," and Martha professes her faith in him as the Messiah, the Son of God. Mary and the other mourners arrive at the scene and Mary, like her sister, makes straight for Jesus. Then, together, they move toward the tomb of Lazarus. There Jesus weeps—not only tears of friendship for his friend, but also tears of anger at the last enemy, death, which he has been sent to destroy.

We can surely feel sympathy for Martha who, having just professed her faith in Jesus, now protests at his command to take away the stone because of her expectation of the stench of four-day death. Like Peter (Matt 16:16), like ourselves, faith can waver when confronted with what seems to be "reality" intrudes with its apparent unpleasant consequences for our lives. Jesus' prayer to his Father and his loud cry: "Lazarus, come out!" tear open both heaven and earth to witness to the truth that, for the glory of God, Jesus will bring us out of death. Lazarus emerges, his face and body still wrapped in his burial cloths, and Jesus commands the watchers to: "Unbind him, and let him go." Soon Jesus himself will be a tomb-dweller for three days, but he will leave his burial cloths in the tomb, will come forth unaided and unveiled by human help as the Risen and Sent One who goes into the presence of his Father.

Although called forth to life by Jesus in our baptism, like Lazarus we need others to help us go free, and during Lent this command to "unbind" one another has a special urgency. The last scrutiny is celebrated today, and with the elect the parish community prays for both their unbinding from sin as they are called to the new life of baptism in two weeks time, and for ourselves, the already baptized, who are still bound in our sinfulness. For all of us, Jesus is our hope of coming forth into the new life of his Easter mysteries.

In the Valley of Dead Bones the prophet Ezekiel is asked to see, through God's eyes, the situation of the Babylonian exiles. Humanly speaking, they were as good as dead because they were so bereft of hope. Ezekiel is challenged to believe in God's promise to open the graves of the people's despair and bring them back to their own land of Israel. The Jewish Nobel Laureate, Elie Wiesel, who experienced the exile and dead bones of the Nazi death camps, comments that every generation needs to hear in its own time that dead bones can live again, needs to look at their lives through God's eyes, see in God a new and possible reality, and dare to hope.[5] In our Sunday assembly, the Liturgy of the Word is the weekly prism for such a vision.

God listens, God forgives, God may often ask us to wait longer than "four days" to be called out of the depths of despair into hope, out of the valley of what seems to be a dry and dismembered life back to a realization that God always dwells with us, out of the dark night into the dawn of faith in the divine mercy and fullness of redemption. This is Psalm 130's cry of encouragement, the assurance that we can count on God's word. In Jesus, this word is most clear and death-defying.

Paul assures the Roman community that those who have no interest in things that are of God, or in how their lives are related to God, are confined in a limiting understanding of their humanity. Their mind-set is hostile to God, and so not life-giving. Those who are baptized should live in the Spirit-centered mind-set, for the Spirit dwells in them. Paul names this Spirit as the "Spirit of God," the "Spirit of Christ," the "Spirit of the One who raised Jesus from the dead." And as God was faithful to Jesus' Spirit-filled humanity in raising him from the dead, so through this same Spirit, God will raise from death those who live in the Spirit.

In the Valley of Dead Bones, at the tomb of Lazarus, in Paul's Roman church, the call is to life, not death. In these last days of Lent the resounding call is to come out from death: from the death of our personal sin; from our contribution to social sin such as terrorism, racial prejudices, the rape of our mothering earth; from our disregard of the truth that we are all subject to physical death. How well are we praying, fasting, almsgiving of ourselves, as well as sharing our material resources, so that we may rejoice in the Easter life to come?

Palm Sunday of the Lord's Passion

Procession Gospel

• Matt 21:1-11

We enter into Holy Week, the Great Week of the liturgical year, with the procession of palms. In ancient times, this Sunday was called "the flowering Pasch," a rightful suggestion that this is not a pageant or a folkloric restaging of what is described in the gospel but an anticipation of what we will celebrate in the days ahead, and especially in the Triduum, the three-day feast of Christ's Pasch: his Passover through death into the life which he shares with all those who die and rise with him. The palms or branches that we wave, the "Hosannas" that we sing, are symbols of Christ's victory, of the sap that flows through the wood of the Cross to flower in us, the branches grafted onto him.

The processional gospel begins near Bethphage on the Mount of Olives, just outside Jerusalem, with the obedience of two of Jesus' disciples who are sent to find the ass and colt on which Jesus will sit. Perhaps the puzzling mention of two animals suggests that the colt was a young animal being pressed into its first service, and so accompanied by a parent. The service it will offer is to carry the Messiah into his own city as the royal Son of David. Jesus will not charge into Jerusalem/Zion on the back of a well-muscled warhorse; he will come humbly, gently, on an animal of the people of the land. This was how Solomon rode into Gihon for his anointing as king (1 Kgs 1:38), a symbolic reminder that the king's main concern was not to make war but to establish peace and defend the poor and disadvantaged. That most of the kings failed in this vocation contributed greatly to the later downfall of the monarchy.

Who were in the crowd that followed Jesus? Immediately before this entry, Matthew has described a large crowd that was joined by the two blind beggars whom Jesus healed (Matt 20:29-34). Matthew seems to suggest that this is the crowd that followed Jesus: a mixed lot of the poor, the healed, the unambitious, the women and children, the sinners whom Matthew's narrative describes as gathering around Jesus. These were the people who had experienced his compassionate love along the way, no doubt joined by those who would come running at the least hint of excitement—and disappear just as quickly when their expectations were not met. They probably didn't have much to spread along the way, no soft runner to roll out, but some laid down their dusty and unglamorous cloaks to make a royal carpet for this conspicuously humble king. Others, perhaps the more excitable, ripped branches off the trees to wave. Matthew deliberately evokes memories of the Old Testament crowd who had hailed kings (1 Kgs 1:32-37; 2 Kgs 9:13) and great leaders (1 Macc 13:51; 2 Macc 10:7) in similar ways.

But crowds are fickle. Today the words are right, but for some the understanding is shallow. In a short time, some of the "Hosannas" will turn to "Crucify him!" Today we hear that the whole city of Jerusalem was shaken by the arrival of the one who was hailed as a Davidic king and a prophet; in a few days there will be another earthquake in Jerusalem as the King and Prophet dies (Matt 27:51-54). We should not be horrified in retrospect, but presently honest about our own fickleness and vacillating commitment to the humble One who comes to us as the crucified and risen Christ for the sake of our salvation.

The Mass

• Isa 50:4-7 • Ps 22:8-9, 17-20, 23-24 • Phil 2:6-11 • Matt 26:14–27:66

The gospel of the procession ended with the people of Jerusalem asking, "Who is this?" of the crowds following Jesus. The reminder that the answer to this question involves suffering comes quickly, with the first reading of the third Suffering Servant Song. During the coming days of Holy Week, the first and second Songs are read, with the culminating Fourth Song always proclaimed on Good Friday. The identity of the Servant is a mystery, variously suggested as Zion/Jerusalem, the exiled people, a prophet, someone who is a contemporary of Isaiah, or someone for whom Isaiah waits and hopes. By the use of this ancient sixth century B.C.E. text in today's liturgy, the church directs our hearts to the memory of the Servant Jesus whom Isaiah never knew, and about whom he could not explicitly write. Today, we are a privileged assembly graced to know that what Isaiah was hoping for became brutally explicit in the passion of Jesus.

The Servant is attentive to the word of God that, morning by morning, wakens his ear. Before any speaking there must be listening with new ears; only then can come the new speech which rouses the Servant to be God's spokesperson. Those to whom the Servant is called to speak are the people about whom God is most concerned: the weary, the downtrodden, the disadvantaged. The Servant's obedient solidarity with them also makes him a target for suffering. Fists fly at the mouth that comforts; those whom the Servant's truthful words enrage insult him and spit out lies about him. But never does the Servant query or rebel against his treatment or regard it as punishment for his own guilt or sinfulness. His maturing and prophetic wisdom accepts that this is simply the result of his obedience to the Lord; he does not lament his suffering. The Servant will never waver because he believes that God never wavers in his support of the Servant. He is nonviolent, calmly confident that in his suffering God is present and proclaimed. This is true for all those who, in every generation and for the sake of justice, speak out for those wearied by vicious political regimes or abused by so many forms of human injustice and degradation. Some we can name; many are nameless like the Isaian Servant. But as Paul will proclaim in the second reading, God has given the name to one Servant that is above every name: Jesus the Christ. The passion and death of Jesus was not unique as an historical execution, but what makes it infinitely more than just a regrettable act of cruel injustice and an apparently tragic failure for one man is the fact that God has opened the ears of this Son and Servant to the cosmic consequences of his obedient love.

With verses from the responsorial Psalm 22 we lament the suffering that so often we do not understand, we speak the truth about our own pain and the pain others experience, we complain—but complain *in faith* to God. And God heals us. Like every one of the laments in the Book of Psalms (except Ps 88), the movement is from despair to hope, from agony to ecstasy, from death to life.

To the Philippians, Paul writes that Christ emptied his divinity *into* our humanity; he did not leave this state of divine equality behind or discard it. Jesus reveals God by what God does in him. Jesus' humanity is the most definitive, most understandable Word that can be spoken about God, revealing God as self-giving love . . . and love is always vulnerable, always unconcerned about power or status. Jesus' vulnerability would take him to the cross, and for this loving obedience to God and humanity the humiliated Servant is raised by God as "Lord" over all creation and is reverenced by heaven and earth. It is a lordship of compassionate love and fidelity. Therefore, we who name ourselves as Christians in Christ are called to lives of obedience, service, selflessness, and humility in our particular personal and communal situations.

The Lectionary begins Matthew's passion narrative with the treacherous approach of Judas to the chief priests. It is regrettable that the anointing of Jesus at Bethany in the house of Simon the leper is not heard. On the threshold of his passion, an anonymous woman comes to table to soothe him and anoint his head with expensive ointment, while the disciples complain about such a waste of money. Jesus affirms her prophetic insight into what lies before him—his death and burial. (Matthew has no post-death anointing in his narrative.) What this woman has done, says Jesus, will be remembered throughout the whole world, wherever the Gospel is proclaimed. Then as a dark foil to the woman's generous love of Jesus, comes Judas' concern with thirty pieces of silver. In Exod 21:32 this was the price named as the recompense to be paid by the owner of an ox that gores a slave. So much for Jesus' worth in some eyes.

For two people, Jesus and Judas, the hour of handing over has arrived. The hands of one man grab silver for himself; the Other's hands will snatch salvation for the whole world, at the costly price of his life. Jesus gathers with his disciples at the sundown table for the Passover feast of freedom, and to the great distress of his disciples he announces at the beginning of the meal that one of them will betray him. And the last Lenten question oozes out into the darkness, out of Judas: "Surely not I, Rabbi?" "You have said so," is Jesus' reply. Horrifying as it may be, Judas' question is one that we must keep asking ourselves. Jesus gives himself to his disciples as food and drink, under the form of bread and wine. Death will be the crushing of the wheat, ground to make the Bread of Life; it will be the trampling of the grapes, poured out as the saving cup that Jesus will drain to its bitter dregs. This will be the last feast before the kingdom feast with his Father. There are great protestations of fidelity to the Shepherd, especially from Peter. Then it is on to Gethsemane.

The passion narrative is a story of many people who, as Paul wrote to the Romans, do not do what they want, but do the very thing they hate, and find it hard to believe that they could act this way (Rom 7:15). Sinfulness is doing what, in our personal depths, we know is evil, because of fear, greed, social pressure, lust for power, or disregard for human life. In the garden of Gethsemane, Peter the Rock crumbles into a soft sand-drift of sleep, and the dozing Zebedee brothers (Matt 20:20-23) no longer seem to care whether they are on the right hand or the left hand places of the man who lies in agony among the olive trees. The traitor's kiss smacks them from their sleep, and the violence spawns a feeble swordplay until the words of Jesus, even in the context of such violence, command peace. Then those who had once left everything to follow Jesus (Matt 4:22) now leave everything to run away from him.

Peter crawls away like a spider into the dark corner of the high priest Caiphas' courtyard. While Jesus is on trial inside, he is spinning his web of lies outside. Impetuous speech has often been Peter's downfall; tragically, tonight it is more deliberate, trapping him three times in what he does not want to do but does, choosing self-survival over faithfulness to his Master. And the terrible anomaly of this is symbolized by the cockcrow that does not herald dawn but deepest night in Peter's soul. But Matthew tells us that Peter will be saved, as we will be, by the remembrance of Jesus' words and by our tears over our betrayals of Jesus.

Jesus is handed over to Pilate, the Roman governor, who is unnerved by Jesus' silence. Pilate would much prefer this Jew to be as slippery as the blood that he suspects he will cause to be shed; wishes that Jesus would wriggle out of Pilate's conscience and this trial. Instead, it is Barabbas that the weak Pilate allows to slip out free. Pilate might not want to hand Jesus over, but again here is someone who compromises himself because of social pressure from the crowd and the fear of losing favor with Caesar. Only Pilate's wife honestly intervenes to try to save Jesus. Just as Matthew's infancy narrative had dreamers like Joseph and the Magi, so here is another dreamer. But a woman's dreams and witness are unacceptable. Pilate washes his hands of the whole dirty matter. Compromise, dismissal of the "dreams" of others, peer pressure, and fear of losing upward social mobility: these can also send our truth as followers of Jesus gurgling down the drain.

So then there is the mockery of stripping, crowning, scourging—and gambling with a life for military amusement before their boredom is relieved by a crucifixion getting underway. Wrapped again in his own garments, Jesus is dispatched to crucifixion, and as he is led away Simon from Cyrene is grabbed by the soldiers and yoked unwillingly to Jesus. Soon they are at Calvary. A chorus of mockers—Jewish leaders, passersby always eager for a bit of drama, and the criminals fixed on crosses beside him— hail the crucified one who is labeled "Jesus of Nazareth, King of the Jews." To show how Jesus thirsted for his Father's presence, Matthew puts on Jesus' lips, in his mother tongue, the beginning of the lamentation of Psalm 22: "My God, my God, why have you forsaken me?" This is not a cry of despair, but of agonizing faith. No one sends out a voice to one whom we believe is not there. As Jesus hands over to his Father the breath from his torn body, we fall down on our knees in silent awe of the mystery of our salvation. The earth also is ripped apart for there are, as we have heard already from Paul, cosmic consequences of Jesus' sacrifice. Worshippers will be able to enter into the temple of the body of Jesus that has been opened to all by his wounds; the places of the dead will be transformed into life. And as an earthquake happens in the centurion's soul, too, there is shaken from him the cry of Gentile faith: "Truly this man was God's Son!"

The faithful women are there, watching and waiting, as women so often do at birth and death. Joseph of Arimathea, rich and courageous, has permission from Pilate to unpin Jesus from his mount, press him gently into linen sheets, and lay him for his Sabbath rest in Joseph's own new garden tomb. But despite the seals and the Roman guards, in three days the New Man will erupt from this tomb.

There is so much here to reflect on and ask ourselves about: friendship, betrayal, forgiveness, our own small and large violences, our too easy and too frequent excuses for our failures in Christian discipleship . . . . And so we, too, wait and watch through this Holy Week.

Notes

1. Elizabeth Jennings, "Dust," *New Collected Poems* (Manchester: Carcanet, 2002) 172.
2. See Vatican II, *The Church Today*, art. 13.
3. William Shakespeare, *The Tragedy of King Richard the Second*, 1.3 in *The Complete Works*, second edition, General Editors Stanley Wells and Gary Taylor (Oxford: Clarendon Press, 2005) 345.
4. *John Newton Diary*, Princeton University, co199, 21 March, 1805.
5. Elie Wiesel, "Ezekiel," *Congregation: Contemporary Writers Read the Jewish Bible*, ed. David Rosenberg (San Diego: Harcourt Brace Jovanovich, 1987) 186.

4

The Season of Easter

The Easter Triduum

From the evening of Holy Thursday to the evening of Easter Sunday we celebrate the Easter Triduum. Deriving from the Latin for "three days" and adding "Easter," it celebrates the proclamation of Jesus' resurrection "on the third day," and helps us to realize that what we celebrate during these days—Jesus' passion, death, and resurrection—is such an immense and awe-inspiring mystery that we need three days to enter into its truth. The liturgy weaves together passion and death, glory and suffering, into the richest of Christological tapestries. On Holy Thursday we gaze on the paschal mystery from the viewpoint of floor, table, and the garden of Gethsemane; on Good Friday from Golgotha and cross; at Easter in another garden and before an empty tomb. There is no attempt to soften either the sadness or the joy.

On these days we do things in church that we do on no other days: wash feet, kiss wood, splash water, kindle fires, turn lights off and on. We listen to the same old stories with, we hope, new ears unplugged and new hearts converted by the Lenten discipline; and on Easter Day, for the first time for forty days, we sing again and again into the night and the dawn the one word which is made holy and exuberant by the tremendous mystery it contains: "Alleluia!"—"Praise Yah!" (YHWH, the Name). Sometimes there is a tune which we say we have "on the brain"; "Alleluia!" is the word that the church has "on her heart" at Easter because, as St. Augustine said, "We are Easter Christians, and Alleluia is our song" in praise of the Crucified and Risen One.

Holy Thursday

Evening Mass of the Lord's Supper

• Exod 12:1-8, 11-14 • Ps 116:12-13, 15-18 • 1 Cor 11:23-26 • John 13:1-15

Tonight we do not hear any of the Synoptic Gospels recounting the institution of the Eucharist. The institution tradition is left to Paul in the second reading from his First Letter to the Corinthians. By proclaiming John's last supper narrative, the Lectionary links this celebration with the Johannine passion that is read on Good Friday and with the Sunday gospels of the Easter season, most of which are from John. But there is more to this choice than textual correspondence. This is the "hour" of radical and privileged decision-making, the return of the tempter in Judas Iscariot, the beginning of Jesus' journey from this world through death to resurrection and his return to his Father.

Jesus celebrates this last meal with his friends, and with a friend become enemy. Tonight Jesus rises and lays aside his garments to perform, unencumbered, an act of service; tomorrow he will lay aside his own life. Tonight he clothes himself with a towel; tomorrow he will be clothed as a fool and stripped naked. The "hour" has come: the hour of Jesus' love for his own to the very end, the hour when the Father has given all things into his hands. John tells us what these "things" are tonight: a towel, a bowl of water, and the feet of his disciples—such ordinary, humble, human realities with which Jesus will show the depths of his love. Tomorrow, the salvation of the world will be put into his hands that are nailed to the wood. And on the third day, Jesus will be clothed in the glory of his risen life.

Tonight Jesus kneels on the floor to wash the feet of his disciples, and we might wonder why this gospel is chosen on the night when we remember the institution of the Eucharist? Perhaps, like John's community at the end of the first century, we are used to celebrating Eucharist, but familiarity may have eroded its meaning for us. John reminds us by the washing of the feet, this "parable in action," that Jesus is Servant, one who is ready to do the dirty jobs, to be at the bottom of the social heap, to take the last place along with all those whom we shove down: the abused, the marginalized, the refugees, the unemployed, those with physical and psychological disabilities. Bearing down on them are those at the top of the pyramid: the powerful, the rich, the successful. Until Vatican II and its recognition that "all the faithful of Christ of whatever rank or status are called to the fullness of Christian life and to the perfection of charity,"[1] even the Church had become a social pyramid, from the papal peak to the largely squashed laity at the bottom.

Peter finds Jesus as Servant hard to accept. He wants a Jesus who is Master, who is above him, and in whom Peter can feel secure. This foot-washing-Jesus will be hard to follow. To put one's feet in another's hands makes one vulnerable. Rather than a powerful Messiah, here is what

Julian of Norwich called "the courtesy (or homeliness) of God."[2] Peter surely suspects that if Jesus is like this, so must his disciples be—and he panics, he objects. When Jesus tells him that unless he allows Jesus to wash his feet, Peter will not share friendship with him, Peter swings, desperate and still uncomprehending, to a wildly quantitative response. Well then, wash not only his feet, but also his hands and his head! But it is not the quantity but the quality of one's life as a servant that will bring salvation. Jesus has also washed Judas' feet; physically, he is clean, but his heart is polluted by betrayal and his rejection of his Master's love. So Jesus tries to explain to his disciples: "Not all of you are clean."

Jesus returns to the table as Lord and Teacher to help his disciples to understand that "you also should do as I have done to you." Some commentators have called these words the Johannine words of institution, for the Eucharist is about sharing the love and life of Jesus who humbled himself, even to death on a cross. In the vulnerability of bread eaten and wine drunk, Jesus asks us to follow his example: to get down, metaphorically, and serve one another, despite the dust and smell and misunderstandings; to be hospitable to our sisters and brothers and in communion with them; to be vulnerable in a society of loving service offered and received when so often we have been encouraged to value self-reliance, autonomy, getting to the top. Then we, too, will have a share in the hospitality of the kingdom.

The Exodus reading describes the preparations that the Hebrew people were to make for their journey from slavery into freedom on the night of the Jewish Passover. The reading concludes with the command to keep a day of liturgical remembrance of this event by which the past is brought into the present, and the present becomes a challenge for the future. Similarly, our Eucharist is a "memorial" in this rich liturgical sense of the word when we celebrate that "Christ has died. Christ is risen. Christ will come again." The ritual as described in Exodus had probably evolved from that of nomadic Bedouins who, on the first full spring moon and under the safe cover of darkness, prepared for a dangerous migration with their flocks to spring pastures. Especially vulnerable were the newborn lambs, and so the nomadic community would sacrifice one of these lambs and mark their tents with its blood, believing that this would ward off evil. Jewish liturgical genius (as does Christian) took elements of an already established ritual and transformed them into the celebration of God's protection and deliverance for the Hebrews who were about to become God's nomads in search of new pastures of freedom. They were to go forth in haste, not delaying to leaven their bread, unencumbered with anything but the bare necessities of staff and sandals to help them on their journey.

The Passover was to become the defining experience for the Jewish people. It testifies to the truth that human beings are meant to be free, and that God is concerned when they are not. But it also shows that God requires an active response from the oppressed people: not passive acceptance of the status quo but a willingness to set out on a dangerous way, trusting in God's protective presence. In every generation, Jews are to celebrate Passover with a remembrance that pulls past, present, and future into a glorious but demanding "now" and a personal and communal "we," just as Christians do when we celebrate the memorial sacrifice of Christ our Passover.

In his First Letter to the Corinthians, Paul proclaims the ancient tradition of the words of the institution of the Eucharist. It too, Paul writes, is a memorial of what was, is, and will be because of Jesus our Passover Lamb. Paul had cause to rebuke his Corinthians over many issues by which they betrayed their communion with Christ, including their disregard for the poor about which Paul writes in the verses immediately preceding tonight's reading (1 Cor 11:17-22). Christ's followers have been baptized into his Body, and as his Body in the world we are to be bread broken for and consumed by others, wine poured out and drunk to quench the thirst of our sisters and brothers.

"Eucharist" (*eucharistía*) means "thanksgiving," and tonight the responsorial Psalm 116 gives us the words to sing our thanks to God for the blessing which the psalmist never saw in its fullness, but which we have been privileged to know in Christ. "Our blessing-cup is a communion with the blood of Christ," we respond. Our gratitude is most genuine when we are a blessing to others, when we fulfill our baptismal vows before all the people, and do as Jesus has done for us.

Good Friday

• Isa 52:13–53:12 • Ps 31:2, 6, 12-13, 15-17, 25 • Heb 4:14-16; 5:7-9 • John 18:1–19:42

In his poem, "The Coming," the Welsh poet R. S. Thomas imagines God holding a small globe in his hands, into which his Son looks. He gazes at the world of light and shadow, of scorched land and rivers, and sees:

> On a bare
> Hill a bare tree saddened
> The sky. Many people
> Held out their thin arms

> To it, as though waiting
> For a vanished April
> To return to its crossed
> Boughs. The son watched
> Them. Let me go there, he said.[3]

Today we celebrate the Son who willingly climbed the tree on the hill of Golgotha, and to whom we thin, needy people, stretch out our arms today. Our paschal faith affirms that the tree of the cross blossomed with Jesus' crucified body, the body that would be laid at the heart of the earth to become fruitful with his resurrection. As on every day of this three-day feast, the light of Christ's resurrection shines through even the darkest day of the church year. John has written in his prologue that: "What has come into being in him was life, and the life was the light of all people. The light shines in the darkness, and the darkness did not overcome it" (John 1:4-5). The paschal mystery is a mystery of death *and* resurrection.

The first reading is the fourth Suffering Servant Song of Isaiah, and in this song Old Testament language is pushed to its limits. The song opens with the announcement of what God promises the Servant: exaltation to great heights. It closes with the reason for this exaltation: the Servant's willingness to suffer for others. In between we have a tragic chorus of voices who tell the story of the one who was "wounded for our transgressions, crushed for our iniquities," those voices who admit their guilt for what has happened to the Servant. The community's disregard of the Servant has added to his dehumanizing pain. The images that Isaiah uses emphasize this: the Servant is like a root pushing up from the dirt, useful for nothing but kicking or falling over, or like a lamb that is led without protest to slaughter. From his disfigurement, the people hide their faces. Yet no word is spoken by the Servant, no retaliation attempted.

We may not be able to explain what we hear but, in the context of today's liturgy as we gaze into the depths of God's Word in the Old Testament, we are grasped by its truth, shaken into a new realization that what God does in the Isaian Servant he continues to do in Jesus. And when we are despised, rejected, crushed, and step into what seems the greatest darkness with no guarantees but our faith in the promises of God, we too will be allotted "a portion with the great," a share in the salvation which makes this Friday "Good." We respond to the first reading with Psalm 31, an expression of hope in helplessness, of trust in betrayal, of possession by God when discarded by everyone else. We profess our faith in the verse that Luke puts on the lips of the dying Jesus: "Father, into your hands I commend my spirit" (Luke 23:46).

Through the lens of the Letter to the Hebrews, Jesus as the High Priest who intercedes for us is brought into sharp focus. On the annual Jewish Day of Atonement, the high priest passed through the veil of the Temple to sprinkle the blood of the sacrificial goat on the mercy seat and make intercession for the people. Through the blood of Christ's sacrifice, our humanity, with all its shared weakness, has been taken into the merciful presence of God. The prayer of Jesus was not always ecstatic. "In the days of his flesh" (see Heb 5:7) Jesus brought his grief, his disappointment, his desolation and confusion before God in prayer that was agonized, and he was heard because of his painful obedience in these circumstances. We have the witness of Jesus himself that the honest prayer that lives closest to our deepest hurts and endures in and through pain, is acceptable to God.

On Good Friday we do well to remind ourselves that Lent is finished and that we are halfway into the Easter Triduum. It is John's passion narrative that is most permeated with the glory of the resurrection of the strong Son of God. The Johannine Jesus is the free man, neither defeated nor disgraced, who has already announced: "No one takes it (my life) from me, but I lay it down of my own accord. I have power to lay it down and I have power to take it up again. I have received this command from my Father" (John 10:18). Artists continue to see something inexhaustible and new in the mystery of the cross—from the 5th-century carvings of crucifixion scenes, through those of the Middle Ages where either outer pain or inner peace predominates, to the modern representations where sculptors have made the cross and corpus from junk material to show that something creative can come from the debris of human living. So it is with the four evangelists. John's portrait of Jesus in his passion is painted in the burnished gold of the holy icons, and his cross is studded with the truth of victory that found artistic expression in the jeweled crosses of the early centuries of church art. As the Passion of John is read, it is as though the eyes of the Church's faith are piercing the darkness of crucifixion almost impatiently, to glimpse the mystery of Christ glorified in death.

At the beginning of today's gospel there is no identifying and treacherous kiss in the garden. Jesus goes forward on his own initiative to meet those who have come to arrest him, announcing himself as "I AM (he)" which causes an ironic and tumbled "prostration" by his enemies. But Jesus announces himself with the holy Name not only to identify himself but also to protect his followers (John 17:12) whom he would not allow to be snatched out of his hands (John 10:28). It is Judas, the disciple of the night and his cohort, who need their artificial torchlight and weapons. True disciples have need only of the "light of the world" (John 8:12) and the farewell supper gift of Jesus' protective peace that overcomes the world, not the violence of Peter's sword play (John 18:10).

Who do we meet in this passion narrative that we can recognize in ourselves and others? And what is our response, as disciples of Jesus, to this recognition?

For his Jewish trial, Jesus is led to Annas, the powerful former high priest, who had managed to insinuate into that role five of his sons and his son-in-law, Caiaphas, the then high priest. He can quickly whip up apparently rational arguments to control damage like a consummate politician. He had trained his son-in-law well, no doubt agreeing with him that it is preferable for one man to die than for a whole nation to perish (John 18:14). Peter scuttles into the high priest's courtyard like a chameleon, taking on the darkness of his environment. In the shadows, by a charcoal fire, he tries to warm himself, but his denial of his Master chills him to the heart.

Jesus is parceled up and sent bound to Caiaphas, the high priest. While Jesus is on trial inside, Peter is on trial outside, sentencing himself by his treachery. Then the cock crows to announce the darkest day that Peter will ever know, and we are shaken at the possibility that such a swift fall from grace is always possible for each one of us.

The cruel shuttling back and forth of Jesus continues as he is taken to his Roman trial before Pilate, the would-be neutral man who becomes a victim of his own compromises. We know what it is like to be Pilate when we disguise our weaknesses with bluster, fear to make a mistake that would put us out of favor with higher authorities, or cause us to lose the little status we have. Pilate suspects that he is being put on trial by Jesus, that Jesus is turning the tables on him in the debate about kingship, authority, and truth, so he decides to make a fool out of "the Jews" in the person of one of them by handing Jesus over to the soldiers for flogging and crowning as a "fool king." "Here is the man!" announces Pilate in his last inside-outside maneuver between Jesus, the crowd, and his own conscience. And we behold again the heights and depths of human possibility in the suffering Servant Jesus. Friend of Jesus or friend of contemporary "Caesars": the choice is ours as well as Pilate's. We are still sadly capable of handing over the body of Christ, sisters and brothers of the Son of Man, to crucifixion.

Self-possessed and undefeated, the Son of God strides toward the accomplishment of his Passover. John has no Simon of Cyrene; Jesus carries his own cross, the cross that belongs to him and which, for that very reason, will be raised up as a sign of victory. On the cross is a description of Jesus' "crime": "Jesus of Nazareth, King of the Jews." Written in Greek (the language of trade and commerce), Latin (the language of Roman government) and in Hebrew (the language of Jesus' own people), John makes a proclamation of Jesus' universal kingship out of what Pilate has written to salve his conscience. On either side of Jesus hang "two others," named neither as criminals nor insurgents. They are merely two attendant shadows who fade into anonymity in the presence of the royal and crucified One.

The drama of dispossession is acted out in three scenes. First, Jesus is dispossessed of his clothing by the soldiers. Then he dispossesses himself of his mother and the beloved disciple, the woman and man who are his ideal disciples. They are silent; there is no Cana comment, no intimate questions. Yet in this hour of pain and separation the evangelist is telling us something about a new communion that will be a model for the Johannine church and every community of the Crucified. Here are women and men as equal disciples, given into each other's care, accepting one another as Jesus' gifts, and all this under the shadow of the cross that is the glory tree. In this silent space we lay down our defenses and try to identify with such discipleship.

Jesus knows that it is all finished, but he proclaims his thirst until the end and is offered sour wine on a sprig of hyssop. John is deliberately evoking the "Lamb of God" memory, for it was with the fern-like hyssop that Exodus 12:22 describes the sprinkling of doorposts with blood on the night of the Hebrew Passover. Unlike the Synoptic evangelists, John sets the crucifixion of Jesus not on the day of Passover but on the day of preparation for this feast. Again to emphasize the Lamb of God perspective, John's narrative situates Jesus' crucifixion at the time when the minor priests in the Jerusalem Temple were beginning to ritually slaughter the Passover lambs to be eaten after sunset at each family's paschal meal.

In this gospel there is no agonized dying cry, only the silent triumph of one who has accomplished that for which he came into the world. As his final dispossession, Jesus hands over his last breath to his Father, the breath which animates the new creation. No bones of this paschal lamb are broken, no cosmic darkness falls upon the earth, but from the pierced side of Jesus flow blood and water, John's signs of Eucharist and Baptism through which all peoples and nations can enter into the new temple of the body of the Crucified and Risen One. He who thirsted becomes in death the source of the living water of the Spirit (John 7:37b-39).

With deliberate irony, John proclaims that it is with the dead body of Jesus in their arms that hesitant Israel comes to faith. Joseph of Arimathea, a secret disciple because of his fear of Jesus' enemies and his own associates, and the night time seeker, Nicodemus, take the body of Jesus and bind it in the swaddling bands of death. They surround him with an extravagant amount of costly spices, for this is a royal cortege and burial. The seed of

Christ's body is buried in the earth, hidden there until it bears fruit on Easter morning.

Silence was God's answer on Golgotha; silence is our answer today when we kneel, or touch, or kiss the cross. Young people welcoming some activity, children interested in this novelty, old people doing what they have done for years, parents carrying their babies, the poor and the disabled heading with determination to what they are so familiar with: together we are the people who hope that this tree will drip its salvation upon us. "Were you there when they crucified my Lord?" we may sing, but there is another question to be answered: "Where are we now in relation to the cross and the Crucified?" When we encounter it with hope and love, we speak its mystery to the world for which Jesus died.

On this day of dispossession, we are dispossessed even of the eucharistic action and receive the hosts that were consecrated on Holy Thursday night. In deep silence we leave the church to move into our own preparation day for the Passover of Jesus, the preparation that will allow Jesus to burst forth from the tombs of our hearts on the night of nights.

The Easter Vigil

• Gen 1:1–2:2 • Gen 22:1-18 • Exod 14:15–15:1 • Isa 54:5-14 • Isa 55:1-11 • Bar 3:9-15, 32–4:4 • Ezek 36:16-28 • Rom 6:3-11 • Matt 28:1-10

Eons ago there was a first time when our ancestors discovered that if lifeless stones were struck together, if fallen twigs or dead wood were rubbed hard and patiently together and a living human breath blown onto these, then a spark of fire would spring forth and a reality of extraordinary potential would be born. This is the night of the Great Firemaker, and we gather eagerly around the Easter fire and column of wax by which the Church symbolizes the truth that Christ is the living spark that springs from the dead wood and stone tomb. Here we will be fire-takers who want Christ's life to warm us and brand us as his disciples: people who will pass on this fire to enlighten the darkness of our world. Above us is the full moon, the cosmic calendar by which each year we calculate the date of Easter. New fire, newly full moon, new people . . . but lest we forget that the Pasch is about the inseparable cross and resurrection, the presider traces the cross on the Easter candle and pierces it with five fragrant "nails" of incense. The date of the current year and the Alpha and Omega are also traced on it, and we commit ourselves again, this year, to the Risen Christ who is the beginning and the end of our lives. Then this wax column of fire leads us into the dark womb of the church for the rebirth of our commitment to Christ.

Having exultantly praised the Light of the World, we sit around the candle's fire to listen to stories from the two Testaments that affirm our identity as God's people, brought from the darkness of sin into light and life. If we are privileged to hear and respond to God's word in the presence of those who are about to receive their new identity in the waters of baptism, tonight's Liturgy of the Word will have added significance.

In the first reading from Genesis (never to be omitted on this night of new creation), the Word of God broods over the primeval chaos and brings forth life to the repeated rhythm of God speaking, naming, seeing, and blessing. Into the world prepared by the Spirit's creativity, God calls forth humanity, male and female, made in the divine image and entrusted with the stewardship of creation. Then on the seventh day, there is the "Sabbath," the day of contemplative, mutual presence of God and creation to one another. This is the day that is "very good," but one day will be infinitely better—in the new creation, in the risen Christ.

Then the Word of God proclaims what does not seem good, what in the Jewish tradition is called "the Binding of Isaac" and is referred to constantly in the liturgy of the Jewish High Holy Days and the daily prayer of Jewish men. But Abraham belongs in this night; he is the pioneer of faith who shows us the way to hope against hope (Rom 4:18) when burdened with immense grief. When told by God to take his only son, Isaac, and make of him a burnt offering on Mount Moriah, Abraham realizes that this means there will be no descendants of himself and Sarah, no numerous stars of the sky or sands of the shore—nothing but ash. And yet because "God said," Abraham replies, "Here I am." He is ready to trust, not in the promises made through Isaac, but in the Promise Maker himself. Abraham believes, as we all must when an incomprehensible disaster occurs, especially when we lose a loved one who seems so necessary to our present and future, that God has ways of keeping his promises that we can never imagine. The Risen Christ, the Son of God in glory, is the realized promise of God and the hope of our future that is beyond our human imagination.

The story of the passage of the Hebrews through the Sea of Reeds is always read on this night, for it is part of the foundational story of the identity of Jesus the Jew and his people, the "rich root of the olive tree" onto which we Christians have been grafted (Rom 11:17). God the liberator leads his people through the waters of chaos. The outstretched arm and staff of Moses, the protection of the angel, the pillar of cloud that is both guide for and buffer between the Hebrews and the Egyptians, all these are instruments of God's deliverance. As we remember these waters, we sing our praise for the great salvation that has been won for us by the flood of death that overwhelmed Jesus, his passage through these waters, his deliverance from their chaos in his resurrection, and our baptism into this mystery of salvation.

Isaiah gives us a moving description of God's fidelity to his people. He uses the imagery (patriarchal in that era) of God as a faithful husband to his bride Israel. Despite Israel's unfaithfulness and the divine disappointment, despite temporary separation, anger, and upheavals, the relationship endures. And not only does it endure, it is transformed. The everlasting love of God builds a more beautiful relationship with his people with the tools of forgiveness, integrity, and peace. This is how Jesus will rebuild our lives after we have failed by our sinfulness to be faithful covenant partners of God.

Again we hear Isaiah speaking of God's love. It is like water for the thirsty, food for the hungry, wine and milk for the poor. Because of such love, the covenant made with David has been extended to embrace all those who listen attentively to God and are open to the mysterious accomplishment of God's will. The Word of God which announces this will goes forth, newly expressed throughout the generations, to bring forth new life, but nowhere and in no one is this will and Word so fully expressed as in Jesus, the Word made flesh, the Covenant Maker with his own body and blood.

The reading from the prophet Baruch, Jeremiah's secretary (Jer 36:4), is a hymn of praise to Wisdom. Wisdom is the gift of God to Israel and, with her assistance, the people are to rebuild their lives on the foundation of God's commandments. This Wisdom is practical, not speculative. She will be the companion who leads the people out of the exile of sin and restores them to the youthful love and peace of their earlier relationship with God. The cosmos itself is a witness to the creativity and wisdom of God that comes with obedience to God's word. "Turn," "seize," "walk": we hear these vigorous words as not only encouraging Israel to make the right choices in life and death situations, but also for our own encouragement. Such right choices were made preeminently by Jesus who reveals God's wisdom made flesh among us (Matt 11:19).

By their infidelity the people of God defiled themselves and desecrated the holy name to which they should have given praise and witness before the nations. God, however, will re-create them in ways that will enable them to do this, and will rescue them from the foreign lands where they have been scattered. The re-creation of the people is described symbolically by the prophet Ezekiel, first as a ritual washing which cleanses them of any defilement, and then as a biblical "heart transplant." Only God can be the skilled surgeon who delicately removes the people's hearts of stone and replaces them with warm and living hearts that will beat with love for and obedience to their God. Then God will resuscitate the exiles with his own spirit/breath to make of them a renewed, regenerated people. For us, as a Christian assembly who are already baptized, and for the elect who are about to enter the baptismal waters, this is the great night of our washing and regeneration.

Paul is explicit about this regeneration. It is in the waters of baptism that we go down into the death of Christ so that we may rise up with him to new life. We *are* baptized, continually called to live this new life of holiness. Through his crucifixion, Christ put to death the slavery of sin for the sake of our freedom; in his descent into the waters of death, he transformed them into the milieu of life. These are the great exodus themes of the Christian story within which we live and through which we find our identity as sons and daughters of God in the Son. When we renew our baptismal promises tonight, we again pronounce our determination to come out of sin and stand in mutually reassuring solidarity with the newly baptized. After this reading, and for the first time in seven weeks, we respond with "Alleluia!" in praise of the love of God that has no end, and the bells and the song return. It is such love that made Jesus, the rejected cornerstone (see responsorial Ps 118:22), into the keystone of the new Temple into which we are built as living stones by our baptism.

Eugen Drewermann comments that it is right that women should be at the center of all the gospel narratives of the resurrection:

> The passion story we heard on Good Friday is only about the works and deeds of men, and it is a gruesome and bloody story. But from old it is the women who are the protectors of life. They had to watch the fire when the men went out to hunt or to war . . . In their maturing, they embodied the earth itself, and in the periodic monthly rhythms of their own bodies, they imaged the mystery of the moon. Theirs from old is the power to create life, and no one could solve the mystery of its beginning.[4]

Matthew tells us that the women had seen the Crucifixion, had watched the burial, had sat contemplating the tomb. After the Sabbath they return again to see the tomb—nothing more, no greater expectation—and to continue their vigil at the grave. We understand; we know how hard it is to leave the place where we have just buried a loved one. There is no anointing in Matthew's account because it had already been done (Matt 26:6-13). There is no thought of rolling away the stone; the Roman guards are still there. But then there is the last of Matthew's earthquakes: an angel descends from heaven, the stone is rolled away, and the messenger of God sits triumphantly on it in front of the women. What the angel proclaims to the women is the emptiness of the tomb, the futility of human attempts to seal in the grave "Jesus of Nazareth who was crucified." There is more seeing for the women to do. As we are tonight, they are called to look at the empty tomb and believe that Jesus is risen and goes before us into new life. At the beginning of his gospel Matthew places a woman, Mary of Nazareth, whose empty, virginal womb would give birth to Jesus, the Savior, conceived by the Holy Spirit. At the end of his gospel, Matthew places Mary Magdalene and the other Mary at the empty tomb where they are told that risen life has been conceived and brought forth. They believe, and they are enlivened. In contrast, the guards are shaken with uncomprehending fear and become as dead men. But there is more: the women are to tell Jesus' disciples this good news of his resurrection and of his going ahead of them to Galilee where the disciples will also see him. As the women hurry away with this mission, Jesus himself comes toward them. It is no chance meeting, but the risen One's personal affirmation of the angel's message. He is no ghost; the women take hold of his feet that yesterday were nailed to a cross and today carry him to their meeting. Jesus announces one change from the angel's message: "his disciples" become "my brothers," forgiven brothers. Jesus is going before them into Galilee—Galilee of the Gentiles, Galilee of the springtime of their call, where the winter of their infidelity will thaw in the presence of the warmth of the forgiving, trustful love of their risen Master, and they will be commissioned by him to make disciples of all nations.

Our faith in the resurrection is built on the Word of God and on the presence and witness of the risen Christ in human experience, in women and men who have received the gift of faith and have had this nourished in the community of believers. This is what the newly baptized tell us tonight; this is the responsibility we have for one another. We will fail; we will be called back to "Galilee" again and again, called to leave the place of the dead and follow Jesus who offers us his new life that will continue to transform us into the image of the crucified and risen One. For all this, we will loudly and constantly sing "Alleluia!" for the next fifty days.

The Sundays of Easter

As Christians, we are not only the people who celebrate the mystery of the death and resurrection of Jesus, we are also people who celebrate that mystery as our own. Even the three great days of the Triduum are not enough for this, so the Church gives us fifty days, from Easter Sunday until Pentecost, to celebrate this season "in joyful exultation as one feast day, or better as one great Sunday."[5] One writer suggests that we think of an eagle, circling endlessly above a hillside, rising and falling on the currents of the wind, surveying the terrain that lies below. The "terrain" of the Lectionary for the Sundays *of* (not *after*) Easter is laid out, and we circle peacefully around it:

> . . . in an atmosphere of joy, born aloft by the power of the Spirit, the church surveys and claims for herself the whole mystery of salvation. It is the "eagle" of the evangelists, John, aided and abetted by the storyteller of the Acts of the Apostles, who inspires the church to spread her wings and fly like this.[6]

This year we see Jesus in our midst as the wounded healer, the stranger who shares stories and bread, the secure and protective gate of the sheepfold, the host at table who lingers to explain the way to our Father's house and to promise us that we are not orphaned by his death. Jesus declares his oneness with his Father and the participation of his disciples in this communion.

In Year A, the second readings are from the First Letter of Peter, written either by Peter using a secretary, or by someone who knew Peter well and is committed to carrying on his heritage in the last two or three decades of the first century. It can be seen to contain elements that could well be an extended and pastoral homily on baptism and its implications, and is therefore most suitable and challenging not only for those who were baptized at the Easter Vigil, but also for the local parish community. Washed, oiled, and fed by Mother Church on the night of nights, the neophytes enter into the time of mystagogy or post-baptismal catechesis, a time of reflection on the mystery of Christ—and the mystery of themselves as members of his Body. If the local parish community is to offer the neophytes support and companionship on this journey of faith after the euphoria of the Easter Vigil, they too need to continue with a mystagogy that will enable them "to grow in deepening their grasp of the paschal mystery and in making it part of their lives through meditation on the gospel, sharing in the Eucharist, and doing the works of charity."[7] Together, we mount up on eagle's wings to gaze on the great mysteries of the coming fifty days from different perspectives of the Sunday Lectionary.

Second Sunday of Easter

• Acts 2:42-47b • Ps 118:2-4, 13-15, 22-24 • 1 Pet 1:3-9 • John 20:19-31

Today's gospel is the same in each of the three yearly cycles, a fact that underlines its significance. It proclaims that the risen Christ is often in our midst in ways that we do not expect, and that even though Jesus is risen, we still have to confront the mystery and the glory of the wounds.

Terrified by the death of Jesus, dispirited and disillusioned over their own failures and their desertion of their Master, the disciples huddle behind closed doors. Mary Magdalene has announced to them that she had seen the Lord and delivered to them his message, but she is just a woman and, according to the socio-religious views of the time, a woman's evidence did not count! So these Jewish disciples, probably a more inclusive group than the Twelve become Eleven through Judas' treachery, lock their doors against "the Jews" (the Johannine terminology for the opponents of Jesus) and barricade their hearts against hope. But for the One who can break the bonds of death, locks are no obstacles. Suddenly the Tomb Breaker is in their midst, and his first gift to them is his peace.

Biblical peace is much more than the absence of war; it is a wholeness and holiness of spirit, soul, and body. Its opposite is chaos, and this community is a community in chaos. To re-create the lives of these vulnerable disciples and bring them out of their chaos and hurt, Jesus then shows them his wounded hands and side. He stands before them in the glorified reality of his humanity, of all that he has become by his life, death, and resurrection—and this includes his wounds. A risen Lord without his wounds would have little to say to the wounded ones in that Jerusalem room, just as he would have little say to us. We can be rather cynical about the devotions of some cultures that seem to delight in processions, images, wayside shrines of a bloodied Christ, judging that they have not learned to go forward to his resurrection. And yet these people are usually the ones who know what it is to suffer with the crucified Christ who by his resurrection is now present with them.

Charles Peguy recounts a story about a man who died and arrived at heaven's gates. The recording angel said to him, "Show me your wounds." "Wounds?" replied the man, "I haven't got any." And the angel asked, "Did you never think that anything was worth fighting for?"[8] The crucified Christ knew that all his sisters and brothers were worth fighting for.

Our wounds tell us something about who we are. The death camp numbers branded on a Jew's arm, the distinctive and advertised scars of the missing person, the scars of lifesaving surgery, the hated or denied wounds to our own hearts: much of our identity lies in our wounds. Some of us allow our life to drain from our wounds; others grow to new life at these broken places, and this is resurrection, this is a call to go and be wounded healers of others.

There is a Jewish wisdom story that distinguishes between those who are so fascinated with their own wounds that they cannot go readily to the assistance of another, and the wounded who are ready to serve a sister or brother:

> Rabbi Joshua ben Levi came upon Elijah standing at the entrance to a cave.
> He said to Elijah, "When will the messiah come?"
> Elijah said, "Go and ask him."
> "And where is he to be found?"
> "At the gates of Rome."
> "And what are his signs?"
>
> "He is sitting among the beggars suffering from sores. They remove and re-make their bandages all at once. But he removes and remakes his one at a time, thinking: 'Should I be required, I shall not delay.'"[9]

Jesus repeats his greeting of peace to his disciples, and then breathed his intimate breath over them. The word used here for "breathed" is used nowhere else in the New Testament. It has all the unique and privileged nuances of the enlivening spirit/breath/wind that hovered over the chaotic void of Genesis; all the wonder of God's inbreathing which raised humanity from the lump of clay with the mission to multiply, fill the earth and stew-ard it. This is a new "first day" of a new "week" of life and mission for those newly created in the risen Christ, and to which the newly baptized witness so powerfully in these Easter weeks. Jesus has no words of recrimination, no harsh reminders of the guilt of his disciples, but he does ask that they be people of forgiveness. In the presence and the power of his wounds and breath, the disciples come to their own moment of self-judgment and healing.

To the absent Thomas, the other disciples announce the resurrection as Mary Magdalene had announced it to them, and with as little success as she had! "We have seen the Lord," they say. Like them, like ourselves, Thomas demands a personal experience of Jesus before he will believe. Thomas has been rather unfairly treated by the tradition that has attached "doubting" to his name. Nowhere in the gospels is he so described. On the news of the death of Lazarus, Thomas is the one who expresses a resigned but deter-mined resolution to go with Jesus to Bethany, even if it means dying with him (John 11:16). He is the honest person who helpfully (or disconcert-ingly) blurts out the question that all probably wanted to ask but hold it back because of embarrassment. At the Last Supper, Thomas is the one to ask Jesus how they can go with him to the "place" that he is talking about when they don't know where it is (John 14:5).

Eight days later, on another "first day" of the week, Jesus again breaks into the house where his disciples are gathered with his greeting of peace and, today, his compassionate concern for the one of them who is still locked in grief, still desperately wanting to believe that life can conquer death. The wounded and risen Jesus and the disciple wounded by his painful doubts stand before one another. Here is the way, the truth and the life that Thomas was seeking (John 14:5-7), and Jesus invites Thomas to stretch out his hand to the wounds of his risen body. But it is not the physical touching (which the gospel does not describe Thomas as doing), but Jesus' personal self-offering and intimate presence to Thomas that touches *him*, demolishing all the disciple's doubts, and causing him to make the most profound and personal assent of faith in all the gospels: "My Lord and my God!" For future generations of disciples like ourselves who will listen to the gospel in the presence of the physically absent Jesus, the Lord then pronounces the last beatitude and the one that is our greatest hope: "Blessed are those who have not seen and yet have come to believe." It is to hand on such lifegiving faith, says John, that he has written his gospel.

Jesus is still offering us his wounded hands and side. Both individually (like Thomas) and as communities (like the Easter eve gathering), we are being called to recognize him in the wounded ones of our world and in our own wounds. Ronald Rolheiser wonders if our Eucharists are too anemic to help us to do this. We come to the Eucharist, he says with the same wounds that we bring to our other tables:

> Worship, then, is meant not to just celebrate our joys, our gratitude; its task is also to break us open, to make us groan in anguish, to lay bear our paranoia and to lessen the jealousies and the distance that sit between us. Here we are asked to be vulnerable before each other, to forgive and embrace each other. Bitterness, hatred and suspicion are supposed to disappear; and liturgy is supposed to help that happen. . . . What is wrong generally is not that people do not sing and dance, but that they do not break down. There is too little anguish in our liturgies.[10]

Out of such anguished faith comes the joy with which we proclaim: Christ has died. Christ is risen. Christ will come again.

The summary statement about the first Christian community seems to describe it as an ideal community, not at all wounded. In what becomes a "foundational" story for all future Christian communities, Luke wants to show the possibility of achieving that peace, unity, and joy that is born of the Spirit after the experience of Pentecost. Soon enough in the Acts of the Apostles, controversies, tensions, and failures will intrude, and there must be an ideal to be remembered as a reference point for their solution. The community is characterized not by fleeting, euphoric enthusiasm, but by persevering (v. 42) fidelity to the teaching of the apostles, by community living and sharing, by the Eucharist (the "breaking of the bread"), and by prayer. The signs and wonders worked by the apostles showed them to be heirs, through the Spirit, to Jesus' healing authority on behalf of wounded people. Common Christian values found external expression in community of goods, in sharing with any who were in need. Seeing themselves as the true Israel and the inheritors of the promises made to their ancestors, the community continues to participate in Temple worship, while joining to this their own domestic church rituals. This model of *koinonía* (community), of common belief, common living, common sharing, and common worship was embraced with the joy of the Spirit that attracted many. Is this what people, especially the young and the wounded, are seeking today? What does the ideal ask of our reality as a local and universal Church?

The newly baptized, obviously, can listen with great joy to the First Letter of Peter as the author praises God for the wonderful mercy that has enabled us to be reborn as God's sons and daughters in Christ. But, as we are continually reminded throughout the Easter weeks, we are *all* people on whom the baptismal waters never dry, people who can hope in the firm promises of God because it is a hope grounded in the resurrection of Jesus which overcomes death. This is a "living hope" that, even in suffering, will give life to the believer. It is a hope that is both present encouragement and future glory.

On those who have been tried by the fire of suffering and found to be faithful, this Letter bestows the beatitude proclaimed by the risen Christ to Thomas. Although the community to whom Peter writes has not seen Christ, they love, believe, and rejoice in the salvation won for them by him. Of course, this will not be true for everyone; the mystery of suffering remains, the paradox of Easter light and darkness, and our own free choices of darkness or light have to be made. As Ernest Hemingway wrote, "Life breaks all of us, but some people grow at the broken places."[11]

Third Sunday of Easter

• Acts 2:14, 22-33 • Ps 16:1-2, 5, 7-11 • 1 Pet 1:17-21 • Luke 24:13-35

In Luke's Gospel, the "same day" of Easter is filled with action: the spice-bearing women go to the tomb and announce the resurrection to the Eleven who consider this "idle tales." Peter at least goes to the tomb, but comes away not sure what he has seen apart from emptiness and linen burial cloths; and two disciples turn their backs on Jerusalem and head for Emmaus. It is a day of journeying, a day when we remember what Luke has told us from the beginning of his gospel and what Vatican II most solemnly proclaimed: that with Jesus we are a journeying, pilgrim people.[12] The Emmaus event is about being "on the road," about the new things that we are called to do by the risen Christ after we have heard the story and shared the broken bread.

For the two disciples of today's gospel, dreams have been destroyed and they have turned their backs on Jerusalem, the city of destiny. From Luke 9:51, Jesus had steadfastly "set his face to go to Jerusalem," and his followers had straggled after him with varying degrees of enthusiasm and insight. To avoid Jerusalem is to refuse to travel with Jesus. But now, for Cleopas and his unnamed companion, it is all over. On the way, and out of their wounded hearts, they are sharing their disappointment, pulling each other deeper and deeper into the mire of disillusionment. Then a Stranger joins them and ministers to them.

In this gospel there are wonderful strategies for our ministry, too, and perhaps the fact that Luke leaves one of the disciples unnamed is an invitation to each one of us to step into the shoes of this anonymous traveler on the way to our own "Emmaus," to the place or activity to which we flee when we want to escape and forget what seems too painful, too demanding, or too soul-destroying. The Stranger does not immediately interrupt the conversation of his disciples; he simply travels with them in silence, listening. When Luke says that their eyes were kept from recognizing Jesus, it is not physical appearance that is at issue. The whole of the New Testament considers that of no importance, because we do not know each other as persons simply by physical appearance. To recognize the truth of a person is a matter of seeing with the heart, of loving the truth of someone quite apart from height, weight, color of eyes or hair. When one's heart is broken, it is hard to focus on anything but personal grief, so for the moment the Stranger knows that communion is more important than communication. At the right time, the Stranger asks the right question and waits for an answer. He neutralizes Cleopas' rather impertinent reply by ignoring it and recognizing it as a desperate expression of pain and disappointment. At least Cleopas is ready to admit association with Jesus of Nazareth, whom they had hoped would be a "prophet mighty in deed and word," but there is delightful irony in his response. The Stranger is really the only person who *does* know the full truth of what has happened in Jerusalem, knows that the "bad news" which the disciples tell him is, in fact, "good news." Without interruption, the Stranger allows the disciples to tell their story as they experience it. They recite a litany of remembrance of Jesus that seems to be influenced more by the socio-political hopes of first century Palestine waiting for a glorious political leader to restore the nation's glory than by the faith of disciples in Jesus. He has turned out to be a failure, a victim, a dead man—and with him their hopes of "a prophet mighty in word and deed" have also died. The "idle tales" of some of the women have been dismissed as inconsequential intrusions into this reality.

In our ministry, timing is always important, as it is on the way to Emmaus. Now comes the moment when the Tomb Breaker needs to shatter the images of the Messiah that all disciples so easily make for themselves, and break open the eyes of their hearts so that they may truly see and believe. Jesus exchanges the "bad news" of the two companions for his own "good news." He inserts his new story into the story of the Hebrew Scriptures: his new exodus and return, his hospitality to death so that it may be hosted into eternal life. Jesus asks all of us the strong question: "Was it not necessary?"—all the suffering so that the Christ should enter into his glory, and is it not necessary for his disciples? Death and suffering do not destroy Jesus' messianic credentials but put them into the widest perspective of God's huge and holy love. Mixed like leaven with their own experience, hope begins to rise in the disciples.

The day is drawing to a close, but faith is about to dawn. As they come near the village, Jesus acts as if to go farther. He will not impose himself on disciples, then or now; he waits for an invitation to stay with them, and when this first response of the travelers to his story is offered, he accepts it readily. Jesus enters the house as guest and becomes the Host. At table he takes, blesses, breaks, and gives the bread. On the road he had already broken the Scriptures for them, and these ritual actions at table complete the revelation. Then he vanishes from their sight. The bread has been eaten, the story has been told, the hospitality has been offered and accepted. Word and Bread and hospitality—these will continue to make Jesus present to and understood in his post-resurrection church.

Emmaus is the place of conversion, of broken people healed by the broken word and the broken bread. Wounded hearts have become burning hearts, disfigured dreams are transfigured, and death is recognized as the way to invincible life. But Emmaus is not the place to stay. The two disciples turn and return to the Jerusalem community, driven on their mission of proclaiming the risen One to the wounded community of the Eleven. There they hear that the forgiving and compassionate Jesus has already appeared to Simon (Peter), the disciple most wounded by his denial of his Master.

Week after week in the Liturgy of the Word, whenever we sit at the eucharistic table, and day after day in our prayerful reading of Scripture, we share in the new story and new hospitality that Jesus offered to the Emmaus disciples. The temptation is to prefer the old story, the old bread of power and violence and exclusion; to prefer the option of escape from suffering rather than seeing it as inevitable in our traveling with Jesus; to rationalize about what is too difficult and too unjust to forgive. But Emmaus challenges us to walk through our daily lives in the company of the Christ who reveals himself in Scripture and Eucharist, and also in the other unexpected "strangers" whom we may meet and who share with us the bread of their lives that proclaim hope in the face of suffering and apparent hopelessness. The climax of the Emmaus narrative does not happen in the house but in the mission that takes the disciples, with burning hearts, back onto the road and to Jerusalem. We hear the story in the liturgical moment in church; we live it outside in our daily lives.

The First Letter of Peter is one of the most pastorally rich writings of the New Testament. It is also a "travel" narrative, as the author sees all Christians as pilgrims and sojourners, living in exile from our true home in heaven but traveling toward it. The Letter was written to encourage and strengthen Christians for their journey of discipleship, especially in times of distress when it is difficult to persevere in faith and hope because of the scorn of their neighbors or persecution. At Easter we remember the Lamb of God who gave himself as a sacrificial offering, and so Christians too will be called to the obedience of self-sacrifice. We can choose "silver and gold," perishable realities and contemporary "idols," or the gift of our redemption that is offered to us by Christ crucified. This is the good news that proclaims this most precious and imperishable gift. When accepted at baptism, it is a gift that brings with it the responsibility of following what we sing in the responsorial Psalm 16: "the path of life and the fullness of joy in God's presence"—a joy that was unimaginable to the psalmist, and may be as unexpected and demanding as it was to the disciples on the way to Emmaus, to the recipients of Peter's letter, or to us.

Peter's first speech after Pentecost is today's second reading. After Pentecost, Peter too has the holy fire burning hotly in his heart, and he stands up to tell the story of Jesus' death and resurrection with urgency and boldness. It is a poignant note that again Luke writes that Peter does this "with the Eleven." Matthias has been elected to take the place of Judas, but the wounds from the betrayal and cowardice of the disciples are still raw, especially for Peter. Taking the words of Psalm 16, Peter transplants them into the mystery to which he is a witness. Jesus was not abandoned to death; in his resurrection he shows humanity the path to eternal life; in the Spirit he is the most joyful and intimate presence to us. For Luke, the author also of the Acts of the Apostles, Pentecost is the beginning of the new story, the new era of the church and the time of the beginning of the fulfillment that had begun "with Moses and all the prophets" (Luke 24:27). It is now our responsibility to stand up and proclaim this same good news with our lives.

Fourth Sunday of Easter

• Acts 2:14a, 36-41 • Ps 23:1-6 • 1 Pet 2:20b-25 • John 10:1-10

The audience in today's gospel is the same as that which witnessed the healing of the man born blind in the previous ninth chapter of John. There it was the Pharisees who had ended up as the "blind" ones (John 9:39-41) because of their arrogant disbelief in the sign of Jesus' healing. They are the leaders who are shepherds blind to the needs of their people, failing in their duty of pastoral care, and ancestors of the unhappy line of some religious leaders that stretches down to our own day. The pastoral situation in the Johannine community at the end of the first century may be that which is reflected in 1 John 2:18-23. There it appears that some members of the community had become disenchanted with Jesus as Messiah and had "gone out from us," drawing others with them. Proclaimed in our assembly, this gospel has a sharp edge for today's pseudo-saviors, those who can see no possibility of salvation unless it corresponds perfectly with their own distorted vision; those leaders who are traitors—or in the language of this gospel, "thieves" and "bandits"—to their people's trust; or those who are just too lazy as presiders or homilists to enable the Christian assembly, the gathered "flock" of Jesus, to claim their rightful inheritance of Word and sacrament.

The shepherd tradition in the Old Testament was both positive and negative. "The Lord is my shepherd," we respond today in the responsorial Psalm 23, probably the best known in the Psalter. The shepherd kings, above all David, were to reflect this divine image by protecting the flock of their people, especially the poor and weak, suffering the burdens of office on their behalf, and leading them to a better life. By these criteria there were a few successful shepherd kings in God's eyes, but many more unsuccessful. On these latter the prophets called down bitter woes (Jer 23:1-4; Ezek 34), announcing that God will be the Good Shepherd who will intervene personally to save the flock. In the image used in today's gospel, Jesus himself is the shepherd to whom God has entrusted authorized access to and care of the sheepfold.

The relationship of shepherd to sheep may be difficult for people if flocks are in the thousands and herders, motor bikes, and dogs are today in control of these animals that seem to be unmotivated and rather stupid! But in the Palestine of Jesus' day, and still in many other countries, there is an intimacy of naming, calling, and leading between the shepherd and his sheep, and the shepherd needs his sheep for his livelihood. Pet nicknames, special whistling or tonal calls enable the sheep that have been herded into a common sheepfold and guarded by a night gatekeeper to respond to their own shepherd and follow him out to morning pastures. It was on Easter morning, when Mary Magdalene heard the one most personal word—her own name, "Mary!"—called by the risen Shepherd, that she responded to the One who called her by naming him: "My Master!" Familiarity with Jesus' voice demands that we hear it today: in our prayerful *lectio divina*, in our study of Scripture, often in our small parish and home groups, in our attentive and mindful listening to the Liturgy of the Word and, hopefully, the homilies that break it open for us.

The pastoral image of leaders of the church has been damaged in recent years, especially by the sexual abuse committed by some of its shepherds. But there are also those many leaders who know and love their flock despite great personal suffering, like those bishops who visited the families of all the victims of sexual abuse in their dioceses, knelt down before them, and asked to be allowed to wash their feet.

There are many voices of "thieves and bandits" shouting at us today. Not only are they the voices of the drug dealers who are stealing life from so many of our young people, or the economic rationalists who are enticing us into selfish materialism and consumerism. Some of the harshest voices are those of the ultraconservative critics in the sheepfold itself who are busily robbing the flock of their Vatican II inheritance and doing subtle violence to anyone who differs from their self-righteous positions.

In the second section of the gospel, Jesus makes another of his solemn "I AM" proclamations: "I AM the gate for the sheep . . ." The sheep must pass through this Gate if they are to find abundant life. The identity of Jesus and his "little flock" (Luke 12:32) are intimately related. The late Cardinal Joseph Bernardin of Chicago was a shepherd who, having weathered the storm of false accusations of sexually abusing a young man, was soon to learn that he had terminal cancer. Because Jesus was for him the gate through which he knew he would soon pass into the green pastures of eternal life (that we sing of in the responsorial Palm 23), Bernardin also wanted to be a "gate" for a different and more inclusive flock of other cancer sufferers. As he explained to Henri Nouwen:

> As I go to the hospital for treatment, I do not want to go through the side door directly to the doctor's office. No, I want to visit the other patients who have cancer and are afraid to die, and I want to be with them as a brother and friend who can offer some consolation and comfort. I have a whole new ministry since I became ill, and I am deeply grateful for that.[13]

In front of the Jerusalem crowds Peter burns hotly with Pentecost fire as he proclaims that salvation comes through the Shepherd whose body was ravaged on the cross and who rose again as Lord and Christ of God. Peter's words cut into the hearts of his listeners, and their response to his words is a question from the heart: "What should we do?" From his own wounded experience of his betrayal of Jesus, cauterized now by the Spirit's fire, Peter knows only too well what is needed: repentance, and its ritual expression in baptism. This echoes the challenge of John the Baptist (Luke 3:10), but now Easter and Pentecost have happened, and the baptism is not only one of water for repentance but baptism in the Spirit and fire kindled by the resurrection of Jesus and so "in his name." The repentance is not just "being sorry," but is an act of *metánoia*, of radical conversion of heart and mind that turns one's life to Christ. Beyond those to whom Peter spoke, the promise of the gift of the Holy Spirit is also for those who are as "far away" as ourselves who have responded to the voice of the Lord who calls us. Numbers are a symbolic rather than a real concern of the Scriptures; whatever was the exact number of those baptized in response to Peter's sermon, Luke's aim is to show us that the large number is a wonderful and foundational restoration of the people of God within historic Judaism, and at its heart in Jerusalem. The joy and enthusiasm will be contagious. Is it still contagious so that people ask us: "What then should we do?" Perhaps the response to the Rite of Christian Initiation (RCIA) in our parishes is an indicator?

The image of the Suffering Servant continues to be woven into the reading from the First Letter of Peter. Today's reading might almost be called a Christian meditation on the fourth Song of Isaiah (see Isa 53:4-9) that we heard on Good Friday. Again there is the imagery of sheep and shepherd. Christ is described as the shepherd and guardian of our souls, as one who was unjustly insulted, tortured, and wounded for our sins, dying so that we, his flock, might live. This example of Christ is the strength of all who suffer injustice. As we have just sung, even if we are called to walk in the valley of such darkness, we need have no fear, for the Shepherd's rod and staff are there to comfort and protect us, as well as gently prod us on.

Fifth Sunday of Easter

• Acts 6:1-7 • Ps 33:1-2, 4-5, 18-19 • 1 Pet 2:4-9 • John 14:1-12

When Marshall McLuhan once commented that we drive into the future looking through the rear vision mirror, he was rephrasing in more contemporary language the observation of the nineteenth-century Danish philosopher, Kierkegaard, that we live forward but understand backward.

We have all experienced that truth: of not realizing at the time the signifi-cance of some event, and of the joy and amazement, or sorrow and regret, as we look back a long or short time later. All the New Testament authors wrote out of a faith that looked back to Christ's life, death, and resurrection in order to drive their own and all Christian communities into the future hope of reaching the true home of our one Father in heaven. Jesus speaks about that homecoming in today's gospel from John's Last Supper farewell narrative.

To be homeless is a human tragedy that is defined not only physically in terms of living on the street, under bridges, in empty buildings, in boxes, or in refugee centers. Homelessness is also about the deep personal sense of "not belonging"—sometimes for a moment, or sometimes constantly and tragically, even in the most affluent situation or in the midst of the happiest crowd. This gospel is often proclaimed at funeral liturgies, where it reflects our abiding Easter faith and hope that at the end of our life's journey we will be welcomed into the many dwelling places of our Father's house.

Gathered as a eucharistic community, we go "backwards" into the early part of the Last Supper narrative with a sense of both the timelessness of this table discourse and its celebration in time at every Eucharist. By plac-ing this gospel after Easter, the Church wants us to hear again some of the most treasured words of Jesus, the full significance of which is only re-vealed in the light of his resurrection. There is a gentle urgency about the first words of this gospel: "Do not let your hearts be troubled. Believe in God, believe also in me." This is a rallying cry to faithfulness as Jesus draws near to his passion and death through which he will return to his Father's house. It is a rallying cry to all his disciples who will also go into death—but with the confidence that is born out of Jesus' resurrection from the dead. The "Father's house" is not spatial but relational, and so there is room for everyone who abides in Jesus as he abides "near to the Father's heart" (John 1:18). Jesus does not deny that anxiety is looming and absence is threaten-ing as he speaks, but his departure will only be that of a good host who ex-cuses himself for "a little while" (John 14:19) in order to make rooms ready for the guests who have been invited to his Father's house.

And yet Thomas' question haunts us. "Lord, we do not know where you are going. How can we know the way?" In even the most faithful life, there may come a time when we seem either to stumble suddenly into darkness or gradually wander away from old certainties. We would all like a simple, clearly marked road to direct us to the Father's house through what is often the dark wood of our lives. What we are offered is not a map but a *person*, Jesus Christ, who replies to Thomas' question with another solemn "I AM the way, and the truth, and the life" (John 14:6). When we journey along a well-traveled road, we trust the road because we know it has been made and used by others who have been there before us, putting in bridges, median strips, detours where necessary. Others have traveled this way safely. When both the way and the Traveler who has gone before us is Jesus, we should journey with the greatest confidence.

On display in Auschwitz there is a large map clearly marked with the rail systems that carried over two million people, especially Jews, from all over Europe to this place of death. At the Yad Vashem Holocaust Museum in Jerusalem, a memorial to those transported is a rail wagon hanging on a piece of broken track over a gap into the valley below. Jesus is the map that we follow to life, the way across the gap to those who fear that his leaving them will mean abandonment, and the truth that will carry us to life not death.

For the Jewish people, the prohibition against making images of God flows from the Genesis tradition that humanity, male and female together, reflects the image of God (Gen 1:26). So the answer that Jesus gives to Philip's question is, in one sense, the traditional Jewish answer: Jesus shows his disciples the face of God in his own humanity (2 Cor 4:6). In another sense, it is radically different because, in words and works, Jesus is the unique and saving revelation of God, one with God.

The "greater works" of which Jesus speaks are the new challenges to and responses of the Christian communities. These will demand the translation of the words and works of Jesus into language and witness that can be understood by future generations. If the words and works of Jesus are not spoken by lives lived practically in the power of his Spirit, they become unintelligible and unattractive. The first reading shows such a response already happening in the first Jerusalem community. In no community, then or now, does everything go smoothly all the time! Problems arise among those who have been ideally described as of one heart and mind, with provision made for everyone according to need (Acts 4:32). Diversity in membership inevitably brings tensions that can either pull a community positively forward or pull it negatively apart. What the Hellenists (Greek-speaking Jews) consider the unfair treatment of their vulnerable widows in the daily food distribution, as compared with the Hebrew widows, is a serious threat to the unity of the community. This justice issue is resolved in a way that offers a model for contemporary problems. It respects the ecclesial principle of collegiality through the initiative and discernment of the Twelve who call both Hellenists and Hebrews together and outline the problem. The principle of subsidiarity, of allowing a task to be performed at the lowest appropriate level, is respected by handing over to the community the choice of seven men who will serve them by distributing the daily food.[14] By the prayer and laying on of hands by the apostles, the choice of seven Hellenists (going by their Greek names) is affirmed. This is a wise and pastoral comment on a process that allows the original complainants to take forward the ministry in the context of difficulties wisely resolved, and unity is restored. The seven are chosen not for what they have done, but for who they are, according to the criteria proposed by the Twelve: men "of good community standing, full of the Spirit and wisdom" (Acts 6:3). Commenting on this text in his encyclical, *Deus Caritas Est*, Benedict XVI reminds us that the work of distribution of food was not purely mechanical. "In other words, the social service which they were meant to provide was absolutely concrete, yet at the same time it was also a spiritual service."[15] Our contemporary church structures could well reflect on this ecclesial experience when administration becomes so burdensome to the ordained ministers that new infrastructures are needed, and serious consideration must be given to the possibility of handing tasks over to competent lay people who are likewise "full of the Spirit and of wisdom." Like the apostles, pastors might then be more able to devote themselves to their own particular and special pastoral service. Luke adds that after the early Jerusalem community had reached "inwards" to resolve this crisis, its outreach flourished and its numbers increased, including even a large number of Jewish priests. What might be the result of following these ecclesial principles and structural changes today?

Our Father's house is not the only spiritual building referred to in today's Liturgy of the Word. The First Letter of Peter images the Christian community as constructed from the "living stones" of those who have been baptized into Christ. Stones that are quarried and dumped in piles have no use or significance until they are used for a building project. The author of this Letter forges links in the chain of memory: from the wonderful deeds of which Isaiah speaks to the laying down of the foundation stone of the Temple inscribed with the words "One who trusts will not panic," through Psalm 118:22 and its reference to the rejected cornerstone (see also Matt 21:42-44, Luke 20:17), and onto Christ, the cornerstone and foundation of the Christian community of stones that live because of their relationship with him. Built on Christ, we are the community which is "a chosen race, a royal priesthood, a consecrated people, a people set apart to sing the praises of God," taking forward the identity and mission of God's people. For those who knowingly and deliberately reject Christ, he is not the cornerstone but a stumbling block. At every Eucharist we gather as a community of praise and thanksgiving, as we sing in today's responsorial Psalm 33. We praise God for the most faithful Word that, in the fullness of time, he spoke in his Son; we give thanks for the wisdom of the early Jerusalem Church which listened and discerned and spread this Word; and we rejoice in our own privileged baptismal life as living stones built on Christ the cornerstone and supporting one another as the new temple of his body.

Sixth Sunday of Easter

• Acts 8:5-8, 14-17 • Ps 66:1-7, 16-20 • 1 Pet 3:15-18 • John 14:15-21

> We must be still and still moving
> Into another intensity
> For a further union,
> A deeper communion . . .

T. S. Eliot writes these words in *Four Quartets*.[16] The communion that we hear proclaimed in today's gospel is the deepest, most intense and personal of unions, prefaced repeatedly by "in . . . ." It is the indwelling of the Paraclete who is "in you (disciples)"; of Jesus, who says he is "in my Father"; of the disciples who are gathered "you in me and I in you." This indwelling happens through mutual love which frames the reading in its first and last verses.

Our TV screens are tragically full of images of contemporary orphans of war, of HIV/AIDS, of natural disasters. We see how the untimely death of their parents has left some children in deep sorrow and with feelings of abandonment. Jesus' leaving of his disciples is not "untimely"; it is part of his "hour" which reveals the fullness of his mystery. To help them understand this, to enable them to move from fear to faith, Jesus promises his disciples "another" Advocate. This is only one translation of *parákletos*, a word rich in its various meanings of Comforter, Encourager, Counselor. We admire those generous, if too rare, men and women who advocate in our courts of law (often without charging legal fees) for the downtrodden, the dispossessed. We can become enthralled in courtroom dramas on television or in a gripping novel. The Advocate whom Jesus will send will care for the disciples who are "dispossessed" of the human presence of Jesus and will be the real drama of their lives, as Luke will show in the Acts of the Apostles.

This Advocate will do what Jesus did, but in "another" way, through the Spirit of Jesus abiding in his disciples. If they want to cling to the Jesus they knew on this side of death, they will never know him as the risen Lord who shares new life with them. This was the Easter command of Jesus to Mary Magdalene that is proclaimed during the Easter Octave (on Easter Tuesday): "Do not hold on to me" (John 20:17).

It is all a work of love, and not love that is a private relationship with Jesus, but love that is as communal as that between the Father and Son and the Spirit of them both; love that reflects the communion between disciples and is expressed in works of love; love that reflects the life, death, and resurrection of Jesus; love that is the empowering reason for the obedience of disciples to Jesus' words and works.

For each one of us there will come a time of "farewell discourse" as we face the prospect of our own biological death. Pierre Teilhard de Chardin writes powerfully of the ultimate indwelling of God in us that can come only through death, as it did for Jesus:

> . . . and above all at that last moment when I feel I am losing hold of myself and am absolutely passive within the hands of the great unknown forces that have formed me; in all those dark moments, O God, grant that I may understand (provided only my faith is strong enough) that it is you who are painfully parting the fibres of my being in order to penetrate to the very marrow of my substance and bear me away within yourself.[17]

It is unfortunate that the Lectionary does not commence the reading from the Acts of the Apostles a few verses earlier so that Philip's mission to Samaria (he is one of the seven Hellenists we met last week) is put into the context of the persecution of the Jerusalem church and the scattering of Jesus' followers throughout Judea and Samaria. Persecution does not stop the proclamation of the gospel; it adds urgency to it, and so the mission of the church spreads, and spreads to the marginalized, to those to whom Jesus was so present in his words and works. In this instance, the marginalized are the Samaritans who were regarded by traditional Jews as "half-breed" traitors and outcasts because, for example, they raised their own temple on Mount Gerizim, committed acts of desecration of the Jerusalem Temple, and accepted only the first five books of the Hebrew bible. In going to the Samaritans, Philip is reaching out to them in a "shocking" mission, as did Jesus with the Samaritan woman and her townspeople (John 4:1-42). Peter and John come down from Jerusalem to Samaria to confirm the preaching and healing ministry of Philip, not to usurp or belittle it. Just as Philip and his six companions ensured the fair distribution of bread among the Hellenist and Hebrew widows so, with apostolic authority, Peter and John, two of the Twelve, "redistribute" the Holy Spirit among the Samaritans to ensure that they, too, like the Jerusalem church, share all things in common, especially the gift of the Spirit and the mission entrusted to them by Jesus. Again the witness is there for us: to take the Good News, to offer the healing of Jesus to those on the margins, to those held in contempt by people and prejudiced by structures, and to do this in the power of the Spirit of Jesus. Peter and John lay hands on the Samaritans to gift them with the Spirit. Who has laid hands on us—in friendship, for comfort, with encouragement—and by these simple acts has given us something of the Spirit of Jesus? And when did we last do this for someone else?

The responsorial Psalm 66 invites the assembly to "Come and see the works of God" that have been, and continue to be, worked throughout the earth. When we sing this psalm we become the joyous people of God, astonished at what has been done for us in the new exodus by which Jesus leads us from death to life, and which we celebrate as a worshipping community.

The First Letter of Peter recognizes that Christians may be put on trial because of their commitment to Christ not necessarily or often in a court situation but, rather, in the encounters with those who abuse or slander them in everyday encounters. It is Christ's acceptance of suffering, dying, and rising that is to be the example and hope of every Christian. If others ask about this hope, disciples are to respond, but in nonviolent ways. Nonviolence is not to be equated with nonresistance. We have only to look to modern martyrs such as Martin Luther King or Archbishop Oscar Romero to appreciate what they resisted and risked as people of faith, as followers of Jesus who spoke passionately and lived daringly in the face of opposition from their enemies. As Jesus did, his disciples are to speak out boldly, but with courtesy, respect, and integrity.

In 1968, Martin Luther King spoke about the nonviolent demonstrations for justice in Birmingham, Alabama, and how fire hoses were turned on the marchers to stop them. But they just kept on marching, he said, because they knew the fire within them could not be put out, and they knew water that flowed not from hoses but from their baptism. In that memory and conviction they marched on for freedom. The fire and the water of Easter are our strength for the march through the year ahead.

The Ascension of the Lord

Seventh Sunday of Easter

• Acts 1:1-11 • Ps 47:2-3, 6-9 • Eph 1:17-23 • Matt 28:16-20

The French have a proverb: "To leave is to die a little." That is what we experience when we leave a house, a community, a place full of memories, when we say good-bye to adult children as they leave home, or when we have to cope with new geographical distances between ourselves and our friends; often something in us dies. And when we offer our final farewell to our loved ones in death, there is so much pain. But out of these deaths the new can be born. After the death of his mother, Henri Nouwen wrote:

> The deeper I entered into my own grief, the more I became aware that something new was being born, something that I had not known before. I began to wonder if Jesus does not send his Spirit every time someone with whom we are connected by bonds of love leaves us . . . . by letting her go I did not lose her. Rather, I found that she is closer to me than ever. In and through the Spirit of Christ, she is indeed becoming a part of my very being.[18]

Today's feast celebrates the truth of the promise that Jesus makes to his disciples and is so integral to the Easter mystery: that only after they have stopped clinging to his physical presence, only after he has ascended to his Father, can the promise of the Father, the Holy Spirit, descend into their hearts. "Be sure to keep in touch!" These are familiar words we speak to our friends when they are leaving us, and their response is always something like, "Of course, promise!" But often, and regretfully, we fail to keep the promise. The Ascension is about promises kept through the gift of the Spirit who enables us to be always, intimately, "in touch" with Jesus.

In the first reading from the Acts of the Apostles, Luke briefly summarizes the narrative of his "Part 1" of the good news, his gospel. He then shows us the apostles wrestling for forty days with the words, the appearances and the promises of the risen Christ. The symbolism of "forty days," rather than the chronology, is what is important. It recalls the forty years of the Hebrew's wandering in the wilderness and God's tutoring them to be his people, Moses' forty days on Sinai (Exod 34:28), Elijah's forty-day journey to this same mountain of God (1 Kgs 19:8), the crossing of the Jordan after forty years of wilderness wandering. After these "forty" experiences, there is a transition to something new—a new freedom, a new covenant, a new experience of God in "thin" silence, a new land. The Ascension of Jesus proclaims a new aspect of his Easter mystery and the last task of the Incarnation. Jesus is no resuscitated corpse or pale immaterial wraith. His return to the Father, his messianic enthronement, will be as one living in the power of his resurrection and sharing this power with his disciples through the Holy Spirit who will come upon them. His followers are to wait in Jerusalem for this new promise. From Jerusalem, the hub of Israel's holiness, there will be a new transition as their mission to witness to Jesus radiates out "in all Judea and Samaria, and to the ends of the earth."

There is no place, therefore, for disciples who stand gazing up into the heavens as Jesus is lifted up and embraced by a cloud. Again, we need to be sensitive to the biblical symbolism of this account. This is no space launch with a NASA background; Luke wants us to remember the ascension of the prophet Elijah (2 Kgs 2:11) and perhaps the non-biblical tradition of Moses' ascension found in the writings of the Jewish historian Josephus (ca. 37-100) and the eclectic Jewish thinker and exegete Philo (ca. 20-50). The two men in white robes who speak to the disciples recall both the presence of Moses and Elijah and the enveloping cloud of God's presence at Jesus' transfiguration, as well as the Easter morning question of the two men in dazzling clothes to the women: "Why do you look for the living among the dead?" Jesus has not abandoned his disciples; he has lifted us up into the mystery of his ascended body, "the fullness of him who fills all," as the second reading from the Letter to the Ephesians expresses it. The cloud wraps Jesus in the rich glory of God that was with his disciples in human flesh for only a few years of our human history. The Ascension is not the time nor the season for gazing into the heavens in what seems to be "false expectation, dawdling, missing the point, longing for the quick solution."[19]

But the disciples needed to see Jesus ascending. Just as Elisha was only able to inherit Elijah's prophetic mantle after he had seen his master taken up into heaven (2 Kgs 2:9-14) and then cross the parted waters of the Jordan that he had struck with the mantle, so the disciples must now prepare to cross over into their prophetic ministry when they are clothed with the promised Spirit. And so they return to Jerusalem for the days of different waiting: a gathering which Luke will describe (in the verses following today's reading) as one of about a hundred and twenty sisters and brothers in pregnant, prayerful expectancy, with Mary, the mother of Jesus at its heart, waiting for the new to be born.

The conclusion to Matthew's gospel is chosen for this feast in Year A. Even though it does not describe any ascension, it confirms Jesus' promise to be always with his disciples. At the beginning of his gospel, Matthew has named Jesus as "Emmanuel," "God is with us" (Matt 1:23), and at the end he repeats the promise to be "with you always, to the end of the age" (Matt 28:20). It is only in the context of this promise that there can be any hope of fragile disciples fulfilling the imperatives of their great commissioning to "Go! . . . baptize! . . . make disciples! . . . teach! All this is spoken to the Eleven who, in Matthew's Gospel, we last saw forsaking Jesus when he was arrested (Matt 26:31-35). They had struggled through to enough belief in what the women had told them—that Jesus was going before them into Galilee and would meet them there—to get themselves to Galilee.

Why Galilee? Matthew's concern is not with geographical exactitude, which never brought anyone to faith. Rather, he makes geography serve his theology. The Eleven have passed through the harsh winter of their disillusionment with themselves and the pain of Jesus' passion and death. What more appropriate setting for a second spring of discipleship than Galilee, the place of their first call, first enthusiasms, first mission? In the eyes of Jewish orthodoxy, Galilee was also a marginalized region, less sophisticated and more populated by Gentiles than was Jerusalem. What Matthew is announcing to his own and future communities like our own is that we too are being called again and again, with new responsibilities, to our "Galilees": the world of the less privileged, the place and time of new beginnings of our discipleship, and that here is the starting point for the proclamation of the Gospel. The Galilee setting is also Matthew's subtle way of emphasizing the identity between the earthly and risen Jesus. For Matthew, mountains are important as places of temptation (Matt 4:8), teaching (Matt 5–7), and transfiguration (Matt 17:1-8). Here, in this last scene of his gospel, the final teaching is given, healing forgiveness is offered in Jesus' approach to and acceptance of the disciples in their brokenness, and the Eleven are transfigured into teachers, evangelizers, and baptizers in the name of the Father, the Son, and the Holy Spirit.

When the disciples see Jesus, "they worshipped him, but some doubted." The mixture of post-resurrection faith and doubt is not so much skepticism or disbelief as the fearful doubt of, for example, a Moses or Jeremiah or Peter who struggle to accept the call and its responsibility, knowing only too well their own weakness. The only other time that Matthew describes the disciples as worshipping Jesus is after the calming of the storm on the Sea of Galilee and Jesus' rescue of Peter from the waves when his faith in Jesus falters. We can easily see ourselves, individually and communally, in the same mix of worshipping faith and doubt. True discipleship does not exclude doubt, but takes it before God and into the mystery of Christ in whose absent presence we fall down and worship.

Jesus is the great boundary crosser. Having crossed the greatest divide from life into the realm of death and conquered this, he returns with freedom and authority to his disciples to call them to do what he has done. They are to stand on dangerous edges and do new things to make disciples of "all nations" and form inclusive communities where ethnicity or race or gender is no barrier to belonging. The encounter of Jesus and the Canaanite woman is to be the repeated and normative experience of the Christian community. Disciples are to minister a new initiation rite—baptism in the name of the Father, the Son, and the Holy Spirit—which no doubt reflects the developing liturgical tradition of Matthew's communities over two generations of searching faith. The Eleven are entrusted by Jesus with the teaching ministry that was withheld from them in Matthew's earlier missionary discourse (Matt 10). Now that they have experienced his life, death, and resurrection, they are able to proclaim the whole truth about Jesus.

Whether the author of the Letter to the Ephesians is Paul or a later Christian leader familiar with Paul's insights, the Pauline mystery of God's saving plan in Christ is the Letter's large background. The author prays that this church may remain constant in the hope that has come to them through the wisdom, knowledge, and insight that enlighten "the eyes of your heart." This enlightenment, therefore, is not just intellectual, but is a deeply personal and core commitment to Christ, a gift of the Father, and a share in the risen power of the Son. The opening prayer of today's Mass sums up the hope of the second reading: "You have raised us up with him: where he, the head, has preceded us in glory, there we, the body, are called in hope." It is a huge and holy hope in Christ whose glory fills the whole universe. What have we made of this hope? How has it shaped our lives?

The responsorial Psalm 47 gathers up the mood of this feast with shouts of praise and applause of God. Kings may not be popular today, but what we praise with this imagery is the Lord whose kingdom is not established by military might but by the weapons of the Gospel and the authority of the risen Christ, and is part of our inheritance. For all this we can "Sing praise!" with so much more heartfelt thanks than the psalmist who did not share our privileges.

Pentecost Sunday

(The Gospel of the Day Mass in Year A is basically the same as that of the Second Sunday of Easter; therefore, the following is a reflection on the rich Liturgy of the Word for the Pentecost Vigil.)

• Gen 11:1-9 • Exod 19:3-8 • Ezek 37:1-14 • Joel 3:1-5 • Rom 8:22-27 • John 7:37-39

Even if we do not go to the Vigil, we could well read and reflect on the extended readings from the Old (four of the possible seven are chosen here) and New Testaments, for in these the creating Word of God continues to breathe over the assembly. In their circular letter, *Preparing and Celebrating the Paschal Feasts* (January 16, 1988), the Congregation for Divine Worship wrote:

> Encouragement should be given to the prolonged celebration of Mass in the form of a vigil whose character is not baptismal as in the Easter Vigil, but is one of urgent prayer, after the example of the apostles and disciples, who

persevered in prayer with Mary, the mother of Jesus, as they awaited the Holy Spirit.[20]

All the readings focus on the Spirit who has been present and active in creation and in significant moments in the history of God's people. In Jesus is the fullness of the Spirit which he continues to pour forth on his Church and its mission to the ends of the earth, the focus of the Pentecost feast.

The story of Babel is an inspired symbol story of human attempts to build a self-sufficient world without God, in which human beings will rule. It is a reflection on lived human experience, a story of tragic ambition to pierce the heavens and make men and women equal to God, an attempt to "make a name for ourselves" with what is insubstantial—the bricks and cement of the narrative. The builders do make a name for themselves, but "Babel" becomes a symbol of confusion, not creation, with no communication possible between them, and no human solidarity. With delightful irony, God is depicted as coming down to see the tower that from a human perspective seems so tall but to God is insignificant. The biblical author wants us to hear God's laugh at the arrogance of human beings!

Babel has profound lessons for our world, for as Jonathan Sacks, the chief rabbi of Britain and the Commonwealth writes:

> By aspiring to reach heaven by technological prowess rather than moral conduct, the builders of Babylon discovered that not only do we fail to reach heaven, we lose our compact nature, our unity, on earth.
>
> Babel is a profound commentary on the human desire to take the place of God.[21]

On a smaller scale, we can still be guilty of the same ambitions: to be accountable to no one but ourselves or myself; to weaken by our personal animosities the fabric of human relations that is bonded by mutual love and respect. Tonight we pray that the descent of the holy fire of the Spirit will destroy our Babels, our global and personal babbling and stammering confusion, our secular and religious megalomanias, and fuse us into a reconciled people. Tomorrow and into the future, beyond the liturgical moment, we are called by God's word to live what we pray.

The reading from the Book of Exodus recounts the giving of the teaching (Torah/Law) to Moses on Mount Sinai fifty days after the exodus from Egypt and the Hebrew's Passover from slavery to freedom. It reads like a liturgy: Moses, the mediator, ascends to the holy place for a covenant-making with God that will give special identity to the Hebrews as God's beloved people, who will be carried by God as a parent eagle carries the fledgling on its wings, teaching it to fly by tossing it into the abyss of air but always ready to swoop down and bear it up on parental wings until the day when it can fly free and strong by itself. Israel is to be a consecrated people, God's priestly servants, and so Moses gathers the people to receive this word of God. To capture the emotion and reality of the event, images and symbols are needed. Luke will use the same images of "something like" fire and wind and shaking to describe the Christian Pentecost event that establishes the identity of the church and shakes the disciples out into the world with fiery enthusiasm to spread the good news of the risen Christ—the good news that we are to proclaim with zeal, knowing that even when we fail, God will catch us on the "eagle's wings" of his love and carry us until we are strong enough to fly.

"Our bones are dried up, and our hope is lost; we are cut off completely" (Ezek 37:11). This cry in the valley of dead bones is the complaint of the Jewish exiles in Babylon when they were tempted to give up on life, on their future, on their God. But even though death abounds, so does the vivifying spirit/breath of God which God commands the prophet to breathe over the symbolic "dead bones" of the exiles. Exile and return, the rhythm of Jewish history, is achieved in this spirit. Almost six centuries later, the dead bones of Jesus would be raised by this Spirit after his three-day exile in death, and through his Spirit the dead hopes of the first Christian community will revive. In every generation, the cry of the dead bones becomes the cry of all the wretched of our earth: the victims of war, the famine-driven refugees, the unknown multitudes of victims of the corrupt and powerful. Their hope lies in today's prophets who will breathe the Spirit of God into them and over their lands. Our baptism has made prophets of us all, and it is our responsibility to exercise this prophetic role however we can: at the ballot box, by participation in justice efforts on behalf of today's exiles, and by assuring that our own lives are a hopeful witness to those who have no hope.

In his first post-Pentecost sermon, Peter quotes from the prophet Joel whose words we hear tonight. In the name of the Lord, Joel proclaims that the spirit that God will pour forth on humanity will transform people into dreamers and visionaries of new possibilities: of a new equality between young and old, men and women, slave and free. God's spirit is no respecter of social distinctions, but becomes a danger to domination by age, gender, or wealth. In the "last days," the days of cosmic signs of fire and smoke, of darkened sun and bloodred moon, the people who "call on the name of the Lord," that is, those who confess God's wonders, will be saved. In Acts 2:38, Peter promises that those who believe in Jesus will inherit the fulfillment of Joel's prophesy in the new age of the Spirit and the "last age" of the church.

When people are seized by God's Spirit they hear the sigh that goes through the world, and they begin to become newly and sensitively aware of the longing for life that is as small as the human heart and as large as the cosmos. "The whole of creation is on tiptoe with excitement, waiting for God's children to be revealed as who they really are."[22] Something new is coming to birth, and in the labor pains of the church, in the midst of the pains of the world, the Spirit of God sustains and inspires us. We cannot abandon the world to ecological destruction, but must bring to it "now" something of the final healing and transformation, which is the "not yet" reality of the kingdom of the world that will become the kingdom of the Lord and his Messiah (Rev 11:15). Nor can we be struck dumb with grief at the apparent failures of our hope, cosmic or personal, for it is at these very times that we need to surrender to the Spirit within us who intercedes for us "with sighs too deep for words" and so gives our groaning, birthing world a silent and most articulate voice before God. To realize this is a privilege that is beautifully expressed in an Easter commentary: "The Spirit is sleeping in the rock, dreams in the flower, awakens in the animal, and knows that it is awake in the human being."[23]

The vigil readings culminate with the words of John 7:37-39. The backdrop to this chapter is the Jewish feast of Sukkot or Booths (see John 7:2). In the time of Christ, a water-drawing ceremony was part of its celebration in Jerusalem. A torchlight procession with musicians and dancers accompanied the priests to the Spring of Gihon, the main water source of the city. The start of the rainy season usually coincided with this feast, and in a land where water was scarce and precious, prayer for plentiful rains were offered. The "first water" of the season was drawn from the spring, carried in procession to the Temple, and poured out on the ground to symbolize the people's overflowing joy in and hope for this gift of God. On the last day of the feast, says John, Jesus stands up and proclaims that those who are thirsty should come to him and drink. Out of the heart of the believer will then flow the saving witness to Jesus who is the source of life and light. After Jesus is glorified in his resurrection it would flow over "about three thousand souls" on the Lukan day of Pentecost (Acts 2:41), and over every baptized person until the end of time.

Pentecost is a continuing event that dares us: dares us to become a community of fire who will keep the flame of passion for God, and for the world God loves so much, burning strongly, even in the darkest nights. It dares us to become a community of strong wind that blows the good news of the risen Christ through the cracks and crevices of our fractured world. If we, too, persevere in prayer and community, the Spirit will enable us to speak in intelligible tongues to contemporary men and women, young and old. We will make mistakes, but God will never fail us; the Spirit will never allow the community of believers to suffocate. As the poet prays to this Holy Spirit:

> Engender upon our souls your sacred rhythms; inspire
> The trembling breath of the flute, the exultant cosmic psalm,
> The dance that breaks into flower beneath the storm-voiced mountain;
> Array in your dazzling intricate plumage the swaying choir.[24]

Notes

1. Vatican II, *Dogmatic Constitution on the Church*, art. 40.

2. Julian of Norwich, *Showings (Long Text)*, The Classics of Western Spirituality (New York: Paulist Press, 1978) 189.

3. R. S. Thomas, "The Coming," *Collected Poems 1945-1990* (London: Phoenix, 2002) 234.

4. Eugen Drewermann, *Dying We Live: Meditations for Lent and Easter*, trans. Linda M. Maloney and John Drury (Maryknoll, NY: Orbis Books, 1994) 101.

5. *General Norms for the Liturgical Year and Calendar*, no. 22.

6. Tom Knowles, s.s.s., "The Fifty Days: Easter," *The Cross, Our Glory*, ed. Frank O'Loughlin (East Melbourne: Diocesan Liturgical Centre, n.d.) 52.

7. *Rite of Christian Initiation of Adults*, no. 234.

8. Quoted in Timothy Radcliffe, o.p., *What is the Point of Being a Christian?* (New York: Burns & Oates, A Continuum Imprint, 2005) 75.

9. Shared at a Jewish-Christian meeting of table conversation and storytelling.

10. Ronald Rolheiser, o.m.i., *Forgotten Among the Lilies: Learning to Live Beyond Our Fears* (New York: Doubleday, 2005) 182.

11. Quoted in Daniel O'Leary, "Glory of the Wounds," *The Tablet*, (February 18, 2006) 14.

12. Vatican II, *Dogmatic Constitution on the Church*, art. 48.

13. Henri J. M. Nouwen, *Sabbatical Journey: The Diary of His Final Year* (New York: The Crossroad Publishing Company, 1998) 9.

14. Cf. Vatican II, *Pastoral Constitution on the Church in the Modern World*, art. 86c. The principle of subsidiarity was first formulated by Pius XI in his 1931 encyclical, *Quadragesimo Anno*, pars. 79–80.

15. Benedict XVI, Encyclical Letter, *Deus Caritas Est*, art. 21.

16. T. S. Eliot, *The Complete Poems and Plays* (London: Faber and Faber, 2004) 183.

17. Pierre Teilhard de Chardin, *Le Milieu Divin: An Essay on the Interior Life* (London: Collins, Fontana Books, 1967) 89–90.

18. Henri J. M. Nouwen, *In Memoriam* (Notre Dame, IN: Ave Maria Press, 1980) 59–60.

19. Daniel Berrigan, s.j., *Whereon to Stand: The Acts of the Apostles and Ourselves* (Baltimore, MD: Fortkamp Publishing Company, 1991) 8.

20. Quoted in Normand Bonneau, o.m.i., *The Sunday Lectionary: Ritual Word, Paschal Shape* (Collegeville: The Liturgical Press, 1998) 93.

21. Jonathan Sacks, *To Heal a Fractured World: The Ethics of Responsibility* (London: Continuum, 2005) 143–44.

22. N. T. Wright, "The Letter to the Romans," *The New Interpreter's Bible*, Vol. X (Nashville, TN: Abingdon Press, 2002) 596.

23. Quoted in Leonardo Boff, *Cry of the Earth, Cry of the Poor*, trans. Phillip Berryman (Maryknoll, NY: Orbis Books, 1997) 169.

24. James McAuley, "To the Holy Spirit," *Collected Poems 1936-1970* (Sydney: Angus and Robertson Publishers, 1971) 69.

5

The Season of Ordinary Time

The Season of Ordinary Time is a "split time" of the *per annum* or "through the year" weeks between the Baptism of the Lord and Ash Wednesday and the weeks after Pentecost. They are the ordered weeks, from 1–34, that progress more or less continuously with the companionship of the Gospel of Matthew in this Year A of the three-year cycle. To call the weeks "ordinary" should not imply that this is a dull and uneventful season. Every Sunday is a celebration of the paschal mystery, but the Sundays of the festal season of Advent, Christmas, Lent, and Easter focus on specific aspects of Christ's mystery. The Sundays of Ordinary Time embody the ancient tradition of the Church's celebration of the Lord's Day before the development of the cycle of solemnities and feasts.

These are the weeks of persistent faith: of the call to the disciples and their response to Jesus, of seed-planting and harvest, of storytelling, of yeast-mixing and thirst-quenching, of cross-carrying and yoke-bearing, of discovering the new possibilities for our discipleship as ordinary people who are touched by the extraordinary grace of God within the demands of our daily life. Sunday after Sunday, therefore, we gather: to listen to God's proclaimed Word, to take the Easter bread in our hands and drink the Easter cup, and to keep alive the Easter fire in our hearts.

Matthew's Gospel is structured around five discourses: the Sermon on the Mount (Matt 5–7), the Mission Discourse (Matt 10), the Parable Discourse (Matt 13), the Sermon on the Church (Matt 18), and the Discourse on the End Time (Matt 23–25). In these Jesus is the great teacher, the Messiah of the word, but what he teaches he also does as Messiah of the deed—in the narratives of his miracles, his relationships, and above all in his passion, death, and resurrection. For Matthew, writing for a predominantly but not exclusively Jewish Christian community about the years 85–90, the Hebrew Scriptures were a precious part of the treasure that the scribe who was trained for the kingdom would bring to the community (see Matt 13:52). The treasure of Jesus' teaching was that it did not disregard the "old" but gave it "new" and ultimate significance.

The unity between the Old and New Testaments governs the choice of the first reading. Correspondence between the first and the gospel reading may rest on a mention of a place, a similar event or deed, or a related and complementary viewpoint. The main concern of those who made the Lectionary choices was to expose the worshipping assembly to a representative sample of the riches of God's word that proclaims God's personal, saving relationships with men and women not so different from us.

The semi-continuous second readings in Year A are from the Letters of Paul: to the communities of Corinth, Rome, Philippi, and Thessalonika. We hear of the successes and failure, the joys and sorrows, the creative and destructive tensions of these early churches as they struggled "to put on the Lord Jesus Christ" (Rom 13:14) in their daily lives. The same struggle is ours.

On the two Sundays following Pentecost we celebrate the overflow of the Easter season into Ordinary Time with the Solemnities of the Most Holy Trinity and the Body and Blood of Christ. Both feasts, introduced into the liturgical calendar in the second millennium, celebrate a later doctrinal development in our understanding of Christ in his mysteries.

Our hope for the transforming effect of our Sunday worship "through the year" is described by Eugene Peterson:

> When we walk out of the place of worship we walk with fresh, recognizing eyes and a re-created, obedient heart into the world in which we are God's image participating in God's creation work. Everything we see, touch, feel, and taste carries with it the rhythms of "And God said . . . and it was so . . . and it was good." We become adept at discerning the Jesus-signs and picking up on the Jesus-words that reveal the presence and the glory. We are more deeply at home in the creation than ever.[1]

This is our challenge for thirty-four weeks.

The Most Holy Trinity

• Exod 34:4-6, 8-9 • Dan 3:52-55 • 2 Cor 13:11-13 • John 3:16-18

It is a huge mystery, this "unnumbered three" of whom George Herbert wrote:

> Whose sparkling light access denies:
> 　Therefore thou dost not show

> This fully to us, till death blow
>   The dust into our eyes:
> For by that powder thou wilt make us see.[2]

When we trace the sign of the cross on the forehead of a loved one into whose eyes this dust of death has blown, we profess our faith in the Father, Son, and Holy Spirit in whose communion we believe our dead now see fully. At our baptism we were named and claimed for the Trinity; at the beginning and end of every Mass, when we bless our children, the food on our table, or "furrow our forehead" (Tertullian) with the sign of the cross, we acknowledge the Trinity by word and gesture. But familiarity may make us mindless about the name and relationship we profess. It is a relationship of love that is meant to "furrow" not just our foreheads but also our hearts, plowing its mystery deeply into this core of our being.

The mystery of God which all three readings proclaim is love—and love is never solitary, never static nor finished. Theology has tried to express this idea in the word *perichorésis* or "dance/choreography."

Choreography suggests dynamic, mobile partnership: encircling, encompassing, permeating, enveloping, outstretching. As Catherine Mowry LaCugna writes:

> There are neither leaders nor followers in the divine dance, only an eternal movement of reciprocal giving and receiving, giving again and receiving again . . . . The divine dance is fully personal and interpersonal, expressing the essence and unity of God. The image of the dance forbids us to think of God as solitary.[3]

We have come to know the God who is One through the Holy Lord who partnered Israel (first reading), the humanity of the Son who embraces the world (gospel), and the Spirit who stretches out to be the bond of love in the church with the Father and Son (second reading). It is this name, this personal relationship with the Trinity, that we are greeted with, and dismissed from, at every Eucharist. Every Eucharist, therefore, sends us out on a mission of love.

In the first reading, Moses is summoned by God to return to Mount Sinai with the two tablets of stone. More accurately we could say with the "second" tablets, for this encounter comes after Moses has smashed the first tablets in anger when he finds the impatient Hebrews had made and worshipped a golden calf with the encouragement of Aaron, Moses' brother (Exod 32:19-20). It is not hard to imagine the fear and trepidation that Moses felt when he went to keep this next appointment with God after his people's idolatry. Hidden in a crevice of the rock, Moses hears the Lord pass before him in a cloud, a symbol of divine revelation. And the name that is spoken by God is not one of a harsh judge but of a God "merciful and gracious, slow to anger, and abounding in steadfast love and faithfulness." This is a God of compassionate womb-love (the Hebrew word for "compassion" derives from the word for "womb"), never vengeful or wrathful, and always faithful to covenant partners. Before this God, Moses can bow down with confidence in divine forgiveness, for this is a God who loves and wants to be loved.

The responsorial psalm is taken from the canticle of praise Daniel and his companions sang after they were saved by God from the fiery furnace. Like Moses, like Paul, like Nicodemus in today's readings, and like ourselves, life is threatened by our personal and communal weaknesses: our sinfulness, our fear, our failures, our obtuseness. Out of all these dangers God will rescue us if we have the fidelity and trust of Daniel and his two companions. In such joyful faith we are enabled to praise the love of God—shown us most fully in the Jesus that Daniel never knew—rather than to focus on the "flames" that surround us.

In the book, *The Color Purple*, by Alice Walker, a battered and exploited woman, Celie, meets the exotic and free-spirited Shug. She tells Celie that mutual love should be the reality behind all our relationships; that love transfigures and brutality disfigures; that it's not only pleasing God that matters, because God is always trying to please us back with surprises—just as Shug, the mistress of Celie's cold, distant husband, is a surprise for Celie.[4]

The biggest "surprise" that God has sprung on the world is the love which takes flesh and comes among us in the Son. The gospel of today's feast again proclaims that God is not intent on judging and condemning the world, but judgment will happen—not as a future event but as a present reality for which we ourselves are responsible when we accept or reject the Son. Like Nicodemus, whose encounter with Jesus begins in the verses immediately preceding today's gospel (which most regard as continuing the dialogue between him and Jesus), we are so often "night visitors" to the mystery of God, afraid to come into the light, wanting to keep our acceptance and understanding of God within the confines of our own manageable and limited experiences. Today's feast invites us to remember God's most gracious hospitality, most free and generous love for all created reality. Through Christ and the Spirit, in whom our humanity is born again when the womb waters of baptism break over us, we are a precious and privileged part of this creation.

It will often be a struggle to live what we are, and we need the encouragement that Paul gives to the Corinthians in his Second Letter. This is a Letter in which Paul has to deal with the pain of attacks on his apostolic credentials, not from without but from within the community. He has admitted his weakness which can be his strength only in Christ, and has needed to write strong criticism to this often cantankerous church which he still loves dearly. In his closing words, Paul bids the Corinthians farewell with words that encourage them to live in joy, peace, and love for one another, because this is the life that reflects their God. Liturgically, this is shown by the "holy kiss" (of peace). Paul ends with the blessing that we would now describe as Trinitarian: the grace that is received through the gift of Jesus Christ, the all-embracing love of God, and the communion of the Holy Spirit. This is the dynamism that binds together every Christian community. It is also the challenge to love, to comfort, to live in peace with one another.

As Augustine wrote, "If you see charity, you see the Trinity."[5] Over and above all theological speculation, the best way of meditating on and understanding something of the extraordinary mystery of the Trinity is to reflect on the love that we ordinary Christians show in our daily lives. Beautiful though this may be, it is only the faintest image of the love of Father, Son, and Spirit, whose communion is the source not only of our responsibility to one another but also to the whole interdependent cosmos.

The Body and Blood of Christ

• Deut 8:2-3, 14-16 • Ps 147:12-15, 19-20 • 1 Cor 10:16-17 • John 6:51-58

This is the day when we acknowledge that we have Christ in our blood; that we are the people for whom the Word takes flesh, the people who are hungry and thirsty for God. It recalls Holy Thursday, the first day of the Triduum, and the God who feeds us with the real eucharistic presence of Jesus. On the Sunday after we have celebrated the mystery of the Most Holy Trinity and the communion between Father, Son, and Holy Spirit, we remember that we enter most intimately into this communion in the Eucharist. This is beautifully expressed with the artist's graphic and religious insight in the well-known icon, *The Holy Trinity*, painted by Andrei Rublev (ca. 1420). It was inspired by the revelation at the Oak of Mamre where Abraham and Sarah offer hospitality to three strangers who become the one Lord of covenant promises. The unity in diversity of the three figures and their communion in mutual, hospitable love is suggested by the illuminated haloes, the heads inclined to one another, and their countenances of eternal youthfulness. In one hand each holds a staff of authority while the other hand gestures to the sacrificial cup that rests on the altar around which they sit, and which is at the center of their attentive gazing.

Today the emphasis is no longer on processions with the Blessed Sacrament but on participation in the mystery which, as St. Augustine says in one of his Easter Sermons (227) enables us to say "Amen" to what *we are*: the body of Christ, head and members. This is what gives us the strength not just to walk behind the Sacrament on this day, but to walk in the power of Christ's eucharistic presence day after day, aware of our dignity, our communion with and responsibility for one another.

Near the end of the Bread of Life Discourse of John 6, the gospel reading in Year A, Jesus' proclamation that his flesh is to be eaten and his blood drunk shocks his Jewish audience. His words are meant to shock us, too, into hearing with new ears and understanding with new and open hearts. In the prologue to his gospel (John 1:14), as in this reading, John uses the word *sarx* (flesh), instead of *sōma* (body). The latter meant a body tangible to our human senses, while *sarx* implies human nature in its completeness. The phrase "flesh and blood" is a common way of referring to or characterizing a human being. In positioning this solemnity so soon after the close of the Easter Season, we are reminded that the resurrection spills over into the Eucharist and is central to its reality. What we receive is the risen Christ who is now present to his church, and so to eat and drink, to accept his whole risen sacramental presence of flesh and blood and to abide in its mystery, is a pledge of sharing in Christ's resurrection.

In the wilderness, Jesus' ancestors experienced the new and unexpected gift of the manna. God gave them this when they were hungering after the bread of Pharaoh, even though that tasted of injustice. Better, they cried to Moses, the stomach full of slavery than the empty hunger of desert freedom. In that dangerous, vulnerable moment, God tested the people to see if they would commit themselves to doing things God's way. Jesus reminds the people around him of this past complaint (John 6:49) because to accept Jesus as broken bread to be eaten and wine to be poured out is to take the "manna risk" of the new covenant. Today when we hold out our hands and accept the broken bread, we are daring to take hold of a body that was broken in death and rose for freedom and justice. When we drink the cup, we pledge ourselves to solidarity—especially with the losers, the powerless, the have-nots, the "dregs" of society, the sinners—for whom Jesus drained the cup of suffering. This solemnity, therefore, should focus our attention on what we can so easily forget: that every Eucharist should create in us a great sense of unease about disunity, discrimination, and hypocrisy in the body of Christ. No matter how liturgically correct or ritually beautiful our celebration, much is missing from the "full, conscious and active participation" of the assembly[6] if we do not do this in memory of the Just Servant. Liturgical memory is not a nostalgic or romantic recall of the past, but a present reality that demands that, in Jesus' name, we do justice now and in the future. The Eucharist is a gathering place and a stopping place for us nomads on our own exodus way toward the kingdom of justice and peace.

In the first reading from the Book of Deuteronomy, the ancestors of Jesus are urged never to forget the loving providence of God during the wilderness years. Deuteronomy means "second law," a recalling and a reinterpretation of the Mosaic Law/Teaching/Torah in a later time. We might also think of it as a "seconding" of the Mosaic Law in the sense that we "second" a motion or affirm and endorse an original proposal. Today's reading is part of what is structured as a speech of Moses in which he urges the people to remember God's providence in the vulnerable wilderness years. There God tested their hearts, and they were humbled when found to be deceitful and petulant people with meager resources of their own. When they were hungry and thirsty during their wandering, God fed them with manna and water. But when they came out of the wilderness, in times of greater abundance and a more settled lifestyle, the temptation was to forget this gift-giving God, to become complacent, full of their own achievements, and lose their hunger and thirst for God. Times of success and prosperity bring their own subtle temptations in every age and place. As the late rabbi Abraham Heschel once remarked, the contemporary concern in many affluent societies is not how to keep faith in the underground but above ground in our condominiums and corporations.

"One does not live by bread alone, but by every word that comes from the mouth of the Lord" (Deut 8:3) is the biblical quotation from this rich Deuteronomic heritage that Matthew puts on the lips of Jesus in his wilderness temptation (Matt 4:4). Our hunger is fed by the Liturgy of the Word and by prayerful reading of the Scriptures during the "forty years" (a symbolic biblical number of fullness), our lifetime of wandering and temptation. When are we faithful to and when are we forgetful of the God who gifts us not only with the biblical word, but also with the Word made flesh and made living bread so that we may eat and draw everlasting life from Jesus?

Paul says it boldly to his church at Corinth. Through our communion in the cup of blessing and the broken bread we not only become one with Christ, we become one with one another. We are called to be nourishment for our sisters and brothers, to be living bread for them in their wilderness, ready to be broken, given, and consumed by them.

An Irish priest recalled how he had arrived at his new African mission a few days before today's solemnity. He worked hard at the preparation of his first homily and on the day stood up to preach with enthusiasm and confidence and a great desire to make a good impression. But he found it distracting and difficult to make himself heard, not because the church had no public address system, but because in the small, intimate, and poor worship space there was a loud sucking and gurgling of about a hundred babies being fed and pacified at their mothers' breasts! Suddenly the priest realized that the truth of what he wanted to preach was being imaged before him: sacrificial love, life poured out as food and given for the sake of another. As he later remarked, "I told those women that they were preaching Eucharist to me, and that, as mothers, they surely understood so much about the supreme self-giving and sacrificial love of Jesus which is the foundation of their own love."[7]

Second Sunday in Ordinary Time

• Isa 49:3, 5-6 • Ps 40:2, 4, 7-10 • 1 Cor 1:1-3 • John 1:29-34

The readings for this Sunday are rather like a hinged door. The Lectionary pushes it open to allow us to gaze backward at the significant figure of John the Baptist who points to the One we have celebrated as coming among us in the flesh in the Advent and Christmas seasons. And the readings also direct our gaze forward to our ongoing call to be servants of God among the nations for the long haul of Ordinary Time. The number of Sundays between the Baptism of the Lord (also called the First Sunday in Ordinary Time) and the First Sunday of Lent varies each year, depending on the date on which Lent commences.

What is stressed in today's readings is appropriate as we move out of festal highpoints: we are called, in all seasons, every day, to live what we are by the grace of God—chosen and gifted people. Paul says it so succinctly in the first three verses of his Letter to the Corinthians that we read semi-continuously from this Sunday through to the eighth Sunday of this year. He introduces himself and his brother worker, Sosthenes, as called by the will of God to minister to the Corinthians. The initiative is always God's; the response is ours. The Corinthians, likewise, are called to be saints in the Pauline way of understanding this identity. It is an identity not reserved to those who might be perceived as almost unattainably holy "peak-dwellers," remote for those of us trudging across the plains. Paul sees being a saint as responding in every season of our life, in its heights and depths, to God's longing for each of us. The supreme expression of this longing was Jesus Christ into whom we are baptized, in whom we become "church" in Corinth, and in every place in every age. Because it is so easy for a church in any one place to become insular and concerned with its own particular successes and failures, Paul is careful to remind his Corinthian church that they belong to the larger community of the holy people of God: all the saints who call on the name of Jesus Christ and who depend on and trust in him.

As we will see as the year's readings continue, the Corinthians were a boisterous church in a society with a well-established pecking order between rich and poor, slave and free. Most Christians were poor, but some problems arose with the attitudes of the rich members of the church; other difficulties stemmed from the predominant Gentile membership and Paul's need to "re-socialize" them into familiarity with the Jewish Scriptures and traditions of Israel, while at the same time recognizing that in Christ they have become "the Israel of God" (see Gal 6:16). In all these situations, unity was Paul's great concern—but unity that respected the diverse individual situations and gifts of the Corinthians. At the beginning of his letter, therefore, Paul wishes his church grace and peace so that having received the blessing of their calling from God in Jesus Christ, they may be a blessing to one another. In his introduction to the 2004 edition of Donald Nicholls' book, *Holiness*, Gerard Hughes, s.j. describes how Donald, a highly respected international academic recently returned to England from his position as rector of the Ecumenical Institute for Theological Studies at Tantur, Jerusalem, came home exhausted from a university meeting:

> "It was a dreadful meeting," he said. "We all had to sit down and introduce ourselves. People introduced themselves as professors, readers, lecturers, doctors, etc. When it came my turn, all I wanted to say was, 'My name is Donald. I am a unique manifestation of God.'"[8]

In the background, listen to Paul's applause!

In the gospel we meet John the Baptist who also knew his place in salvation history. He sees Jesus coming toward him and points him out as "the Lamb of God who takes away the sin of the world." Those listening to John, including those sent from the Pharisees (John 1:24), would be sensitive to the Hebrew biblical, cultic, and liturgical symbol of the lamb which recalled both the messianic Suffering Servant tradition (Isa 53:7) and the Passover lamb (Exod 12:1-13) in the history of Israel's deliverance. Gathered as a eucharistic assembly, we affirm our faith in the One to whom John pointed, who is coming to us not on the Jordan banks but as the center of our liturgy: the Lamb of God who, by his life, death, and resurrection, has taken away the sin of the world. The gospel refers to "sin," to the collective brokenness and sinfulness of the world, not to individual sins, and to the collective social and structural evil that will be arrayed against Jesus by his enemies. As human beings we have solidarity in this sin.

The evangelist introduces us to John the Baptist in his Prologue (John 1:6-9) because the vision of the Prologue is what we hear John is sent to proclaim: Jesus as the pre-existent Word, the Spirit-filled one, the Son of God.

Today's reading suggests that John recognized Jesus when he came to him for baptism, unreported in this gospel. At Jesus' baptism, explains the Baptist, the Holy Spirit descended on and now remains with Jesus. John the Baptist's mission was always to point to Jesus, never to himself. The last words that the Baptist speaks later in the Fourth Gospel sum up his calling: "He must increase, but I must decrease" (John 3:30). Our discipleship, too, without possessiveness, without blocking the view of Jesus, must point others to the One who is "coming toward" them. We all need the humility of John the Baptist that recognizes that when we are acting prophetically it is not our cause, our actions, our self-image, but God's about which we are witnessing.

The Servant of the second Servant Song of Isaiah is also a "called one," as he himself testifies. (Given the various opinions on the identity of the Servant, in this liturgical context it is more important to concentrate on the mission.) The Servant accepts the role of being a light to the nations so that God may be glorified beyond Israel. Light is needed only in darkness, and Israel is enduring dark days at the hand of other nations, yet its own survival is dependent on outreach to them and not withdrawal into a self-protective cocoon. It is puzzling why the Lectionary omits the fourth verse which shows that the suffering and apparent failure of the Servant also give witness to God.

The Servant cannot allow Israel's God to be too small nor its mission too confined. Vatican II makes the same point about the servant church in the *Decree on the Missionary Activity of the Church*. By promoting human dignity and unity and cooperating with state and other religious agencies, especially in situations of war, famine, ignorance, and disease, Christ's disciples are:

> . . . teaching those religious and moral truths which Christ illumined with His light. In this way they are gradually opening a wider approach to God. Thus they help men and women to attain to salvation by love for God and neighbor. In this mystery the new person has appeared, created according to God (cf. Eph 4:24). In it the love of God is revealed (art. 12).

Our servant mission and witness are also much closer to home: to affirm others so that they are able to believe that they, too, are saints, "unique manifestations of God"; to be a light in the dark days in the lives of our sisters and brothers that helps them to see through us to the love of God for them; to create peace and bring the saving grace of God into our own relationships.

The Isaian Servant, Paul, and John the Baptist, all respond to God's calling with lives that are offered in obedient praise. When we sing the words of Psalm 40: "Here I am, Lord; I come to do your will," we are praying that such may be our response to our calling as disciples of Jesus. As a eucharistic assembly, the psalm becomes our prayer for unplugged ears that can hear the call of God's word, for willingness to live a sacrificial lifestyle, for lips that will proclaim the justice that is truly deep in our hearts. It is a strong and urgent call to discipleship at the beginning of Ordinary Time.

Third Sunday in Ordinary Time

• Isa 8:23–9:3 • Ps 27:1, 4, 13-14 • 1 Cor 1:10-13, 17 • Matt 4:12-23

The Incarnation took place in a certain time and certain place, and Jesus humbly accepted these limitations when he "emptied" himself into our humanity (Phil 2:7). Matthew situates the place where Jesus' mission begins as Capernaum in the region of Galilee; the time is after John the Baptist has been "handed over" and imprisoned as one day Jesus will be. Matthew is explicit about where Jesus' ministry began, naming the northern parts of Israel that, as we hear in the first reading from Isaiah, were annexed by Tiglath-Pileser III in the eighth century B.C.E. and incorporated into the Assyrian provincial system with the consequent deportation and disappearance of the people from their own lands. Just as they hoped for a light in their darkness, so Matthew proclaims the public appearance of Jesus and his call to repentance, to radical conversion of heart and life for the sake of the kingdom, as the great light which dawns over the land. In Jesus the reigning presence of God is established fully, but it is not yet established over humanity and all creation. Matthew interprets the Old Testament text in the light of current events at the beginning of Jesus' public ministry; he does this not to denigrate or dispose of the Old Testament, the precious Scriptures that Jesus himself read and prayed, but because, as Donald Senior explains:

> For Matthew, Jesus is the flowering of the history of God's people; Jesus and his mission are God's response to the promises of salvation given to Israel. Therefore, all the expectations and longings condensed within the Hebrew Scriptures find their outpouring and ultimate resolution in Jesus.[9]

Jesus begins to call those who are willing to allow him to rule over their hearts and so spread the reigning presence of God and "make disciples of all nations" (Matt 28:19). His first call is to four fishermen at the Sea of Galilee, a place of a thriving fishing industry and located on international trade routes, at a sufficient distance from Jerusalem. Significantly, Jesus' first call is to people who have something to leave behind, not to poor men who might jump at the chance of following Jesus to better themselves. He sees the brothers, Peter and Andrew, casting their nets into the lake, not indulging in a recreational hook and line type of fishing. Casting nets is a labor-intensive job, demanding strength, long hours, unpredictable results, knowledge of what fish to keep and what to toss back (see Matt 4:18-22), and persistent dedication. To such men comes Jesus' invitation to follow him and use all their skills in a different kind of fishing: fishing for people. We are not told if there had been any previous contact between Jesus and these fishermen, nor is their obedient response elaborated. What Matthew wants to stress is the initiative and the personal impact of Jesus, and Peter's and Andrew's readiness to follow him immediately.

Jesus then moves on to call two other brothers, James and John. In this first call of two pairs of brothers, there already may be a suggestion of the "brotherliness" (and "sisterliness") in the following of Jesus that will be not only of blood ties, but also of the Spirit. James and John are intent on other skills that are necessary for fishing: mending nets that, along with their boats, need to be kept in good repair. Jesus calls, and these two also respond to him. None of these first disciples can stay put. Peter and Andrew leave what appears to be their own established business; James and John disrupt accepted social conventions by leaving their father's business and family ties. Their apprenticeship begins with hearing Jesus teach in the synagogues throughout Galilee and proclaim the good news of the kingdom. Messiah of the word and deed, he also heals the sick. These are all ministries in which the community of disciples will also be involved, in Jesus' name.

No matter what our own lifestyle or social situation, as disciples of Jesus we are all called at various times to leave something behind so that we can follow him. We, too, cannot stay put in an immature understanding of Jesus, cannot remain in enterprises that contradict our baptismal calling, or accept social structures that are contrary to the gospel ethic of love and respect for human dignity. Each of us has to name for ourselves, in our own time and place, how we radically turn our hearts to the following of Jesus.

The reading from the prophet Isaiah is chosen because of geographical correspondence with the gospel, and in order to bring out the unity between the two Testaments of which Donald Senior spoke above. Social, political, and religious disintegration because of corruption and intrigue in high places, and the resulting poverty of the underprivileged, made Northern Israel a rotten fruit that only too easily fell into the Assyrian basket. But Isaiah holds out hope that one day the anguish of this part of the land will be healed and returned to its former glory. Isaiah depicts this reversal of fortune in striking and contrasting images that feed the imagination: light will shine in the darkness, celebration will replace oppression, and harvest will succeed plunder. Without ignoring or obscuring this historical reality of the eighth century B.C.E., we listen to the prophet in the knowledge that his hope was realized when a descendant of David rose as a new dawn over Galilee to offer a light yoke that would free the people from their burdens and afflictions.

In Psalm 27 the psalmist expresses confidence in the Lord who is the people's light, salvation, and refuge. Even in situations that are as devastating as those which Isaiah has described, in the battle of contemporary superpowers, or the violence which is as global as terrorism or as local as abused families, we are encouraged to hope in God's deliverance—deliverance that God may work through the surprising presence of our sisters and brothers.

We hear today that all is obviously not brotherly or sisterly in Paul's Corinthian church. Some members have diverged from the following of Christ into factionalism and partisan allegiances, and the consequent infighting threatens the unity of the community. This unity depends not on Paul, or Apollos, or Cephas (Peter), but on the baptism of the Corinthians into the death and resurrection of Christ. The danger of partisanship can undermine any Christian community. Both progressives and conservatives in today's church can sometimes be so fascinated with what they consider their own "good news" that they lose sight of the Christ who is this good news and whom they are called to follow. There is to be respect for the different gifts of a community and for a harmonious "agreement to disagree," but attitudes that blind us to anything but our own opinions are part of what we must leave in order to follow Christ.

Fourth Sunday in Ordinary Time

• Zeph 2:3; 3:12-13 • Ps 146:6-10 • 1 Cor 1:26-31 • Matt 5:1-12a

Vargas is an illiterate carpenter living on a garbage dump in Venezuela. All around him the land has been devastated by pollution. As well as eking out a bare living by his carpentry, he also paints pictures bursting with life: green trees laden with fruit, brilliant birds soaring into a clear, unpolluted blue sky, animals frolicking joyfully. Nobody can afford to buy them, but that doesn't worry Vargas. He is a prophet who paints not the world that he knows but the world that he hopes for and believes in. He paints his protest about his present world and his hope for a world that he believes will come.

The crowd that is described at the end of Matthew's fourth chapter is rather like the "garbage dump" people among whom Vargas lives. They were the ones who had come to Jesus hoping for a cure from physical and mental illnesses, and his healing compassion had reached out to them. That did not mean that their physical, social, and spiritual disadvantages disappeared overnight, but it did mean that they glimpsed in and through Jesus another world of possibilities. It is these people who gather with Jesus on a mountain where he will give the first of the five great discourses in Matthew's Gospel. In both the Old and New Testaments, the mountain is a privileged place of revelation. On a mountain not only can we physically see farther and need to breathe more deeply, but for Jesus, as for Moses when he received the Torah, it is a symbolic place of wider spiritual vision, of looking at this world, certainly, but also at the kingdom of heaven and the possibilities of the reign of God over physical, social, and spiritual realities.

Sitting down in the posture of a rabbinic teacher, Jesus calls his disciples to himself. The crowd is certainly not excluded from what Jesus is saying, but his disciples are at the heart of the people to whom they are called to minister. As we heard last week, only four disciples have been called so far, so it is not the Twelve but the community of disciples, the church to which we belong, that Jesus is addressing in this gospel. Our eyes need to look out and be directed by Jesus' words to the wider "mountain view"—not just to those more immediately around us, but also to our larger society and world.

The radical significance of what we refer to as "the Beatitudes" can be diluted and sanitized by familiarity. Christian intuition is right to recognize the importance of this text as a program of identity and action for Jesus' disciples, but this has often made it a lifesaving raft to which we cling when unable to think of what gospel passage to use, for example, at a funeral, wedding, or school Mass. "Let's have the Beatitudes," seems safe. In fact, this gospel is dangerous, more like a high-powered motorboat that carries us into deep waters of discipleship. In the religious context, the Greek word *makários* or "happy" has the sense of being blessed by God with grace and joy because of one's fidelity to God (Ps 84:4-6) rather than any subjective feeling that puts a fixed smile on one's face. For this reason, "blessed" is the preferred translation because our happiness comes from the joy of having died and risen with Christ. It is not superficial optimism that can be wiped out by the hard realities of life. In the Germany of the 1930's, Dietrich Bonhoeffer wrote passionately that the Beatitudes are nothing about good behavior, but are an absolute demand that brings a disciple before the face of the living God and the cost of the life, death, and resurrection of Jesus.[10]

As the responsorial psalm often does, Psalm 146 sums up the theme of this Sunday: praising God who is worthy of our trust and keeping faith forever with those who are oppressed—the hungry, the prisoner, the blind, the stranger, the widow and orphan. Being oppressed or being disadvantaged is not blessed, it is an evil; what is blessed is the hope of vulnerable people in a God of faithful love, a God who will bring them into the kingdom of heaven if they respond with fidelity to this divine love. Trust in human leaders and social institutions can be misplaced and their existence transitory; only God, who is with us from age to age, is ultimately worthy of our trust. The fidelity of God is the "bookends" of faith that Matthew would later put around his gospel: from his early naming of Emmanuel, God-with-us (Matt 1:23), to the last commissioning of the disciples by the risen Jesus who will be with his community "to the end of the age" (Matt 28:20).

What Jesus offers in the Beatitudes is an alternative view of a world that is worthy to become the kingdom of God. It is a world in which alienating and dehumanizing forces are destroyed and people are not anesthetized but energized by their trust in God. It is a world of both "is," the present reality, and "will," the not yet. Perhaps as we listen to the beginning of the Sermon on the Mount we should remind ourselves of its last verse in Matt 7:29 where the people come to recognize that Jesus "taught them as one having authority, and not as their scribes," an authority of his own integrity, compassion, and trust in God.

The poor are conscious of their own neediness, of being ground down in body, spirit, and social status, and yet Jesus wants to put them in touch with their blessedness, with their persistent hope in God. They are nothing, have nothing, except their God. Those who mourn are not those in the depths of private grief, but those who passionately lament the suffering of the world, those who can speak the language of tears to God, to their brothers and sisters, and to the church. They move the world toward the comforting of the kingdom. The meek are not "very 'umble," insincere, like the groveling Dickensian Uriah Heep, but those who are meek as Jesus will later describe himself, the "gentle and humble in heart" (Matt 11:29) who renounce violence and stand in solidarity with the little ones of this world, often unobtrusively, but always persistently. A Chinese wisdom saying recognizes that "Rigidity and hardness are the companions of death. Softness and tenderness are companions of life." The life that this Beatitude promises is life in the kingdom of God. The hunger and thirst for righteousness (or justice) embrace aspects of the other Beatitudes. It is the active longing for right relationships with God, with one another, with all creation. It is not the failure but the aspiration, not the achievement but the yearning. We must commit ourselves to working for as well as hoping for justice if we are to find it in the kingdom. God's call for "mercy, not sacrifice" echoes in both Testaments (see Hos 6:6; Matt 9:13, 12:7). The disciple who trusts in the mercy of God and despises legalisms, empty rituals, and arrogant judgments of others will be judged fit for the kingdom of God. The blessing on the pure of heart has nothing to do with the sixth or ninth commandment, and everything to do with the ability to focus on the presence of God and recognize God in expected and unexpected people, places, and events, so that one day God will be seen in fully revealed glory. The Franciscan mother superior of five exiled nuns who drowned on the way to America and were the subjects of Gerard Manley Hopkins' poem, "The Wreck of the Deutschland," had the purity of heart that could recognize Christ even in the doom of shipwreck:

> Ah! there was a heart right!
> There was single eye!
> Read the unshapeable shock night
> And knew the who and the why; . . .
> of the Christ who would soon come to her.[11]

The disciples who struggle to recognize "the who and the why" in life's threatening storms are assured of the kingdom vision of God.

The peacemakers are the reconcilers, those who try to heal the disruption of relationships: the conflicts that may be as hidden yet violent as those in a family, as divisive as those in a Christian community (think "parish"?), and as far-reaching as racial tensions or ethnic prejudices on a national or international scale. And the peacemakers, says Jesus, will be called children of God, heirs to the *shalom*, the peace of heaven.

To live the Beatitudes will bring persecution, the opposition of those who do not want their comfortable, predictable world turned upside down. But such persecution will mark disciples as prophets and members of the eschatological community, the people who wait in joyful hope for the coming of the reign of God. Etty Hillesum was a Dutch Jew who after working for Jews in transit to Auschwitz was herself transported and died there at the age of twenty-nine. She felt a deep call to open herself to what she called "cosmic sadness," and in her diary she wrote:

> Give your sorrow all the space and shelter in yourself that is its due, for if everyone bears his grief honestly and courageously, the sorrow that now fills the world will abate. But if you do not clear a decent shelter for your sorrow, and instead reserve most of the space inside yourself for hatred and thoughts of revenge—from which new sorrows will be born for others—then sorrow will never ease in this world and will multiply.[12]

Blessed are the persecuted.

The late seventh century B.C.E., prophet Zephaniah three times calls urgently to the "humble of the land," the *anawim*, the faithful remnant, to "seek . . . seek . . . seek": to seek God in righteousness and humility, and so prepare themselves for imminent catastrophe when, for these seekers, God will be a strong refuge. In the last verses, Zephaniah speaks words of hope. As with the Beatitudes, there is the promise of God's deliverance out of suffering and a new age of *shalom*.

Paul writes words of affirmation and encouragement to the ordinary "little people" of Corinth in about 53–54 C.E. Corinth was a city that was a geographically important port for trade, but whose population was, for the most part, socially mobile and culturally superficial and no stranger to the moral issues of a port society. Those who were called by God to the Christian community were mainly poor rather than rich, the powerless people without any significant social status. But once again we are given an example of how God can turn an established society upside down and inside out, and make the poor, the weak, the despised rejoice in the life that comes to them in and through Christ. About this they can "boast," not in the sense of haughty self-congratulation, but in praise of the blessedness God has worked in them.

From week to week, Ordinary Time will challenge our discipleship: to remain God's faithful remnant, to find our personal and social significance in Christ, to make the Beatitudes a frequent and radical review of our living for the kingdom which is now, but not yet fully established in our hearts and communities.

Fifth Sunday in Ordinary Time

• Isa 58:7-10 • Ps 112:4-9 • 1 Cor 2:1-5 • Matt 5:13-16

Disciples who live the Beatitudes that we heard proclaimed last Sunday are salt and light, says Jesus, in the continuation of the Sermon on the Mount. He says it directly, forcefully: "*You are . . .*" Good teacher that he is, Jesus compares discipleship with these two things that were familiar to and essential for his listeners.

For the people of Jesus' day, salt had great importance, both socially and religiously. Some of its uses persist today. It was a food preservative and a food seasoning. Salt added to food made it more tasty, added to incense it preserved its fragrance and holiness (Exod 30:35). Newborn babies were rubbed with salt in the belief that this was good for their health and could also have some symbolic religious significance of preservation and incorruptibility. Salt was applied to the skin to heal wounds. It was used in covenant-making rituals as a symbol of the fidelity to or "preserving" of the covenant (Num 18:19; 2 Chr 13:5). To describe people's speech as "seasoned with salt" (Col 4:6) was to suggest that their words were "tasty"— wise and graciously witty. Although some salt is needed for fertile soil, an excess is harmful, and so in a symbolic gesture of judgment, those who razed a city might scatter or "sow" it with salt (Judg 9:45) to express the hope that nothing would grow there again (Jer 17:6).

When Jesus calls his disciples "the salt of the earth" he is suggesting by this metaphor that they are the people with a responsibility for savoring the world with God's love, making it more to "God's taste" (see 2 Kgs 2:19-22), healing its wounds. What is the contemporary corruption that we need to name and challenge so that our Christian "saltiness" contributes to humanity, society, our church, and our planet being preserved, healed, and enabled for the kingdom of God in Christ? Salt is not sweet and sugary, and neither can our Christian discipleship be. Put salt on a sore spot and it stings as well as heals. The Beatitudes ended last Sunday with Jesus' encouragement to fidelity when persecution wounds both individuals and communities, and Matthew's community may well have known persecution and the need for painful application of the "salt" that is the acceptance of a share in the sufferings of Christ so that they might be healed and preserved for a share in his resurrection. Perhaps such persecution was not dramatic but rather a persistent pressure to accommodate their Christianity to dominant cultural influences. To compromise our following of Jesus because of the social pressures of materialism, "keeping up with the Joneses," or addictions of many kinds, is still a real challenge today that can inflict cultural wounds that need the healing touch of the "salt" of Jesus' words and the support of other Christians.

Loyalty to our baptismal covenant, loyalty to the precious covenant of friendship with Jesus (see John 15:13-15), is part of the "saltiness" of a disciple. So how can salt become so tasteless that, as Jesus says, it is good for nothing but being discarded and trampled under foot? Once again, like a good teacher, Jesus is using the everyday life experience of the people to whom he is speaking to make a point. The cheap and readily available fuel for their outside clay ovens was camel or donkey dung, known still in some poorer parts of the world. One of the domestic duties of a young girl was to make patties of this dung, mix them with salt, and leave them in the sun to dry. A slab of salt was placed at the bottom of the oven and the dung patties placed on it. The salt acted as a catalyst for the burning, but eventually it lost this property and was thrown out, sometimes onto muddy streets to

make an easier walking surface. John J. Pilch comments that in both Hebrew and Aramaic, Jesus' mother tongue, the word for "earth" and "clay-
oven" is the same.[13] If our commitment to Jesus becomes so "worn out," so
diluted by cultural compromise or so insipid that we have no taste for his
gospel, then we are no longer a catalyst that, when mixed with our society,
can set others on fire with the love of Jesus. We have become useless and
tasteless disciples.

The other comparison that Jesus makes is to light. Disciples *are* the
light of the world as the ritual of baptism declares by the presentation of the
burning candle. Like salt, so with fire: both exist not for themselves, but to
give taste, warmth, or illumination to something beyond themselves. Not
the powerful Roman Empire of the first century or the superpower of any
age, but life lived according to the Beatitudes is what will give light to the
world. This is to be a communal endeavor, as obvious as a well-lighted city
on a hilltop. Vatican II's image of the church was summed up in the very
first words of the *Dogmatic Constitution on the Church*. The church is called
to be the community which sheds on all peoples the radiance of the light of
Christ. The telling title that the United States Conference of Catholic Bishops gave to their 1993 reflection on parish social ministry was *Communities of Salt and Light: Reflections on the Social Mission of the Parish*. In it
they reflected that:

> The central message is simple: our faith is profoundly social. We cannot be
> called truly "Catholic" unless we hear and heed the Church's call to serve
> those in need and work for justice and peace. We cannot call ourselves fol-
> lowers of Jesus unless we take up his mission of bringing "good news to the
> poor, liberty to captives, and new sight to the blind" (cf. Luke 4:18).

Just as salt is used to make food tasty, so a lamp was lit in the one-
roomed house of most of Jesus' listeners in order to illuminate the whole
living space. It is interesting that lamp lighting, like salt mixing, was primarily women's work. Disciples who are salt and light do not draw attention to themselves, but to God. They declare that, through their commitment
to the way of life to which Jesus calls his disciples and his sustaining grace,
the reign of God is coming into our world.

The reading from the prophet Isaiah is specific about how light will rise
in the darkness of a community that has returned from exile and must now
rebuild itself according to the word of the Lord. This rebuilding will not be
effected through the blazing glory of triumphant political victories or re-
splendent liturgies, but through the radiance of justice for the most helpless
and disadvantaged people. The basic human needs of food, shelter, clothing

must be served, not only out of one's surplus or through an anonymous "third party," but personally: sharing the bread on the table with the poor, offering living space in our own home and something of our own clothing to the naked whenever they cross our path. To do this, says Isaiah, is to walk in the all-enveloping presence of God and to turn shadows into noontime light. People of the covenant must also be concerned with and informed about the social structures underlying poverty: economic oppression, war-mongering, malicious rumors, and false accusations. Over two and a half millennia after Isaiah, it is not difficult to put names to people and organizations, especially in politics and mass media, who are still creating shadows rather than light in our world.

The people who cause light to rise in the darkness are praised in the responsorial Psalm 112. In the first verse of the psalm (which we do not pray today), such people have been called "blessed," and as such, give praise to the Lord. Again, within the context of the liturgy, we are challenged to live a beatitude life beyond this liturgy.

Paul is a great comfort to us! When it might seem too impossibly hard to love such a life or give such a witness, he assures us that it is the power of God working in us that will show forth the light of Christ, and a Christ who was crucified, who seemed to be a failure. But in this failure the power of the resurrection is most radically witnessed. Paul himself does not come among his communities as a brilliant philosopher or a brilliant orator. In fact, to preach Christ crucified was "scandalous foolishness" for many who heard him, but a risk that Paul was willing to take. As we have already heard Paul proclaim on the last two Sundays, such is the paradoxical wisdom of God. For his Corinthian church, politically, ethnically, and socially diverse, but with the majority of its members with little to boast about in any of these spheres, the death and resurrection of Christ into which they have been baptized is the source of their union. In making nothing but this his boast, Paul stands in solidarity with his church; he wants nothing he says or does to block the light of Christ. The success that Christ asks of us will be the discernment to recognize and act compassionately for those in need who cross the paths of our ordinary lives everyday, and the kind word or deed that comforts and encourages—all of which can sometimes make extraordinary demands.

Sixth Sunday in Ordinary Time

• Sir 15:15-21 • Ps 119:1-2, 4-5, 17-18, 33-34 • 1 Cor 2:6-10 • Matt 5:17-37

The Old Testament and New Testaments have always been affirmed as inseparable.[14] Today's gospel offers us an example of the "rereading" of the Old

Testament, the scriptures that nourished the faith and discernment of Jesus. The rereading of biblical texts, not to deny them but to quarry new meanings from their original riches, was well known in Judaism. For example, the meaning of the gift of the manna that fed the people in the wilderness is "reread" to embrace "every word that comes from the mouth of God" (see Deut 8:2-3). The Pontifical Biblical Commission's document referred to above comments that the relationship between the two testaments is reciprocal:

> . . . on the one hand, the New Testament demands to be read in the light of the Old, but it also invites a "rereading" of the Old in the light of Christ (cf. Luke 24:45). . . . Although the Christian reader is aware that the internal dynamism of the Old Testament finds its goal in Jesus, this is a retrospective perception whose point of departure is not in the text as such, but in the events of the New Testament proclaimed by the apostolic preaching. It cannot be said, therefore, that the Jews do not see what has been proclaimed in the text, but that the Christian, in the light of Christ and in the Spirit, discovers an additional meaning that was hidden there.[15]

As he says, Jesus does not come to abolish the Law or the Prophets but to carry forward to its fulfillment the movement of transcending, interiorizing, stripping away empty externals and legalistic minutiae that had distorted God's revelation. Some of the scribes and Pharisees, the Scripture scholars and lay leaders of their day, bore responsibility for this when they were so arrogantly sure of their interpretation that they could see no farther than their own narrow point of view. The Pharisees had a fierce dedication to carrying out God's will, but this could lead them to place unattainable burdens on others and themselves, with the consequence that their own failures might result in hypocritical and vehement cover-ups. We also need to remember that the gospel writers were well aware that neither of these groups is historically self-contained. In every Christian community there are also "scribes and Pharisees": learned but self-serving people, and hypocrites whose external religious masks can hide an irreligious heart.

So Jesus focuses not so much on the evils of murder, adultery, or lying, but on the way these take root in the human heart. In other words, he proposes a radical reinterpretation of the teaching. We can look askance at the end point of the continuum of evil and yet not recognize the subtle and dangerous first point when we begin to orient our lives in that direction. Anger, hostility, and insults do not belong in the Christian community, for these are the seedbed of the sin of murder that destroys God's sacred gift of life to another human being. We have seen the drastic outcomes of a religiously insulting cartoon, ethnic prejudice, the first verbal or physical blows of domestic violence.

In his autobiography, *Long Walk to Freedom*, Nelson Mandela writes about the wardens who guarded him and the other prisoners and their essential humanity. He believed that hostility toward them was self-defeating, and that everyone, even our enemies, can change. On February 11, 1990, the day that Mandela was to be released from prison after twenty-seven and a half years, the crowd that had gathered outside and the millions throughout the world who were watching on TV became anxious as the time for his release was well past. Would he not walk free after all? But he did, and the reason for the long delay was because he was saying an emotional good-bye and thank-you to his guards. In his freedom speech that night, Mandela reminded the world that we can all imprison ourselves behind the bars of prejudice and narrow-mindedness.

Sexuality also is a gift from God, and not to be abused. Jesus names male lusting for and oppressive attitudes toward women as adultery in the heart (see Job 31:1). Sexual drives cannot dominate a person's life but need to be integrated into a life which is lived according to gospel values. To show the seriousness of this, Jesus uses the literary device (not literal advice!) of exaggeration, the plucking out of an eye or the cutting off of a hand which is to be preferred to the mutilating effect of unbridled sexual abuse. Jesus is critical of the easy divorce, based on self-interest, that men could often obtain from their wives. In the first century C.E., the school of Shammai, which was conservative on most issues, claimed that the Torah permitted divorce only on grounds *ervat davar*, or "indecency," usually interpreted as adultery. The more liberal school of Hillel (usually closer to Jesus' teaching) in this case interpreted the phrase very liberally as "anything unseemly" which disrupted domestic tranquility. Women had no reciprocal rights with regard to their husbands, and the woman who had been cast aside by her husband often needed to find another man if she was to survive. Jesus also holds as guilty of adultery those men who, by the writ of divorce, force this desperate situation on a woman. Our sexuality is not just a private possession; it involves others, especially in the family. Biblical scholars debate what the sexual irregularity (*porneía* in Matthew's text) was that made divorce permissible. The contemporary status of divorced people in today's church and the most pastoral way of ministering to them is still one of our most pressing questions and quests.

Jesus shares the Hebrew horror at the abuse of calling on God to bolster the claims of a false oath (see Lev 19:12). There should be such integrity and truthfulness in the Christian community that there is no need to bring God into the situation as an additional and "reliable" witness to the too-much-protesting. A straightforward "yes" or "no," with no oath taking at all, should be sufficient.

The reading from the Book of Sirach (or Ecclesiasticus), dating from ca. 185 B.C.E., maintains that men and women can make a free choice between the two ways: between good or evil, order or chaos, life or death. Sirach uses the imagery of destructive fire or regenerating water to describe these options. Although the wisdom of God is all-seeing to the depths of the human heart, God is not a puppeteer who makes us dance to the pull of the divine strings. God is the risk taker who leaves us room to be human, able to make choices instead of living according to our instincts; humanity is the new creation that can be moral or immoral. In the Sermon on the Mount, Jesus reveals the mind of God and understanding of God's will that will enable us to be wisdom people who choose life rather than death (see Deut 30:15, 19-20).

The responsorial Psalm 119, the longest of the psalms, is written in an acrostic form. Beginning with the first letter of the Hebrew alphabet (*aleph*) and continuing through the alphabet until the last (*tav*), eight verses begin with the same letter. Everything from *aleph* to *tav* (or as we would say, "from A to Z") is under the wisdom of God's Law. The verses chosen for today's liturgy proclaim the blessedness or happiness of those who live according to this. Such obedience is of the heart, to a God who loves us, not an external, obsequious, or fearful obedience to a manipulative tyrant. Like the verses with which we respond today, nearly every one of the 178 verses of Psalm 119 contain synonyms for "law": "will," "precepts," "statutes," "word." What this means will be most clearly revealed in the One who is the Word made flesh, the One who comes to do the will of his Father among his sisters and brothers and reveal how much God loved the world.

Paul also speaks about two ways: the way of worldly wisdom "of this age," and the wisdom of those who are mature in faith and believe in what can only be discerned in the power of the Spirit—the kingdom world beyond this one that is now but not yet fully revealed. It has been prepared for those who love God and can live with mystery that is greater than any human imagination or insight. Christ incarnate, crucified and risen, is a revelation of the mysterious wisdom of God.

Harold Kushner, a Jewish rabbi, was faced with the mysterious wisdom of God when his three-year old son, Aaron, was diagnosed with progeria, the terminal illness of "rapid aging." Developing like a little old man in childhood, he died in his early teens. In his book, *When Bad Things Happen to Good People*, Kushner writes of this and other tragedies:

> We can't explain it any more than we can explain life itself. We can't control it, or sometimes even postpone it. All we can do is try to rise beyond the

question "why did it happen?" and begin to ask the question "what can I do now it has happened?"[16]

Kushner turns again and again to the Book of Job. We can also turn to the Gospel of the crucified and risen Christ and the wisdom this witnesses: that in the midst of pain God is still on our side.

Seventh Sunday in Ordinary Time

• Lev 19:1-2, 17-18 • Ps 103:1-4, 8, 10, 12-13 • 1 Cor 3:16-23 • Matt 5:38-48

We live in a world where retaliation seems almost an automatic response—from the playground to the floors of government. When speaking about the Old Testament response of "an eye for an eye and a tooth for a tooth" (Exod 21:24; Deut 19:21; Lev 24:20), Jesus is not trying to drive a wedge between what is wrongly judged as the Old Testament harshness and the New Testament love ethic—a false dichotomy. The *lex talionis*, or "law of retaliation," was formulated in both the pagan and Jewish world as a principle of proportionate retribution, and therefore a moral advance over unbridled and excessive revenge or "payback" in tribal societies. What Jesus proclaims is again a radical reinterpretation of the Law, and with something of the dramatic skill of a great teacher he presents his audience with some "case studies" or critical incidents to make his point.

If someone strikes a disciple, or "backhands" as we might say, this is not only a physical blow but also an insult such as would be offered to a subordinate. Instead of retaliating, the disciple should offer the left cheek as well. If a debtor is taken to court and ordered to surrender his cloak as collateral for the loan, the disciple should also surrender his tunic as well. No doubt Palestinian eyebrows would be raised at the memorable mental picture of the debtor disciple standing publicly naked in the court, bereft of both his under and outer garments, the latter often used also as a blanket at night! The third example is that of a disciple's response to what could be legally demanded by a Roman soldier: that a Palestinian carry the soldier's heavy pack for a mile (1,000 paces). As one trudged past the milestone, not to dump the pack but offer to go another mile with the occupying enemy would seem absolute foolishness. Likewise, to give to anyone who wants to borrow seems extreme.

But God is so generous, and a disciple should be so secure in this love, that there is no need to insist on one's rights. Writing his gospel through the prism of the death and resurrection of Jesus, Matthew sees the light of Jesus' response to love broken into the colors of the generous, practical, and radical. For the sake of others, even enemies, Jesus went the "extra mile" to his death, did not retaliate against the blows during his passion, and was stripped naked, not only of clothes but of life itself.

The final command is the most radical: to extend love even to our enemies. The first reading today from the Book of Leviticus concludes with the command to love one's neighbor as oneself. "Neighbor" in this context means one's kin or fellow Israelite. Nowhere in the Old Testament is "hating" the enemy commanded in the sense of personal vindictiveness and revenge; when this attitude is mentioned it is in the sense of:

> . . . the religious rejection of those who do not belong to God's people and do not keep God's law . . . . Judaism should not be caricatured as though it was always narrow and exclusive; there were elements and tendencies toward love for all people, including enemies.[17]

Jesus "makes love of enemies" specific and concrete. In its absoluteness and concreteness it is without parallel in paganism or Judaism. But how to understand the words: "Be perfect, therefore, as your heavenly Father is perfect" in a way that does not seem impossibly unattainable? The meaning of "perfect" here is "wholeness," (Heb *tamim* or Greek *télios*) or "maturity." God will still be God and we will still be human, but a disciple is called to act wholeheartedly, maturely, focused on God's universal, generous, and impartial love for all that God has created. This response is much the same as the earlier mention of "purity of heart" in the Beatitudes (Matt 5:8). Our love is to be a countercultural, kingdom response to the love of God. Perhaps at times we can only struggle, as the psalmists did with the "enemies" that are scattered plentifully throughout their prayer, and thank God for what he loves in those we find it hard to love—as we go on struggling to do just that.

After the death of her twenty-four-year-old daughter in the London terrorist bombings of July 2005, Julie Nicholson resigned from her ministry as an Anglican priest because she felt unable to lead her congregation in the words of the Eucharist when she was so far from forgiveness and reconciliation. She said, "I have laid forgiveness to one side and it's (forgiveness) up to God at the moment. It's beyond my human capacity to deal with." Whatever the future decision Julie Nicholson may make, her experience is a poignant example of the struggle for integrity between life and liturgy, prayer and practice. And above all it witnesses to what she found it hard to accept: that there are times when we must painfully surrender—often after a long and blessed struggle—to the belief that forgiveness and reconciliation are the work of a generously loving and infinitely forgiving God in us. It is this compassionate and merciful God who is praised in the responsorial Psalm 103.

The reading from Leviticus is also a call to the people of Israel to be holy as God is holy. This divine holiness is both motivation and model, personal and concrete. Faith in this, and the ethics that flow from such belief, are two sides of the one coin. The reading was obviously chosen for today's Liturgy of the Word because it culminates in what we have come to call the "Golden Rule": you shall love your neighbor as yourself. Disputes between people are to be resolved through open and honest dialogue that does not allow a wounded relationship to fester into hatred. Revenge and grudging piousness have no place in children of a generous and loving God. This chapter of Leviticus is a significant part of the Jewish liturgy of the Day of Atonement (Yom Kippur) that celebrates the restoration not only of the individual but also the reconciliation of the community before God (see Lev 16:30). Although omitted in today's reading in order to highlight the correspondence between the Leviticus portion and the gospel, it is important to note that the verses preceding vv. 17-18 emphasize laws related to social justice: help for the poor, honesty in transactions, wages and words, and respect for human life. In practice, this is what love of neighbor is all about, then and now. This is what our holy God expects of a holy people, as the responsorial Psalm also proclaims.

Paul reminds us that it is not only those who are unreconciled and unforgiving who can cause division in a community. Those who have inflated opinions of themselves and their personal wisdom and are dismissive of others, deceive themselves, and are foolish before God. God dwells in the Christian community, and so it is like a holy temple. Even more importantly, the community is not just the general temple precincts but the sanctuary (*naós*), the "holy of holies," with every member a building block of that most sacred precinct. In Corinth, with its many pagan temples, the obligation to respect the holiness of temple sites was very familiar to Gentile Christians, and for Jewish Christians there was the memory of the Jerusalem Temple. How much more, argues Paul, should Christians reverence one another and not weaken the fabric of the community that is founded on Christ and in which the Spirit moves. Paul warns the Corinthians not to overestimate themselves or indulge in "hero worship" of anyone, even Paul himself or Apollos or Cephas, because everyone and everything and every age belongs to Christ and Christ belongs to God. Paul challenges the Corinthian church; how would our local parish church measure up to the same challenge?

Eighth Sunday in Ordinary Time

• Isa 49:14-15 • Ps 62:2-3, 6-9 • 1 Cor 4:1-5 • Matt 6:24-34

Today Isaiah gives us one of the most beautiful and memorable images of God: as a nursing mother. There is no image of trust that is more ordinary and extraordinary than the child, new from the womb and nourished at the mother's breast. The word that the Hebrews used for the tenderness or compassion of God derives from the word for womb, for the womb is what sustains, nourishes, and births life. Isaiah images the exiled people (Zion) lamenting their abandonment by God until God assures them of her love, a love that will always be present to them and for them. Unlikely though it may be, it is still possible that a mother might abandon her child; not so with God who will never forget her child, Israel.

Writing nearly two centuries after Isaiah, in a world lamenting the Black Death and a church in schism with two popes, the anchorite Julian of Norwich (1342–ca. 1416) also saw God as a mother: "And so in our making, God almighty is our loving Father, and God all wisdom is our loving Mother, with the love and goodness of the Holy Spirit, which is all one God, one Lord."[18] And of Jesus our mother, she writes: "The mother can give her child to suck of her milk, but our precious Mother, Jesus, can feed us with himself, and does, most courteously and most tenderly with the blessed sacrament, which is the precious food of true life."[19] Contemporary Christian feminists continue to explore this rich and deep concept from very different life experiences.[20]

In contrast to the intimate and feminine image of God as a nursing mother, the responsorial Psalm does not use Psalm 131 to continue this imagery, but Psalm 62. Although the images are of a stronghold, a fortress, a rock, the psalmist's message is the same as Isaiah's: it is God in whom we can confidently put our trust. Three times this is emphasized by the word "alone": God alone is the one in whom we hope and before whom we pour out our hearts in prayer.

Early in *She Who Is*, Elizabeth Johnson writes:

> As the focus of absolute trust, one to whom you can give yourself without fear of betrayal, the holy mystery of God undergirds and implicitly gives direction to all of a believing person's enterprises, principles, choices, system of values, and relationship.[21]

It is such a God that Jesus speaks about in today's gospel. Not many rich people would have been hanging around on the mountain listening to this itinerant preacher. The majority of his audience would have been typical of the society: those living from hand to mouth, probably some unemployed or sick, with consequent and immediate anxieties about food and clothing for themselves and their families. Whereas the rich are worried about money, either because they fear losing it or want to make more, the poor can also be worried about money because they have none. For both groups, therefore, money can be a consuming passion. It is not possible, says Jesus, to be so attached to two competing masters, and so a choice has to be made between God and money. Jesus is not denying legitimate and responsible concern for material goods, but his concern is the integration of this into everyday life in a way that does not enslave the people.

Jesus then continues to speak as a wisdom teacher and poet. He shares his imaginative vision of God's care and providence for all that God has made, and the right response of disciples to the gift of life. When Jesus speaks of the birds of the air and the lilies of the field, he is no impossible romantic. He is not proposing an understanding of God as a great "Bird Feeder" and "Floral Seamstress," but is following the rabbinic principle of preaching "from the lesser to the greater." If God's providence takes care of the birds and lilies, we can have absolute confidence in God's care for us. Matthew's imagery balances the activities of men, sowing and reaping, with those of women, spinning and weaving. Birds and flowers are concerned with neither; they are present to God simply as themselves.

Those who do not know the provident Father of Jesus may worry about food and drink and clothing, but Jesus wants the seed of his word to touch people, even in their arid lives, so that their trust in God will take wing and their hopes will flower. What disciples are to set their hearts on is "righteousness," the Torah (Law) as interpreted by Jesus, that will enable them to place their lives under God's compassionate rule.

Paul is also eager for his Corinthians to have a proper Christian perspective on life. They have been entrusted by God with knowledge of the divine mysteries, and to steward this precious trust means to serve God in the proclamation of Christ's death and resurrection, as we heard three weeks ago (see 1 Cor 2:1-5). Paul is not concerned about his status or what others think about him. Trust in God is again emphasized: Paul's trust in the judgment of God at the decisive moment when the truth of all our hearts will be revealed.

So much lack of trust surrounds us today: with politicians, with the world of high finance, with our often fragile personal relationships. Young people hesitate to make lifetime commitments in married life, wondering if they will be able to trust one another enough. And the church is not exempt, especially because of the disillusionment caused by the sexual abuse perpetrated by priests and religious in whom great trust was invested. The thirteenth century mystic Mechtilde of Magdeburg echoes the hopeful words and image of Isaiah that we so need to remember when she reminds us that when we are really down, "God is also a mother who lifts Her loved child from the ground to Her knee."[22]

Ninth Sunday in Ordinary Time

• Deut 11:18, 26-28, 32 • Ps 31:2-4, 17, 25 • Rom 3:21-25, 28 • Matt 7:21-27

Today's gospel is the conclusion of the Sermon on the Mount, and Jesus tells his listeners that having heard his words it is now time for them to make choices. A lasting relationship with Jesus will never be built on lip service or pious words such as "Lord, Lord," from those who claim Jesus as their teacher. A true relationship with him is established by putting Jesus' teaching into practice. We may profess we love the poor, are forgiving people, have nothing to do with contemporary demons; we may acclaim Jesus as Lord in our liturgy, but does his rule over our lives extend beyond this assembly? When did we last associate with or serve a poor person? When did we have the courage to say, "I'm sorry" to a brother or sister? When did we do something to exorcise our demons of materialism, addiction, social climbing, or status seeking? To enter the kingdom of heaven we must do "the will of my Father in heaven," says Jesus. And the Father's will is love and life for all that is created and that flows from the radical action of Jesus' life, death, and resurrection. What Jesus teaches, his words and interpretation of Torah/Law, are in perfect harmony with what he does. Anyone who lacks this integrity is "lawless." These words of Jesus' first great discourse in Matthew's Gospel will be re-echoed in the concluding parable of the last discourse (Matt 24–25) on the end of human history and the final judgment. In the "Parable of the Sheep and Goats" (Matt 25:31-46), before Jesus enters into his passion, a time when his teaching is urgent, he again challenges his disciples to be people of integrity, committed in both word and deed.

Jesus ends the Sermon on the Mount with the parable of the Two Builders. The comparison he makes between the successful building on rock and the disastrous building on sand would have been very familiar to his listeners. Much of Israel's topography has areas of sandstone, basalt, chalky rock, and limestone. As a carpenter, Jesus and his audience, through either successful or bitter experience, know the importance of a house's foundations. To dig deeply down to rock level ensures that the house will withstand storms and calamities. Jesus' words pound the ears of his listeners with the staccato force of rain, floods, and gales. In both the Old and New Testaments the image of rock is personalized as in today's responsorial Psalm 31, where the psalmist confidently names God as "rock," "stronghold," and safe "refuge" in times of danger. Paul, for example, tells his Corinthians that by his "master builder" ministry, God has enabled him to lay down the foundation stone of Jesus Christ on whom their community has been built; and for Peter, too, Jesus is the living stone once rejected, but now the keystone which holds together the Christian community of living stones (1 Pet 2:4-5). To build on the words of Jesus is to be founded on him. But it takes strong and deep action, and mature reflection to raise such discipleship. The temptation is always there to "jerry-build": to shallow digging, to satisfaction with the sandy rather than the rock level, and the quick fixing of the foundations. This might seem adequate in the Palestinian dry season, but when the rains and storms inevitably come, the house will fall.

The houses of both the wise and the foolish builder were buffeted by storms. Jesus' disciples are not exempt from calamities: from the human, physical pain of illness and accidents; from personal disillusionment with others and with oneself; from social and ecclesial injustice; from failures in ministry and misunderstandings of authority. But being built on the foundation of Jesus and continually sinking one's life deeply into his Word will enable the disciple who is a wise builder to stand firm and withstand the turbulence. This is much more than just propping up the individual disciple or the community of disciples, and it might make us reflect on what is being propped up in our own lives or in the church at the present time . . . and enable us to ask how wise it is to do that according to the wisdom of Jesus the teacher.

In the reading from the Book of Deuteronomy, Moses has been teaching the people the commandments, the words of God, and now he presents God's people with a choice: between the blessing of obedience if they are faithful to the covenant, or the curse (punishment) for their disobedience. As a visible sign of their fidelity to the covenant, a threefold ritual is commanded which involves the male members of the community in the action of binding on the *tefillin* or phylacteries. These are still worn at morning prayer every day, except on the Sabbath and holy days, by observant male Jews from the time they become a "son of the commandment" (*bar mitzvah*) at the age of thirteen. They now take the form of small leather cubes containing portions of the Torah, including the "Listen, O Israel" (the *Shema*) of Deut 6:4. Wrapped around the forehead, the *tefillin* concretize the injunction to keep the Word of God constantly in one's mind; bound on the biceps of the left arm, near the heart, the reminder is to guard the commandments of God in one's heart. When the people came into the land of Canaan there would be temptation to follow other gods; loyalty to the God of the covenant and responsibility to bind themselves in heart, mind, and action to their God would be the blessed choice.

"But now . . . !" Paul is excited about the "unveiling" of the new things that have been revealed by Jesus' interpretation of the Hebrew Scriptures. So radically and completely free and faithful were the choices that Jesus made for God that they have cosmic significance for the whole world, Jew and Gentile included. Redemption is a gift of God accomplished through Christ, and from this gift flows the ability to make the choice for God. In his own way, Paul repeats today's gospel reminder: disciples are not to boast about anything good that they do, but discern and be humbly grateful for God's grace which works through them because of the death and resurrection of Jesus Christ.

Tenth Sunday in Ordinary Time

• Hos 6:3-6 • Ps 50:1, 8, 12-15 • Rom 4:18-25 • Matt 9:9-13

After the Sermon on the Mount, Jesus begins to do as he taught. The gospel that we hear today is in the middle of a narrative section about the healing mercy of Jesus for the sick—men and women, Jew and Gentile, those both physically and mentally ill. It is also about the healing forgiveness that Jesus offers to Matthew, the toll collector, and his call to discipleship. Toll collectors were socially and religiously marginal people in first century Palestine. Employed by the Romans, they were ostracized by Jews who regarded them as collaborators with the enemy. As a toll collector, Matthew would not have been in the higher echelon of employees; in fact, many toll collectors were men so desperate to earn a livelihood for themselves and their families, and so ready to take any job, that it would not matter what reputation it earned them. The struggle to survive was also the reason why many toll collectors skimmed off a small profit for themselves by charging a little extra for the tolls, which added to their unpopularity. Religiously, their unavoidable dealings with Gentiles made them ritually unclean, regarded as unfit for Temple worship, and so in the ranks of "tax collectors and sinners."

People on the margins, outcasts and sinners, were Jesus' special concern, and so while Matthew is involved in his unpopular trade Jesus takes the initiative and calls him to follow him. Matthew accepts being found; to allow ourselves to be found by Jesus is a prerequisite for forgiveness and for discipleship. Where Matthew follows Jesus is to a dinner, presumably at Jesus' house, with a number of other tax collectors and sinners. That Jesus should openly sit at table with such people is considered an occasion of scandalous hospitality in the eyes of those who considered themselves observant keepers of the Law, for to share food together is to share life, and these people reclining with Jesus should be excluded according to the rules of purity. But for the excluded of every age, this inclusion affirms that those who seek and follow Jesus will also sit at the banquet table of the eternal kingdom. As Vatican II taught, the Church:

> encompasses with love all those who are afflicted with human weakness . . . the Church embracing sinners in her bosom, is at the same time holy and always in need of being purified, and incessantly pursues the path of penance and renewal.[23]

The Pharisees cannot accept the obvious fact that Jesus embraces sinners. For them, the world of religion and morality is black and white: people are either righteous (in the sense of keeping the Law), ritually clean and worthy of association, or sinners, ritually unclean and to be shunned. Such an attitude is not restricted to first century "Pharisees." Perhaps we should look around our assembly today, reflect on who is sitting with us at table and ask the questions that the church is still struggling to answer: "With whom should we eat?" "Who is missing from table . . . and why?" In a subtly insulting way, the Pharisees dissociate themselves from Jesus, and direct their questions to his disciples, asking them why Jesus eats with such people. But Jesus hears the question, and perhaps to save his rather nonplussed disciples, he himself responds with proverbial wisdom. Brendan Byrne comments:

> The Pharisees, who complain about this to the disciples (v. 11), think that the only way for the righteous to deal with sinners is to shun them. For Jesus, that would be to act like a doctor who avoided sick people rather than tending them to cure them (v. 12).[24]

Then Jesus speaks words that are important not only for the Pharisees but for all of us. In the tradition of the rabbis who encouraged their disciples to go and search the Scriptures and learn there the wisdom of God, Jesus tells his critics to: "Go and learn what this means, 'I desire mercy, not sacrifice.' For I have come to call not the righteous but sinners." The Pharisees should reflect on their own Scriptures (e.g., Hos 6:6; Amos 5:21-24; Mic 6:6-8) and hear the call not to exclude sacrifice but, as Jesus taught in the Sermon on the Mount (Matt 5:23-24), to give mercy priority over it. Matthew reminds his mainly Jewish Christian community that, in Christ, God extends mercy to all humanity, and so all interpretations of the Law must now be seen through the prism of his life, death, and resurrection. Our righteousness, our obedience to God, can so easily deteriorate into self-righteousness which considers our own opinions and interpretations of Christian living to be the only right ones, and leaves Jesus on the margins—where, in the gospel, he is usually found.

The first reading, from the northern kingdom prophet Hosea, is obviously twinned with the gospel because Jesus himself quotes its words about mercy and sacrifice. Israel of the eighth century B.C.E. had turned to covert corruption in high places, political assassinations, the exploitation of the poor in a society that created a huge gap between them and the rich, and a highly debatable foreign policy—none of which may seem unfamiliar to our twenty-first century ears. Worship of Ba'al and the fertility cult had undermined true worship. Hosea calls the people to repentance and the renewal of the covenant with God that will be the source of true fruitfulness. The prophet uses familiar images to help him communicate the truth of God's steadfast love and kindness. If the people repent and believe in him, God will come to them as surely as dawn comes out of night and a fruitful agricultural season comes out of the spring rains that fall. Insincere sorrow and uncommitted covenantal love is like a morning cloud that soon drifts away, or morning dew that evaporates in the heat of the day. The tribes of Ephraim and Judah are put on trial for their inconstancy and hypocrisy. God sees that they are more concerned with legalisms than love, with empty, external rituals rather than the sacrificial obedience of their hearts that will also lead them to sacrifice themselves for others. It is not sacrifice in itself that is condemned, but the dishonesty and hypocrisy of worshippers. In this sense, as Jesus does in the gospel, God calls the people to "mercy, not sacrifice."

Contemporary Christians are not exempt from this hypocrisy and lack of love for God and their sisters and brothers. The community of a Catholic church in the heart of a prosperous central business district has a wonderful formation program to help people with intellectual disabilities become special ministers of the Eucharist. They are on the roster for this ministry at a weekly midday Mass, and for most of them it is the highlight of their week. After the Mass, always very well attended, there is an open invitation to the pastoral center next to the church to share a free cup of tea or coffee and a make-it-yourself sandwich. Overheard at one such Mass was the comment from a well-dressed businessman as he prepared his meal: "Well, I won't be coming to this Mass again, with all those idiots up on the altar!" With just, prophetic anger, those around him "devoured" not their sandwiches but the speaker, a person who apparently had no idea of the connection between the sacramental Communion he had just received and communion with his sisters and brothers, especially the poor and disadvantaged. Fitting is the response we make in the words of the responsorial Psalm 50: "To the upright I will show the saving power of God."

Paul tells his church at Rome that neither age nor God's long delay in fulfilling the promise of many descendants weakened Abraham's faith.

Even though his body was aged and Sarah's body was beyond child-bearing, Abraham was not an old man—if we define "old age" as the time when we believe there is more behind us than in front of us. For this man of faith and hope, the new lay ahead. Abraham would not doubt or deny the promises of his faithful God. Paul, "a Hebrew born of Hebrews, and as to the law, a Pharisee" (Phil 3:5), had been called to "go and learn" what the mystery of Christ meant for the church, which is his body. Paul, too, knew how important it was to keep going forward to the future that has been promised to us in the death and resurrection of Jesus. The example of Abraham's faith should encourage us to believe in a promised future that is infinitely more wonderful and more demanding than the raising of descendants from the "dead" bodies of two aged parents. As Benedict XVI said at his papal inauguration, our call, especially as parish communities, is to give witness to a church that is alive, young, and shows each of us the way to the future.[25]

Eleventh Sunday in Ordinary Time

• Exod 19:2-6a • Ps 100:1-3, 5 • Rom 5:6-11 • Matt 9:36–10:8

After the Sermon on the Mount, Matthew has shown us that Jesus, the teacher, lived what he taught. In the two chapters preceding today's gospel Jesus has healed bodies, brought peace to tortured psyches, and raised from the dead. Men and women, Jew and Gentile, have been included in the ministry of the one who is Messiah in word and deed. Now the disciples are to be apprenticed to Jesus by their involvement in his mission. Before this, Jesus urges the disciples to pray to the Lord of the harvest that laborers would be sent to the abandoned, dispirited crowd to gather them into the caring love denied to them by those who should have been shepherds of "the congregation of the Lord," as Moses charged Joshua (Num 27:17). But the hopes of the people have been plundered by religious leaders who abandoned their sheep, an image that recalls the prophetic indictments of the religious leaders who were unfaithful to their calling (see Jer 23:1-6; Ezek 34). Jesus is the definitive answer to this prayer for harvesters but, perhaps to the surprise of the disciples, twelve of them are also to be part of the answer. It is an urgent call, for fruit or crops not harvested will rot, and between the mission of Jesus and his community there is an urgent and intimate connection.

Jesus' mission is born out of compassion that in the biblical text is a verb, a "doing of compassion," with the meaning of the womb contracting or the gut feeling when one is deeply stirred. In the gospels it is a word that is used only of Jesus, or by Jesus in two of his parables (Luke 10:33; 15:20). Compassion will be Jesus' gift to his disciples to enable them to share his mission.

And so the twelve apostles are called and personally named. This is the only occasion that Matthew uses the word "apostle," "sent one," to describe the follower of Jesus. Whereas the meaning of "disciple" is "learner," in today's gospel the emphasis is on the sending out of those whom Jesus has chosen. They are individuals; about some of them we know their background and the circumstances of their calling, while others are named here and then simply become part of "the Twelve." That is enough to encourage us about the possibility of becoming a community around Jesus. If fishermen (two sets of brothers, with the family dynamics that might involve), a tax collector, a hot-headed revolutionary Zealot, a traitor, and the rest, could be chosen and harvested by Jesus as the first laborers in the field, then surely there is hope for the disparate humanity that is our local or universal church today. Jesus had to work hard, and not always successfully, with these apprentices. The fact that they are twelve is an important symbolic statement. Just as there were the twelve tribes of God's people in the Old Testament, so in the New Testament we again have the twelve. Rather than any replacement or supersessionist concept, we might look at the wonderful description in the Book of Revelation—again highly symbolic—of the holy city, the new Jerusalem. Its twelve gates are inscribed with "the names of the twelve tribes of the Israelites," and the twelve foundations of the city are inscribed with "the twelve names of the twelve apostles of the Lamb" (Rev 21:10-14).

Like all apprenticeships, it was "on the job" training, and the Twelve are immediately sent out on mission to those for whom Jesus wishes to show his compassion. That Jesus sends his apostles only to "the lost sheep of the house of Israel," with instruction to avoid the Gentiles and Samaritans, may disconcert us. Jesus himself has already ministered with compassion to the Gentiles: the Roman centurion's servant (Matt 8:5-13) and the Gadarene demoniacs (Matt 8:28-34). Soon he will meet the Canaanite woman (Matt 15:21-28), and praise her faith in front of the objecting disciples, but it is not until after the resurrection that Jesus will commission the disciples themselves to go to all nations (Matt 28:19), a mission which Matthew had early anticipated by the visit of the Magi to the infant Christ (Matt 2:1-12). After the resurrection they will have been sufficiently, painfully, and joyfully taught by Jesus for their larger mission. The mission of the Twelve at this stage is urgent, and limited to the region and culture with which they are most familiar. Here they are to do what they have seen Jesus doing. Matthew's community of mainly Jewish Christians can identify with this priority, but must also learn the often difficult acceptance of the Gentiles who were joining the early church. Here, in our own life situations, we are to try and do the same: minister with the gift of faith and Christ's compassion to the sick in mind and body, raise people from death-dealing despair, cast out the addictions that so destructively take hold of our sisters and brothers. Baptized into Christ, God has loved us at no charge; now we have to love the unlovable, without recompense.

The reading from the Book of Exodus is another call story. While the people are encamped in front of the mountain, waiting for some word or revelation of their God, Moses is called by God to ascend Mount Sinai, a place where earth and heaven seem to meet, and therefore considered a place of holy presence. There God speaks with Moses and gives him a message, based on remembering, to take back to the people, which may well have been the basis of covenant renewal liturgies. Mountains are also the haunt of eagles, and we hear the beautiful comparison of God to the parent eagle who trains the eaglet to fly. She pushes the young one out of the nest onto her outstretched wings, then hurls it off into the sky, catching it when its wings are too weak to hold it up and before it plunges into a death dive. Over and over again, this parenting is repeated until the eaglet flies free. The eagle-winged God has parented the people, carried them as fledglings out of Egyptian slavery, nurtured and sustained them, and brought them to the foot of the holy mountain so that they would come to what is their true destination: "to myself," says God to Moses. And just as the eagle is also an image of soaring power that swoops on its enemies, so God will defend this people (see Deut 28:49; Jer 48:40).

But there are conditions that must be met by God's people if the relationship is to be sealed. Moses is commanded to be quite specific about the people's covenant obligations. "If" they continually listen to God and obey his word, "if" they are faithful to their promises of obedience to God, and "if" they can hold in a creative tension that pulls them closer to God both the truth of their special election and God's concern for all creation, then Israel will be a priestly kingdom and a holy nation. They will be a people involved in the world as a consecrating presence of God. Jesus, the Israelite who was most perfect in his obedience, who made the new covenant in his body and blood, calls us at baptism into this new covenant with the same listening, consecrating mission.

In his Letter to the Romans, Paul sees the sacrifice of Christ for humanity as an extraordinary sign of love: as the incarnate and most clear expression of God's own eternal love in a privileged and decisive moment (*kairós*) of human history. Not even sin is a barrier to such love and, by arguing from the heavier or greater demand (the salvation of sinful humanity) to the lighter or lesser (the salvation of those transformed by life in Christ),

Paul sees Christians who have accepted Christ as being "like travelers with visas fully stamped ('justified'), believers who can confidently expect that God's love will usher them through the final barrier."[26]

In Psalm 100, we sing a processional song as the flock of our God, no longer shepherd-less, no longer huddled at the barrier waiting to have our entry visas stamped, because we have come into the presence of the eternal and faithful love of God in a way that continues and surpasses the psalmist's experience—in the living temple of Christ's body of which we are living stones.

Twelfth Sunday in Ordinary Time

• Jer 20:10-13 • Ps 69:8-10, 14, 17, 33-35 • Rom 5:12-15 • Matt 10:26-33

Today's gospel is part of the second of the Matthean discourses, usually called the Mission Discourse. Before the disciples are sent out to share the mission of Jesus, they must dare to listen to him explain the tough demands of that mission. Three times Jesus tells them not to be afraid: not to fear those who (in the previous verse) malign them, or disregard them as worthless, or can injure and even kill them. Jesus has gathered them as a community of disciples and sown his word in the soil of their hearts so that it may push through this darkness and bear fruit by their proclamation of the gospel.

Just as Jesus trusts his Father, so it is to be with his disciples. Their one Father is so aware of the creation born from his love that he is even aware of the death of the insignificant and dispensable little sparrows that are the cheapest food of the poor. Once again, using the rabbinic way of arguing from the lighter (lesser) matter to the heavier (greater), Jesus says that if God has this concern for sparrows, how much more will he be concerned with the life and death of human beings. This greater concern is imaged as that of a caring parent who knows so much about his children—even the number of the hairs on their head—and will take care of them.

"Everyone therefore . . ." who hears these words of Jesus, each one of us in the Sunday assembly, is called to fearless proclamation of the gospel, to acknowledge Jesus openly and without embarrassment in our families, communities, workplaces, and wider social situations. If we do this, Jesus assures us of an acknowledgment by his Father when we come to our final judgment. But if we deny Jesus, we will also be denied. It is a pastoral challenge for every baptized Christian to find the right words that are more than "church speak"—language that says nothing to the doubts and anxieties, the truth of who people are. What are the difficulties in climbing to the contemporary "rooftops" where the right words can be spoken and heard? Married people struggling with fidelity, young people at war with their hormones, those with disabilities longing to be recognized first of all as people, men and women searching for their sexual identity, the poor and disadvantaged who are ashamed or angry: all of these need Christians to first of all listen to and then respond to their human stories of "grace and disgrace."[27] We do well to remember that it is also the wisdom and imagination of the poets and artists, the filmmakers and musicians, who stretch us beyond the small horizons of our own experiences and give us a new language.

To be able to find new words, the experience and wisdom of the whole people of God is needed, and situations need to be created where this can be heard and shared without fear; for example, that is what happens in a parish which has "open house" one night a week when anyone is welcome to help in the preparation of the homily for the coming Sunday. Sometimes there might be twenty people, sometimes five or six, of different ages and life situations. The priest or a lay leader who has studied the scriptures says a few words, usually about the gospel. Then those gathered are asked what the word of God meant to them, what they would like to hear explained, how they are challenged, bored, or angered by what they have heard. Everyone's response is respected; there is no argument, no judgment. What the priest has dared to listen to, the "grace and disgrace" in the lives and world of his parishioners, can then help him to shape his homily for the following Sunday.

Jeremiah has no fear about shouting to the people the word of God that burned like a fire in his bones and could not be held in. In the late seventh and sixth centuries B.C.E., Jeremiah lived through tumultuous times. The reforms of King Josiah (622 B.C.E.) were good times, but then came the catastrophic exile of many of Jerusalem's and Judah's citizens to Babylon between 597 and 587 B.C.E., and the destruction of the Jerusalem Temple. This is the background to today's reading. Add to Jeremiah's situation the conflicts between the surrounding nations, and Jeremiah's struggles with false prophets, with kings, and with religious leaders of the establishment, and it may not be a surprise that Jeremiah fiercely directs his complaints to God. When Jeremiah is released from the stocks by Pashur, the priest of the establishment who had physically abused him for daring to try to change the status quo, the prophet announces the priest's new name, "Terror-all-around." The terror that he had caused for Jeremiah will, says the prophet, soon rebound on Pashur who will be taken into Babylonian exile (Jer 20:1-6). The persecution of Jeremiah by Pashur, "Terror-all-around," is being talked about by Jeremiah's enemies at the beginning of the first reading. On the edge of despair, the relentless truth-teller still turns to God whom he believes will defend him like a mighty warrior. Only one who has great trust can complain to God so bitterly. Jeremiah does not try to take revenge *himself*, but asks God for *God's justice* for his enemies. With his lamentation spoken before God, his struggling faith professed, Jeremiah's painful prayer from the "pit" takes wings and rises to God as song of praise for his delivery—delivery not so much from his enemies (who are with Jeremiah to the end) but from his own despair. Down the centuries such suffering and deliverance continues to be experienced: for example, by Jesus himself whose faithfulness to God's word brought suffering, by those who "after Auschwitz" wrestled with God, by those who have stood on the edge of suicide and pulled back, or by all those whose lamentation has struggled into praise, their agony into ecstasy, their death into life.

The verses from Psalm 69 that are chosen for the responsorial psalm echo not only distress and solitude, but also the burning zeal and confidence of someone who, like Jeremiah, trusts in God and assures others that God will listen to the cries of the poor. The reason for this confident faith is repeated throughout the psalm: God is a God of loving kindness, steadfast love and compassion. Because this is how God turns to us in our distress, tiny fragments of his creation though we are, we join the psalmist in words of cosmic praise.

Timothy Radcliffe, o.p., comments:

> Humanity's history is like breathing. The vital moments of our history are always moments of humanity's lungs. God breathes into the lungs of Adam at the beginning, then Christ breathes out his last breath at the climax of salvation, and then the Holy Spirit is breathed upon us at Pentecost.[28]

In the second reading we hear what Paul writes to the Roman church about two contrasting eras in our human history: the era of sin and death that Adam (representing humanity before even Moses and the Mosaic law) inaugurated, and the era of reconciliation and life in which Christ, the New Adam, through his life, death, and resurrection, recreates us in his Spirit/Breath. One is the story of dis-grace, a radical revolt, in favor of self and selfishness, against the humanity which is God's gift. The other is the story of grace, of the radical self-sacrifice of Christ who immerses himself in the reality of human sinfulness in order to make incarnate and universal the over-abundant love of God that reconciles everyone and everything to the original design of creation.

The gift that is Jesus Christ will carry us through all the disappointments of our discipleship, will help us endure when we are "in the pits" of our Jeremiah moments, and will give us voices for the rooftop acknowledgment of the New Adam in our families, our local church, our communities, and our workplaces.

Thirteenth Sunday in Ordinary Time

• 2 Kgs 4:8-11, 14-16a • Ps 89:2-3, 16-19 • Rom 6:3-4, 8-11 • Matt 10:37-42

Standing before the Sunday assembly, the parents of the two-month-old-baby held her tenderly and asked for baptism for their child, and the ritual welcome into the Christian community began—with the signing of their daughter with the cross. The month before, her eighty-seven-year-old great-grandmother had been held peacefully in her coffin in the midst of that same community and friends at her vigil. On the bodies of both of these Christians the sign of the cross was traced, the paradoxical sign of belonging to a crucified and risen Christ in whom we are born and reborn. One day the child will have to make personal choices for or against this Christ and may have to live preferences which will plow roughly and deeply through her life and that of her family; on many days her great-grandmother had, no doubt, struggled to plant the seeds of the preferential love of Christ in the midst of all the other demands for her love. Today's gospel, which many find hard to accept, is about preferences that must be made under the shadow of the cross of the crucified and risen Christ.

It is significant that it is after the call to discipleship and Jesus' instruction about how the disciples are to share in his mission that Matthew uses the word "cross" for the first time in his gospel, and talks about taking up the cross in the context of family love. To put anything else above one's family was unthinkable for first century Middle Eastern society. Unlike many of our contemporary societies where young people usually move out of home as young adults, and certainly move out of their kinship group or family when they marry, to leave one's family in Palestinian culture was to forfeit emotional ties, social status and connections, present economic support and future land rights—the situation of the Prodigal Son in Luke 15:11-32. Jesus is not telling his disciples that they must exclude parental and family love from their lives. That is such a precious and God-given relationship that it finds its place as the fourth holy "word" of the "ten words" (or Decalogue) of God that we call the Ten Commandments: "Honor your father and your mother" (Exod 20:12). On the Sixth Sunday in Ordinary Time we heard how Matthew emphasized to his predominantly Jewish Christian community that Jesus had not come to abolish such commandments but to bring their interpretation to fulfillment (Matt 5:17-18). The human life of Jesus also bears witness to both family love and love of God in his obedience to Mary and Joseph, but overarching all his life and death is his first love of and first obedience to "Abba," his Father. The cross that Jesus presents to his disciples stands tall in the bedrock of tensions and apparent contradictions. For them, it is a matter of getting priorities right, of preferring the love of God to the pressures of society, and especially to the basic social relationships of the family when these make demands that erode commitment to the Gospel.

A precious gem of early Christian literature is the *Passion of Perpetua and Felicity*, a contemporary account, possibly with Tertullian as the principal author. Although written in first person style, it tells of the martyrdom (ca. 203) in North Africa of Perpetua, a young married woman of noble Roman birth, and her slave-girl, Felicity. Both were condemned to the arena at Carthage. One part describes Perpetua's pain because of her father's attitude. Weary and exhausted with grief, he tries to make his twenty-two-year-old daughter change her mind, to pity his white hair, remember the desperate love of her family, and especially her baby son whom she was still nursing. Faced with such distress, Hilarion, the administrator, begs her to offer sacrifice for the well-being of the emperors. Perpetua steadfastly refuses, and Hilarion puts to her the deciding question: "Are you a Christian?" When she simply answers, "I am a Christian," her father made a last attempt to try to get his daughter to overthrow her faith. Instead, Hilarion gave the order for him to be thrown down, and beaten with a rod. This pain, said Perpetua, hurt her as if she herself had been struck. Then the judgment was passed: "To the wild beasts."[29]

Today, the simple answer: "Yes, I am a Christian," may not have the dramatic result of martyrdom in many places. In other countries, however, it is still the very real experience of Christians whose faith has to withstand persecution and tyranny or refuse to be conformed to personal, social, or even ecclesial comfort zones. No committed Christian can escape the demanding priorities of the cross in our daily lives. We do not pray for the cross, but we accept its often surprising arrival, trying to recognize it for what it is: a challenge to trust in God and God's future, and discover that self-giving is self-fulfillment.

If we do give priority in our lives to the love of Jesus and his gospel, and if in doing this we have to painfully bid farewell to people who are precious to us, Jesus offers us a great welcome into a new "family" and community. A chain of hospitality (the life-giving Middle Eastern virtue) binds the disciple to Jesus and Jesus to the Father. To welcome one is to welcome the others. We are not all Perpetuas or Felicitys, but if disciples no longer have family structures to support them because of rifts that come with allegiance to Jesus, the Christian community has the obligation of offering hospitality to them. It may be a gesture as small and ordinary as a neighborly "cuppa," or the affirmation (using modern means of communication as well as personal contact) of those prophets and seekers of justice in our midst who may be persecuted not only by those outside the Church but also by those "in their own country and in their own house" (Matt 13:57).

In the first reading we hear of the hospitality offered to the prophet Elisha by the wealthy but childless woman of Shunem. Without regard for her rank or economic status, she hungers for the holiness that she senses in Elisha; without any show of excessive and embarrassing attention, but with a sensitivity proper to true hospitality, she provides the prophet with a simple welcome. Food, a bed, a chair, a lamp, and the opportunity to rest whenever he passed that way: these were the homely and familiar resources the woman made available to Elisha. The prophet is humble enough to welcome the advice of his servant, Gehazi, as to how best to reward the woman and her husband. Gehazi reminds Elisha that the couple is childless, and the prophet promises them the reward of a child within the year, even in her husband's old age. It is with the power of God that Elisha works miracles that are not part of a huge political landscape but belong to the everyday world of ordinary people and families, for the sake of life not death. As individuals and as local church, and as prophetic people by our baptism, what is the hospitality we can offer that is life-giving rather than death-dealing: for example, to refugee strangers that pass our way, to those for whom a simple meal or bed may be a luxury, to newcomers to our parish community?

Paul writes very clearly in his Letter to the Romans that it is baptism that calls us to hospitality, because by baptism we have been welcomed into the death of Jesus so that we might also walk in the newness of his risen life. But Paul is a realist; he knows that the power of sin and death can still exert its pull on the baptized, and that loyalty to Christ will mean dying to self-centeredness so that we may be transformed and "alive to God in Christ Jesus." Every Christian needs to do some sober spiritual accountancy, a reckoning of how practically we are living in response to the loving hospitality of God that invites us into the mystery of Christ. Paul would approve of the practice of a daily "review of life" that recognizes the love of God of which the psalmist sings in the responsorial Psalm 89. We have the privilege of knowing what could not be known by the psalmist: that the light of the Lord in which we walk now shines forth in the glory of the face of Jesus Christ (see 2 Cor 4:6). He is the one who is now in the safekeeping of heaven and who guides us in our walking to that same home.

Fourteenth Sunday in Ordinary Time

• Zech 9:9-10 • Ps 145:1-2, 8-11, 13-14 • Rom 8:9, 11-13 • Matt 11:25-30

He was a young man, and he looked as if he was probably homeless. Each night he turned up at the adult formation scripture sessions that were being offered at the inner city pastoral center, sitting quietly at the back of the room, but disappearing when it came to any group discussion. He always carried a large cardboard box that he placed carefully beside him. On the last night of the course, the facilitator went over to him before he had a chance to escape, asked him his name and invited him to stay for supper. Much to everyone's surprise, the man agreed. After offering his name, Michael, he was introduced to some of the other young people. During supper, the facilitator noticed that Michael had opened his box and placed its contents on one of the tables around which an admiring crowd had gathered. What had been in the box was not food, not a change of clothes, but a skillfully crafted model of a church made from white cardboard. All along the outer walls of the steepled church were sayings of Jesus and the prophets, written in Michael's beautiful calligraphy. Over the front door were the words we hear in today's gospel: "Come to me, all you that are weary and are carrying heavy burdens, and I will give you rest" (Matt 11:28). Beneath these words the front door was closed with a tiny padlock. Michael told the group that, yes, he was homeless and unemployed. He'd lost his job for standing up for an abused workmate. "Sometimes," he said, "when I show people my church they offer to look after it for me." With a small, sad smile he added, "But they don't make the same offer to me . . . only to my cardboard church."

In the verses immediately before today's gospel, Jesus has reproached the cities that rejected him, but then out of this lamentation there erupts his hymn of praise and thanks to his Father for the "little ones," the Michaels of every place and time, who have no status but can recognize in Jesus the One who is "kind and full of compassion, slow to anger, abounding in love," who lifts up the fallen and those who are burdened, as the responsorial Psalm 145 prays. This recognition is God's revelation, a gift of God's grace, for such people have no other way of coming to this response. As Jesus has just told the disciples of John the Baptist, a sign of the messianic times would be the preaching to and welcoming of the good news by the poor and disadvantaged. These words are not only for Jesus' immediate audience or for Matthew's community of powerless "little ones" struggling with the religious authorities fifty years or more after Jesus' death and resurrection; they are also a present and future challenge to those whose theological and religious pretensions or spiritual elitism ignore or downgrade the wisdom and experience of those who have come to know God through simple, but often hard won and faithful commitment.

Matthew then gives us one of our very few glimpses into the prayer of Jesus as experienced and remembered by the tradition. As when he had earlier taught his disciples to pray, Jesus addresses God as "Father," not to idolize a name or gender or metaphor, but to focus on a relationship: the reign of his Abba over his life and the lives of all those who become daughters and sons of this same God by accepting Jesus as the Word and Wisdom of God. There are echoes here of the hymn that closes the Book of Sirach (Sir 51:22-30). Like Lady Wisdom, Jesus offers an invitation to those who are overburdened and weary: "Come to me . . . ." It is Jesus, not the rigorous law enforcers of his day, who will offer rest. Jesus uses the image of his easy "yoke" to encourage the people to accept his invitation. To the Palestinian peasant, the yoke was a familiar farming object. It was a wooden frame, designed to be fitted over the necks of two oxen or horses to distribute evenly the weight of the load that they had to pull. When yoked, plowing animals were more effectively kept in step with one another. It was usually the local carpenter who would make and fit a yoke, with great concern for the individual animal's neck muscles and the maximum direction of its energy. (One wonders how many yokes Jesus and Joseph had made.) "*My* yoke," says Jesus, will be well-fitted to each disciple. It will distribute the weight of our heavy burdens between each one of us and Jesus; and it will keep us in step with the One who is the Way as we plow through life.

In the Old Testament, the yoke was a metaphor coined in different religious contexts and was still understood in those ways in Jesus' day. To break away from God and rebel against the teachings of the Mosaic Law (Torah) was to "break God's yoke" (Jer 2:20). The yoke of the law hitched the Jewish people to 613 commandments that had evolved over the centuries, although there was also the reality of "the joy of the Torah" when the law was lived from the heart. In the hymn of Sirach, the wisdom of God is personified as Lady Wisdom who establishes her school for the untaught where these "little ones" may put their necks under her yoke and their souls receive instruction (Sir 51:26). Disciples will later be referred to as "yoke companions" who labor side by side with Jesus and one another as they plow the world's fields to prepare it to receive the seed of the Gospel (Phil 4:3). Church leaders today need to reflect on and pray this gospel before God and before the heard experience of those for whom life in the Church has become too burdensome. Are there rules and structures that are not the yoke of Jesus but the imposition of a chafing, constricting authority that results in some people being no longer able or willing to walk with the community of disciples—even though their hearts long to do just that?

In the second reading, Paul reminds his Roman community that for those who have been baptized, it is the Spirit of the risen Christ rather than sin that dwells in them as the guiding force of their lives, their new mind-set, and the promise of the destiny that they will share. Just as God was faithful to Jesus in raising him from the dead, so those who live in the Spirit of Jesus can be confident that their bodies, too, will share in the resurrection. As for the church at Rome, so with our free choices: either to choose to walk the way of Christ who will lead us to new and eternal life in the end time, or to follow our human, self-centered inclinations which bring "death," the quenching of the life of the Spirit within us.

In the first reading, the prophet Zechariah announces his vision of the ideal messianic king. In the Jewish tradition this messiah (anointed one) is not God, but the end-time servant of God who comes to prepare the way for the eschatological Day of the Lord. Zechariah envisages him as riding to his people not on a powerful warhorse but on a donkey, a peaceful animal, and an animal of the common people, associated with much of their daily work. Solomon chooses to ride on King David's mule in his enthronement procession (1 Kgs 1:38) because the kings whom God called to be the special protectors of the poor and the defenders of justice could only succeed in this royal calling if they were humble and peaceful. After some good beginnings, most of the kings failed—but the hope remained. When Jesus enters Jerusalem shortly before his passion, Matthew transplants these words of Zechariah into his gospel to announce faith in Jesus, true Messiah and King, servant of the "little ones" whose burdens he will take on himself, even unto death.

A churchman who came humbly among his people was the late Archbishop Hélder Câmara of Recife, Brazil. One of his famous sayings is: "When I gave food to the poor, they called me a saint. When I asked why the poor were hungry, they called me a communist." "They" would prefer to charge on their warhorses and scatter or trample down those who ask uncomfortable questions about reasons for the burdening of the poor.

Fifteenth Sunday in Ordinary Time

• Isa 55:10-11 • Ps 65:10-14 • Rom 8:18-23 • Matt 13:1-23

> "The play's the thing
> Wherein I'll catch the conscience of the King." (*Hamlet*, Act 2, Sc. 2)[30]

Shakespeare puts these words into the mouth of Hamlet, prince of Denmark. In the Scriptures, parables are designed to catch our consciences, to fasten their biblical grappling hooks into our lives and drag us into a response to the Word of God. We can, of course, try to disengage ourselves from this uncomfortable process and listen but never understand, look and never perceive, as Jesus tells his disciples in the words of Isaiah. In the flow of Matthew's Gospel, in the chapter before today's reading, this is what Jesus' opponents have done when they accuse him of having the power of Beelzebub, the prince of demons (Matt 12:24). A rather gentler concept of parable telling might be described as "teasing." The parable teller begins in the audience's known world in the first century Palestinian situation, the world of farmers and fields and seed sowing; and then, just when his audience is feeling comfortable with the familiar, the story is given a surprising turn which "teases" the listeners into an unexpected revelation, a new way of thinking—if they are open to the new, if they have eyes ready to see and ears ready to listen. In the parable we hear today, what begins in Galilean agriculture ends up in hope and promise of the kingdom of heaven.

Palestinian sowing was not the precise, tidy process of modern farming. The Palestinian sower scattered generous handfuls of seed onto the unplowed field and after, not before this sowing, plowed or raked them into the soil. Given this risky method of sowing, the peasant farmers would know that there is no way that a sower could take credit for extraordinary harvests that yielded "in one case a hundredfold, in another sixty, in another thirty," when a fivefold yield was considered a good crop. Such a return boggles the imagination with the prospect of taxes paid, families well fed, and some profit stored away! The only other time when Jesus' audience might have heard of a hundredfold yield was if they remembered how God blessed the fields of Isaac that he sowed in Gerar (Gen 26:12). Such a yield was God's work and blessing. And so Jesus "hooks" or "teases" his listeners into a new understanding: it is God who gives the increase when the seed of the Word of God is planted among people. For Matthew's community there was internal tension and division between Christians grounded in their Jewish heritage and Gentile Christians who knew nothing of this, and external tension between Christians and Jews, and especially with those of the Pharisee party after the destruction of the Jerusalem Temple in 70 C.E. The latter were suspicious of anything or anyone whom they suspected of undermining the already devastated Jewish community. Matthew's community needed to be encouraged by hearing that God was the Lord of the harvest, despite the poor soil, the rocks and thorns that was their church and world. We are in no less need of such encouragement today.

Middle Eastern wisdom has a saying drawn from the world of agriculture: "Every morning I turn my face to the wind. It is not difficult to scatter seeds, but it takes courage to keep facing the wind." As the Sower, Jesus would have to keep facing the winds of controversy and opposition; so would his disciples. It is not the fault of the sower if the seeds do not grow. One of the challenges to our ministry is to fail with joy—joy which springs from following a crucified and risen Sower.

The seed is a wonderful symbol of the kingdom. Small, hard, unattractive to the senses, yet within it lies the future promise and hope of green and growing things, of harvest and bread. But for all its promise it remains only a seed, contained in its outer shell unless it surrenders itself to an environment that can realize its potential. When that happens, the seed grows gently, quietly; there is no instant produce. This is a good parable for Ordinary Time when the festal seasons are behind and before us and we are in the weeks of patient planting and slow germination, of cultivating and fertilizing the Word of God in the soil of our daily lives, persevering in the hope of the coming kingdom.

This parable can be a searching review of how we live our discipleship. At some time, even in the same day, and individually or communally in family, parish, or community, we can be the different "soils" about which Jesus speaks. We can be people who receive the word on the edge of the path, those who skirt the real issues, who are eager for the first distraction that jogs past, disciples of surface commitment and no depth. Or our lives can be rocky soil: enthusiasts of the moment, people of the quick fix and immediate response to the Gospel, who soon lose interest when the demands of the kingdom mean thrusting one's roots down into darkness, despite the rocky obstacles, and waiting patiently in that darkness for further growth. Again, we may offer a patchy, thorn-infested welcome to the seed of the Word, and the potential for its growth is endangered by our entanglement with self-seeking concerns or apathy, and so the seed does not come to maturity and bear fruit. Then there are the times when we are "good soil" for the seed, when we welcome, obey, and witness to the Word, and God enables us to bear a fruitful harvest for the kingdom.

Isaiah also uses the natural world as a metaphor for the fruitful effect of God's Word. Rain and snow fall from the heavens to make the earth fertile, and in this watered earth the seed can be sown and grow to provide the people with food. This is an observable cycle that shows the dependence of humanity upon the natural world rather than an arrogant dominion over it. It is an image, says Isaiah, of the relationship between the Word of God and those to whom it is addressed. We can trust God to send his Word, through the prophets, to fall on the soil of our humanity. If we recognize and welcome God's Word as a gracious gift on which we depend, we will be given all that we need to receive and nurture it. Then the holy cycle of God's call and the return of our obedience to him will continue season after season throughout the life cycle of God's people.

With Paul we enter into the mystery of our relationship with creation that is not just metaphorical. He gives us a personified vision of what we might call today the integrity of creation. Others might hear echoes of the "Gaia hypothesis," the belief that our planet functions as a single organism. For the Christian, however, this vision needs to be embedded in the cosmos that is itself embedded in God. The tradition that is the backdrop to Paul's thinking is the Genesis sense of stewardship of the world. When human relationships with God are ruptured, this affects material creation (see Gen 1:26-28; 3:17-19). When such relationships are restored, there is a consequent transformation of nature that the prophets imaged as the flowering of the wilderness when the exiles journeyed home to Jerusalem (Isa 41:17-20; Ezek 34:25-31). The human exploitation of our planet by the sins of economic greed that reduce forested land to desert, landscapes devastated by war, human populations suffocating and sickening in industrial air pollution, are but a few examples of the way in which we "subject to futility" the creation that God saw was "good." So Paul pictures creation as groaning—a groaning that is like the pangs of birth as it waits for the sons and daughters of God to be midwives with God of a new and reconciled future of creation. As the poet knows, our world "wears man's smudge and shares man's smell," but there is in all of us the restless hope that:

> And for all this, nature is never spent;
>   There lives the dearest freshness deep down things;
> And though the last lights off the black West went
>   Oh, morning, at the brown brink eastward, springs—
> Because the Holy Ghost over the bent
>   World broods with warm breast and with ah! bright wings.[31]

We already have the first fruits of the Spirit; we wait for the final harvest.

Sixteenth Sunday in Ordinary Time

• Wis 12:13, 16-19 • Ps 86:5-6, 9-10, 15-16 • Rom 8:26-27 • Matt 13:24-43

In this Sunday's gospel, Jesus tackles several issues that are as real for us today as they were for Matthew's first century community: patience, perfectionism, and "big is beautiful." What have these to do with our understanding of the kingdom of heaven? Once again, Jesus is the storyteller who uses vivid images as a vehicle to carry the truth of his words to the crowd.

In the first of the three parables, the weed with which the enemy over-seeded the wheat was probably darnel. In its early appearance this is almost indistinguishable from wheat, and it is only when the heads of the plants begin to fruit that the weeds are recognized. If it is harvested and milled with the wheat the flour will be spoiled, so the immediate response of the landowner's slaves is to uproot the weeds. But their master has a shrewd confidence in the ability of his wheat crop to survive competition for nutrition and irrigation with the entangled weeds. He tells his slaves to wait until the harvest time when the reapers will more easily distinguish the weeds from the wheat, and so not only will he have rescued a good harvest, but he will also have a useful supply of fuel from the dried weeds.

Someone once remarked that to explain a parable was rather like chewing up a piece of fruit before offering it to someone else. Possibly the allegorizing and point-by-point explanation that Jesus later gives to his disciples when they withdraw from the crowds into the house (Matt 13:36-43) was added by Matthew because his urban communities found the agricultural experience less familiar, and so it was harder for them to digest and savor the meaning of the parable. The central meaning of the parable is that the kingdom of God takes root in imperfect communities of "wheat and weeds," and in both an imperfect church and world. Even in the Twelve there was good and bad, loyalty and disloyalty, understanding and obtuseness—and we surely recognize this in ourselves as individuals and communities. Unbridled zeal that wants to create a pure and perfect community becomes intolerant fanaticism, which is not how the kingdom is established. The Pharisees and the Qumran community, for example, wanted communities of holy, separated people in which sinners had no place; Jesus himself was criticized for his association with sinners, with those who are "sick" and need him as a healing physician (Matt 9:12-13). Those who think they are the elite, who consider they have a claim to righteousness because they regard themselves as perfect in their keeping of the law as interpreted by Jesus, should heed the warning that at the final judgment Jesus, as the Son of Man, will separate weeds and wheat. Patience is needed until the end-time because the evil in a person's heart may be transformed into good by God's grace; anger may come to be expressed as work for justice, laziness as active patience, or acquisitiveness as generosity. The leaders of a Christian community need the discernment of the Spirit of Jesus to know when and how to emphasize patience and restraint, or warning and judgment. The community's struggle will be a cosmic one, because "the field is the world," and it is in this context that those committed to Jesus ("the children of the kingdom") will have to withstand those who oppose his word.

In the short parable of the mustard seed there is encouragement for the Christian community struggling with its small beginnings or, like today's church, faced in some places with the diminution of what once was "big," such as priestly and religious vocations or well-attended Masses. We no longer sing hymns about "Who is she that stands triumphant." God's kingdom is not imaged as a towering, majestic cedar that Ezekiel describes (Ezek 17:3-10). It is like a tenacious and domestic mustard bush, and unlike the great and towering tree of Nebuchadnezzar's dream that was also full of nesting birds. That dream, interpreted Daniel, was a vision of Nebuchadnezzar himself and his reign that would be cut down (Dan 4:10-14, 20-27). For the reign of the kingdom, says Jesus, small seeds are enough to grow into welcoming bushes.

God is also like a woman with hands in the flour, mixing in "three measures of leaven," enough for an extravagant loaf that would feed about 150 people! This is Matthew's only parable with a female image of God, and the only positive reference to leaven that causes fermentation and so usually symbolizes corruption. And here is the challenge: as Jesus taught, the realm of God is permeated by those whom many "purists" might consider "corrupt"—the poor, the outcast, the marginalized—who will be the active ingredient for the growth of the kingdom. They are welcomed by Jesus who was crucified and rose again to leaven and transform the world, and who still mixes with us in all our weaknesses and sinfulness. This parable not only challenges us to expand our image of God as a woman, but also to reflect on the ministry of women in the growth of the kingdom, and to hope for more and more leavening as women and men mix together in leadership roles.

Paul was aware of his own and our human weakness, and in his Letter to the Romans he encourages us to entrust this weakness to the Spirit. Last Sunday Paul spoke about the "groaning" of creation and our own groaning as we long for salvation; today he writes about the Spirit who "groans" for us within our personal depths. Because of our vulnerability and inability to pray as we should, the Spirit, who is the Searcher of the depths of our hearts, identifies with our weakness and prays in us. In confident hope, we surrender to this Spirit in whom we believe even though we are not conscious of the intercessory prayer that the Spirit offers in and for us. The Spirit's intercession on behalf of the saints, the people of God, is according to the mind of God, and so is always appropriate and effective.

The portion from the Book of Wisdom is structured as an address to God, but its purpose is to show God's people how they should model their behavior on God's. In the parable of the weeds and wheat, the landowner is tolerant of the good mixed with the bad and their coexistence until the final judgment, and so it is with the God of this reading. God is a provident and just God, even toward opponents. God's justice is never exercised as tyranny but as mercy; God's tolerance is not weakness but compassion that allows time for conversion. God's people should be the same in their relationships. Our liturgical response is verses from Psalm 86, a meditation on the identity of God and the divine mercy and forgiveness that is slow to anger. The psalmist's confidence is based not only on his personal experience of his prayer being heard by God, but also on the witness of the ancient tradition and confession of God's people (Exod 34:6). In God's good time, all the nations will come to adore the One whose reign will be the final consummation of human history. We praise our God who is good and forgiving, merciful and compassionate, when we are gathered around the Word. When we scatter to our homes and families and workplaces, do we live the praise of our God?

Seventeenth Sunday in Ordinary Time

• 1 Kgs 3:5, 7-12 • Ps 119:57, 72, 76-77, 127-130 • Rom 8:28-30 • Matt 13:44-52

In the ancient world without access to bank or strongbox storage, burying valuables was a common practice (Matt 25:18, 25), especially under threat of invasion. If the original owner died or was unable to return to his land, if no one had been told the whereabouts of the treasure or if the land was confiscated, the treasure might lie hidden for many years, unknown to the descendants of the original owner or those who subsequently acquired that land. Then someone finds the treasure. Rabbinic lore (later than the first century C.E., but perhaps also customary then) has much discussion about the legality or morality of such finding and keeping, but in the story context of today's gospel the hearers would have little concern with such matters. The human interest aspect of the fortunate discovery and the man's determination to purchase the field predominates. Whether a day laborer or a tenant farmer, it is obvious to him that the owner of the field knows nothing of the treasure. "Finders are keepers" does not apply in Palestinian society unless the field is one's own property, so the one who finds the treasure determines to sell all that he has and buy the field. It is this joy of discovery, the attitude of readiness to give up everything and risk one's future on the transaction in order to obtain the treasure, that should characterize Jesus' disciples to whom God discloses the treasure of the kingdom that is hidden in the words and works of Jesus. This is what happens, for example, in the call and response stories of the first disciples (Matt 4:18-22), of Matthew the tax collector (Matt 9:9), of the two blind men (Matt 20:29-34). God may touch us in unexpected ways, in the midst of our ordinary routines. Perhaps through a friendship, an event at work, a book read, or in the everyday but humanly significant events of birth, sickness, or death, we may stumble on the Unexpected One who transforms our lives and forever makes everything else relative. Then we know the joy of the kingdom.

Twinned with the parable of the buried treasure is the parable of the pearl of great price. The surprise of this parable is not the discovery of the pearl because, unlike the one who found the buried treasure, the traveling merchant was deliberately seeking the precious pearl; the surprise is its great value. Consequently, the merchant sells everything that he owns to purchase the pearl, considered in the ancient world as among the most valuable of goods. The kingdom of God is beyond all price, and even though a person may be seeking it, when God reveals it to the seeker it is beyond all expectations. We need to remember that this is one of the parables that Jesus is telling in the house and to his disciples, not to the crowds (Matt 13:36). In Jesus, they have found the kingdom, the pearl of inestimable value. Now they must commit themselves totally to it. Some people may come upon the kingdom unexpectedly, like the farmer or laborer in the first parable; others, like the merchant, may earnestly seek the kingdom for many years of studying, questing, and questioning before they recognize and surrender to the kingdom. Some disciples may be poor, others rich, but when the kingdom of God is revealed it becomes the first priority in their lives.

There is a Hassidic tale about Rabbi Eisik, son of Rabbi Yekel of Cracow. After many years of great poverty that had never shaken his faith in God, he dreamed for three nights in a row that he should look for a treasure in Prague under the bridge which led to the king's palace, so he decided to do something about his dream. After a long journey he arrived in Prague only to find that the bridge was patrolled day and night by the king's guard. Nevertheless, he went to the bridge every morning and evening. Finally, the captain of the guard who had been watching him asked him kindly if he was looking for someone or something. Rabbi Eisik told the captain about his dream. The captain laughed good-humoredly, and said, "And so to please the dream, you poor fellow, you wore out your shoes to come here! As for having faith in dreams, if I had that, I should have been off to Cracow to dig for a treasure under the stove in the room of a Jew—Eisik, son of Yekel!" Eisik bowed to the laughing captain, traveled home to Cracow, dug up the treasure from under his stove, and built a House of Prayer.[32] The

place where we find the treasure of the kingdom of God may be unexpectedly close at hand, or it may take a long journey to discover, or it may involve something of both.

The third of this Sunday's parables, about the dragnet, is not concerned
with the "now," but the "not yet." A dragnet was a large net supported by
floats and held in place by sinkers, used for surface fishing. Its catch was in-
discriminate: edible and inedible, ritually clean and unclean, marketable or
worthless, the fish would be sorted out by the fishermen when brought
ashore. As with the parable of the weeds and wheat, the dragnet catch is an
image of the Christian community of committed disciples and sinners, of
good and evil—the mix that we can recognize in ourselves. There will,
however, come a moment of end-time judgment when disciples will be finally accountable for their obedience or disobedience to what Jesus has revealed and their readiness or resistance to allow this to rule over them.

The disciples give a perhaps too ready "Yes," when Jesus asks them if
they have understood, and certainly the power of the story telling helps us,
like them, to understand something of the joy and value of the kingdom of
God. But it is our living as kingdom men and women that is our true assent
to Jesus. The last verses about the scribe trained for the kingdom who
knows how to bring what is new and what is old out of his treasure is sometimes considered a word portrait of the evangelist Matthew who could offer
both the riches of his Jewish heritage and their new interpretation by Jesus
to his mixed community of (predominantly) Jewish and Gentile Christians.
But the reference can be even broader and more challenging to disciples of
all times who are to be dedicated to the treasures of the reign of God: people
of discernment who respect the traditions of the "old" and sacred heritage
of Judaism, but see this against the "new" horizon of Jesus' teaching.[33]

There is another "dream" story in today's liturgy. In the Bible a dream is
regarded as a special vehicle of revelation where God's spirit and the dreamer's spirit touch. In his dream, Solomon responds to God's invitation to ask
for what he most desires. Humbly aware of himself as God's servant, as the
one of all David's sons chosen to succeed him, and of his inexperience in
leadership, the young king asks for a listening and discerning heart so that
he will be able to lead with justice the people of God who are entrusted to
his governance. Such a choice was according to God's own heart, and so
God promises this gift to Solomon. The Lectionary cuts out of this reading
the previous two verses (1 Kgs 3:1-2) that describe Solomon's marriage alliance with the Pharaoh's daughter, his preference for building his own house
before the house of the Lord, and his worship on the high and pagan places,
yet if we had heard these verses, we would realize that in Solomon there

were both "weeds and wheat," and that even so God still comes to Solomon with his gracious favor. Although it is Solomon's wisdom that is stressed in the reading, there is the consolation for us that God also responds to imperfect love with generous blessings.

The verses from Psalm 119, a long meditation on wisdom, look back to this first reading as a prayerful affirmation of Solomon's choice, and forward to the parables in the gospel, because God's word and commandments are a greater treasure than silver or gold. Throughout the psalm the love of God for his servant who responds with love is the foundation of obedience.

The reading from Paul's Letter to the Romans follows immediately on last Sunday's portion that described the Spirit groaning, calling with heartfelt love from the personal depths of believers. This is why he can assure his Roman community that they can have the greatest confidence in God's love, even in adverse circumstances and when it is difficult to recognize and understand such love. Our deep trust is to be in God's unfolding plan, the gift for humanity that embraces those who are called to conform themselves to the image of Christ, the Firstborn of the sons and daughters of God. By this conformity we will share in Christ's resurrection and glory.

Eighteenth Sunday in Ordinary Time

• Isa 55:1-3 • Ps 145:8-9, 15-18 • Rom 8:35, 37-39 • Matt 14:13-21

The Parable Discourse is finished, and Matthew again shows us Jesus, the Messiah of word and deed, active among the people. In the flow of this chapter, Matthew places two feeding stories that are in stark contrast. Immediately before this Sunday's reading is the account of the lavish banquet at Herod's palace (Matt 14:1-12). Then follows the lakeside multiplication of the loaves and fishes and the feeding of the five thousand. Jesus lives abundantly and compassionately with little, concerned only for the hungry crowds; Herod lives weakly and bitterly in his palace, anxious only about losing face and status. One feast ends with death-dealing and Herod's fears that the murdered John the Baptist might come back to haunt him; the other feast results in life-giving for the hungry crowd. The unpleasant mother-daughter team of Herodias and Salome combine with the king to distribute death and vengeance; the disciples obey the request of Jesus to distribute bread and hope.

Between these two "feasts" there is a poignant bridge. As soon as Jesus receives the news of John's death, he is overwhelmed with human grief. He withdraws by boat to a lonely place "by himself," with his tears and, it is not hard to imagine, with his premonition of what could be his own violent death. But out of his personal sorrow comes not self-interest but compassion, the meeting of misery and mercy when he sees the crowd that has followed him. Although Jesus longs for solitude, he immediately sets this aside to meet the desperate needs of the sick and disadvantaged. He spends the whole day moving among the crowd, teaching and restoring the broken ones to wholeness, witnessing to us that even when our own hearts are broken we can be ready to surrender personal agendas for the sake of others. Certainly we need times of solitude and healing, but we must never become so absorbed with our own pain that we are oblivious to the suffering of others. From Jesus' pain was born compassion.

In this narrative, Matthew follows his "accustomed pattern of wrapping Jesus in the mantle of Old Testament symbols and typology."[34] The deserted place and the hungry crowd recall God's gift of manna during Israel's wilderness wanderings (Exod 16). Elisha had fed a hundred famine-stricken men with twenty loaves (2 Kgs 4:42-44), and the prophet Isaiah writes of the wonderful vision of the end-time when all God's people will gather for the messianic banquet on Mount Zion (Isa 25:6-10). But the "timeline" of this miracle extends through Jesus' ministry to the last meal of Jesus with his disciples, and on to the eucharistic feeding at which Matthew's community and all future Christian communities will be fed, with the risen Christ present in their midst. And beyond this is the future hope of our gathering and feeding at the banquet in God's kingdom.

When it is evening the disciples emerge from the crowd. When they had arrived, how they had filled in their day, we are not told. To judge by their approach to Jesus it had probably not been a very compassionate day in Jesus' company, because they urge him to send the people away to buy food in the neighboring villages. But sending away is not in Jesus' plans; he prefers giving and gathering—and the involvement of his disciples in this ministry. Of course the people have to be fed, but Jesus responds to the disciples by saying, "*You* give them something to eat *yourselves.*" Possibly in a panic, perhaps to prove that their suggestion was a much better one, the disciples produce a pitiful little heap of five loaves and two fishes. Maybe this was the food they had been planning to eat in an exclusive supper with Jesus. But Jesus is about to teach them something about the extravagant, open hospitality of God; teach all his disciples that although our own personal or communal resources may be so limited, if we bring the "bread and fish" of our lives to Jesus he will transform them into abundant gifts. Whatever the Christian community has, it has in order to give away to those in need.

As host, Jesus tells the people to recline, to take up the Passover position of a free and feasting people. With the same gestures of taking, blessing, breaking, and giving, Jesus will soon preside at his last shared meal at which he will give himself into the hands of his disciples as broken bread for a broken people; will hand them the cup that he will soon drink to the dregs in his passion. Now Jesus takes what the disciples offer him, breaks the bread, and gives it back into their hands for them to distribute to the people. As they feed the people they are to participate with him in the ministry of holy hospitality. The relationship between Jesus and his disciples, between disciples and the hungry of the world, is to be one of giving and receiving, not taking and holding.

This surely has something to say to our contemporary Church. What can we, ordained and non-ordained, share without threat, without possessiveness or fear of loss of identity, so that those who are hungry for the eucharistic bread may be fed? And it is not only the bread of the Eucharist that we are called to share. As Pedro Arrupe, then the Jesuit General, said in 1976:

> The rediscovery of what might be called the "social dimension" of the Eucharist is of tremendous significance today. In the Eucharist . . . we receive not only Christ, the Head of the Body, but its members as well . . . . Wherever there is suffering in the body, wherever members of it are in want or oppressed, we, because we have received the same body are part of it and must be directly involved. We cannot properly receive the Bread of life without sharing bread for life with those in want.[35]

As long as there are starving people in the world, the Eucharist is "incomplete."

"And those who ate were about five thousand men, *besides* women and children." Various translations of this last sentence have been offered: "apart from," "to say nothing of." Probably Matthew's original intention was to emphasize the enormity of the crowd and so heighten wonder at the miracle, but with our contemporary sensitivity to gender inclusion it is difficult not to hear murmurs of exclusion. In Jesus' time, only men were counted *officially*, but for Jesus, women counted very much; he did not "say nothing of" or do nothing for them. It is tragic that in so many instances in society and in church, *officially*, women and children still do not count for very much: when the feminization of poverty is ignored even in countries of abundance and child poverty is far from being "made history," when the high incidence of domestic violence against women and children is subtly tolerated, when women and children are bartered to satisfy the sweat shops and brothels, and when women are excluded from significant aspects of church life and decision-making.

In the first reading from the prophet Isaiah, God is the generous, hospitable provider of free food and drink to strengthen the returning exiles, in much the same way as the Wisdom Woman of Proverbs (Prov 9:1-6) invites those who pass by to share the life-giving gifts of creation that God made "by wisdom." Walter Brueggemann calls the food that God offers "dangerous food," food that is not the nourishment of political ideologies or the junk of consumerism. It is food that is freely given, just as Jesus will freely feed the five thousand. He comments:

> We must eat. On the other hand the food that is eaten is transformed into loyalty, energy, work and care. The one who provides the food we eat governs the loyalties we embrace. The one who supplies our sustenance has claim upon the loyalty of the community. So we must pay attention to what we eat and who feeds us.[36]

God does not offer food that is meant to ingratiate, "imperial bread" that coerces, or junk food of unhealthy momentary satisfaction that results in spiritual eating disorders. Those who come to God for nourishment, who are loyal to God, will be invited to share in the covenant promise made to David. "You open your hand, satisfying the desire of every living thing," we profess with the responsorial Psalm 145, for God is a compassionate God. This compassionate God is most present in Jesus who now feeds his people, not on the grass of Galilee, but in our own eucharistic assembly.

Our greatest hunger is for love, and Paul proclaims to the church at Rome that absolutely nothing can separate us from the most precious and generous love of God. In the gospel the twelve baskets of gathered fragments were an image of God's superabundant love and nourishing compassion in Christ, and this same love will be shown especially when the forces of evil seem to attack the vulnerable Christian community, when it suffers from hunger or nakedness, or from persecution by hostile civil authorities. The Lectionary omits the prophetic Old Testament references which Paul transplants into his Letter to describe the Christians as "accounted as sheep to be slaughtered" (Isa 53:7; Zech 11:4, 7), as was Christ. By this very suffering, therefore, believers will share in the victory of the crucified and risen Christ. No power in the universe, past or present or to come, will loosen God's loving grasp with which Jesus Christ holds us and draws us into his own glory.

Nineteenth Sunday in Ordinary Time

• 1 Kgs 19:9, 11-13 • Ps 85:9-14 • Rom 9:1-5 • Matt 14:22-33

God is the still eye of the storm: that is the underlying good news of each of the three readings in today's Liturgy of the Word. For Elijah at Mount Horeb/Sinai, recovering from his nervous breakdown caused by his fear of Jezebel whose false prophets he had slaughtered on Mount Carmel; for Paul, struggling to reconcile his love for his own Israelite people and his commitment to Christ; for Peter and the fragile community of disciples buffeted by wind and waves in the middle of the Sea of Galilee—for all these, God is present and close at hand.

After the day of healing and feeding the crowds, Jesus sends everyone away and compels the apparently reluctant disciples to make a night crossing of the lake. He seems deliberately to put a distance between them and himself. It is time for both the disciples and their master to be on their own. For Jesus, being "by himself" means going up into the hills surrounding the lake for a time of solitude and prayer that he had denied himself by responding to the needs of the sick and hungry crowd. And yet he is not alone, for at prayer Jesus is in the intimate company of both his God and his disciples whom he holds in his prayer. The physical separation is no barrier to the abiding presence of Jesus with his own, and so he is aware of the plight of the little community in the fragile boat that Matthew describes as "tortured" by the wild winds and waves that sweep down upon them. In the darkest hour of the night, just before dawn, and when they are far from land, Jesus comes to them as he will always come to his storm-tossed church. Matthew describes Jesus for the vulnerable community, the little church of the late first century c.e. and beyond, and many centuries later the faith of the poet described the same Christ who continues to come to those in great need:

> Our passion-plungèd giant risen,
> The Christ of the Father compassionate, fetched in the storm of his strides.[37]

Matthew's concern was that disciples should recognize the presence and true identity of Jesus, especially in the midst of the storms of conflict, opposition, and persecution, so he structures this narrative to witness that Jesus acts and speaks as Emmanuel, "God-with-us" (Matt 1:23; 28:20). Jesus comes across the waters as the prophets and psalmists had described God, the One who "makes a way in the sea, a path through the mighty waters" (Isa 43:16) with "unseen footprints" (Ps 77:19). As if the storm is not enough, the terrified disciples mistake Jesus for a threatening and ghostly apparition, and to calm their fears Jesus assures them that it is he himself who is present to them by naming himself with the name revealed to Moses from the burning bush: "Take heart, it is I ("I AM"); do not be afraid" (Matt 14:27).

It is Peter who responds. "Lord, if it is you, command me to come to you on the water." And what are we to make of this response? Is this Peter the confident risk taker who disregards all that he knows about the dangers of the deep in the lake where he once earned a living? Or is this a painful post-resurrection memory of an overconfident Peter who blusters that his faith would never be overwhelmed by the waves of passion and death, only to sink a few hours later in the storm of his betrayal of Jesus (Matt 26:33-35; 69-75)? Or is this Peter a mixture of both possibilities, the best and the worst, that we so often experience in ourselves? Jesus speaks the simple, single, and commanding word: "Come." And Peter gets out of the boat to cross toward Jesus. But then the reality of the external storm around him overwhelms his inner faith and his daring confidence in Jesus. He becomes one of the "parable people" who does not persevere in faith (see Matt 13:21), and immediately he begins to sink.

To his credit, Peter knows the right response to make to his failure, and he again acknowledges Jesus as "Lord," as he had done before he left the boat, but now he adds the cry for salvation. And Jesus immediately responds, reaching out to him not as a man of no faith, but as one of "little faith." Again Matthew reminds us of the God who so often in the Old Testament is described as reaching out to save his people "with a mighty hand and an outstretched arm" (see Deut 9:29; 26:8). Here, in Jesus the Lord is that saving hand which holds Peter above the threatening waters, the arm which supports Peter as, together, they walk back to the boat. They get into the boat, and the disciples bow down before Jesus and acknowledge him as the Son of God. Out of their traumatic experience new insight about Jesus has emerged, but its significance for them is still to be tested.

It is to the church, to individuals and communities of disciples of "little faith," that the hand of Jesus is always outstretched to save. We too are "water walkers" today when we are enabled to tread the threatening waves or blustering winds that can sweep over us because of our confidence in the presence and power of the storm-striding and compassionate Jesus. Sunday after Sunday we come together to praise and adore God, despite—or perhaps because of—the storms of the past week. We, too, are an assembly of people who have a "little faith" in Jesus mixed with some doubt that he is in the midst of our ordinary and often chaotic lives, people who struggle to keep faithful, people who sometimes risk a great deal for Jesus in terms of relationships and vocations, in the broad sense of our many and different callings.

Yet we come to worship him. The English poet Francis Thompson expressed his faith in the presence of Christ in ordinary places and events in the last stanza of "In No Strange Land" (The Kingdom of God is Within You):

> Yea, in the night, my Soul, my daughter,
> Cry—clinging to Heaven by the hems;
> And lo, Christ walking on the water
> Not of Genesareth, but Thames![38]

Elijah has his own storms with which to contend. He flees from the wrath of Jezebel, the wife of King Ahaz, after his showdown on Mount Carmel with the false prophets she had imported and supported. On that occasion Elijah had been fierce and uncompromising. Now, in fear of royal retribution, Elijah travels back to the source of his people's faith at Mount Horeb (or Sinai). Along the way he collapses into something of a nervous breakdown or, as we might describe it today, ministerial burnout and depression, until urged by a messenger of God he eventually gets up, eats, and journeys on for forty days and forty nights to reach Mount Horeb. There Elijah withdraws into a cave. God does not argue or reproach Elijah for his fanatical zeal in slaughtering the false prophets and considering that he, Elijah, was the only true prophet in Israel despite the action of Obadiah who had hidden a hundred other prophets in caves (1 Kgs 18:4). Argument or reproach is not the best way to deal with depression! God calls Elijah out of the cave to stand in the midst of a storm and there learn something about himself by learning something about God. God may reveal himself in many ways. On Mount Carmel it was in fire; to Moses at Mount Sinai it was in the midst of wind and earth tremors; now God is present in none of these. Elijah needs to learn about the presence of God in gentleness, in "the sound of sheer silence," in quiet and unspectacular events and people. In the birth of a child, the unremarkable death of a faithful old person, the hidden love of caregivers for people who are disabled or disadvantaged, or in the simple kindnesses of ordinary people, the presence of God can be glimpsed through the thin or "sheer" veil of such silent revelations, if we have eyes to see and ears attuned to these sounds of silence. In a world that often seems to be drowning in a downpour of noise, this is not easy.

For this and the next two Sundays we will hear Paul's vision of the relationship between Israel and Christ. In today's reading Paul agonizes over the refusal of many of his own people to accept Christ. He himself is a Hebrew born of Hebrews, an Israelite, a Pharisee, a descendant of Abraham (2 Cor 11:22-23; Phil 3:5). He is emphatic about the truth he speaks: in Christ he does not lie, and the Spirit working in his conscience confirms his brooding sorrow about the disbelief of the majority of his Jewish brothers and sisters in Christ. When Paul says that he wishes that he could be cut off from Christ for the sake of the salvation of his Jewish sisters and brothers, he is using the device of exaggeration to express his profound longing for them to know and accept Christ. Paul enumerates seven gifts that God has bestowed on the Israelites: their adoption as God's people, the revelation of God's glory, the making of the covenants, the Torah/Law, the worship and Temple, the promise of the land, and the patriarchs. For Paul, as for all Christians, the greatest privilege of the people of Israel was that, in his humanity, Christ was born a Jew.

On Good Friday, 1960, John XXIII spontaneously removed from the long General Intercession the word *perfidias*, "faithless," in the intercession for the Jewish people. Vatican II's *Declaration on the Relationship of the Church to Non-Christian Religions* opened the door to mutual acceptance that would have been undreamed of before—except by people like Paul and other visionaries in the Church—and established an ongoing commitment which we continue to seek. Article 4 of the *Declaration* tells the Church to keep in mind the very words that we have heard today from the Letter to the Romans (vv. 4-5). When we now gather on Good Friday we pray the 1970 revised prayer:

> . . . for the Jewish people, the first to hear the word of God, that they may continue to grow in the love of his name and in faithfulness to his covenant.

> . . . Listen to your Church as we pray that the people you first made your own may arrive at the fullness of redemption. We ask this through Christ our Lord. Amen.

Jew and Gentile, we can pray to God with the psalmist in the responsorial Psalm 85, asking that God will show us "your mercy and love, and grant us your salvation," and that our two communities may embrace each other in mercy and faithfulness, in the justice and peace that has eluded us for so many centuries.

Twentieth Sunday in Ordinary Time

• Isa 56:1, 6-7 • Ps 67:2-3, 5-6, 8 • Rom 11:13-15, 29-32 • Matt 15:21-28

Today's gospel is about crossing boundaries into new territory that is not only geographical but also a venture into differences of culture, gender, and religion. Jesus has been struggling with the painful reality that his opponents among the religious leaders of his own beloved Jewish people do not accept him and so, almost as if he wants to have a break from this op-position, he crosses into the pagan region of Tyre and Sidon. It is here that he is accosted by a woman who is also struggling with pain and rejection. Not only does this encounter happen in pagan territory, but Jesus is con-fronted by a Canaanite, a descendant of one of the ancient enemies of Is-rael. She is the mother of a daughter with a disability, whom she describes as "tormented by a demon." Both mother and daughter are no doubt ostra-cized by the ancient and mistaken suspicion that such a disability is the consequence of sin. The stage hardly seems set for an auspicious meeting, which is what the disciples think when they are confronted by this pester-ing and intrusive woman.

No husband or father is mentioned. The woman is devoting her life to the one she loves, with whom her blood ties are unbreakable but, like Jesus, she too is nearly at the end of her tether. Perhaps she has heard about this Jewish healer from the traders of Tyre, as famous for the news they carried as for their shipment of goods; heard how he flouted legalisms and taboos, and even touched women. Because of her profound and passionate love for her daughter she knows, as any parent of a child with a disability knows, that she desperately needs help for herself if she is to be able to continue to care for her child. So, despite the fact that she is a Gentile, she shouts her faith-filled words at Jesus, hailing him as "Lord, Son of David." Jesus' re-sponse to her cry may surprise us. We probably expect him to react to the woman as we want him to respond to us: immediately and positively. But Jesus is silent, struggling with his identity, his mission, his prejudices. If we deny Jesus such struggles we minimize the reality of the Incarnation—the mystery of the Word made flesh, fully sharing our humanity in a certain time and place, with a particular ancestry, ethnicity, and culture—and we deny his relevance for our own struggles. The disciples want to get rid of her; they think they have enough trouble on their hands with a despondent Jesus. Impatient men and distraught women are not a good mix!

Jesus continues to ignore the woman. As though he is thinking aloud, he says not to her but to his disciples, "I was sent only to the lost sheep of the house of Israel." Tenacious and bold, yet humble, the woman gets down into the dust in front of Jesus, kneels where dogs play and crumbs fall, and asks a second time for his help. Matthew has shown us other Gentiles com-ing to Jesus—the Magi kneeling in adoration (Matt 2:11), the centurion desperately pleading for his paralyzed servant (Matt 8:5-6)—but this Gen-tile is challenging him in a new way that is painful for both of them. Jesus asks her if it is fair to take Israelite "bread," the sustaining gift of God's sal-vation, and offer it to the Gentile "dogs"? At least he is now addressing the woman, and she seizes the opportunity for some serious wordplay. Like a dog, she says, she will be content with any scraps of help that Jesus can offer her from the table of the children of Israel. And Jesus, who had to learn to read the signs of the times in the Hebrew Scriptures, in prayer, in events, and in people, reads this woman. Last week we heard Peter described as a man of "little faith" in the midst of the storm on the Sea of Galilee (Matt 14:31); today, this Canaanite woman, stranger and Gentile, is described by Jesus as having "great faith" in the midst of the storm of her desperation for healing for her daughter.

Impelled by this faith, Jesus crosses into new territory of understanding of himself and his mission to the nations. After his resurrection, the salvation first offered to the Jews through Jesus will be the gift that the community of disciples must offer to all the nations (Matt 28:20). As Matthew's predominantly Jewish Christian community struggled with the increasing number of Gentile Christians who were joining then, it was significant that the evangelist could point to this incident and say, "Behold," (the word in the original Greek text, usually weakened to "just then"), see how *Jesus himself* had to struggle with a Gentile—and see how he recognized her great faith. Not only Matthew's first century community needs to look carefully. It is also our own racism, sexism, cultural superiority that we see reflected in this gospel. As long as there are "dogs under the table," people in misery, people on the margins of or excluded from the church, we are challenged to cross boundaries and offer them the crumbs of our compassion.

The choice between inclusion and exclusion is also the focus of the first reading. Something new is stirring in the post-exilic community of Israel, and it is overarched by God's repeated reminder to the people of the covenant demands of social responsibility. They are called to do justice and relate to God and one another with integrity. In Isa 2:1-5 the first Isaiah has the prophetic vision of the nations streaming to Mount Zion to receive and share in God's teaching. Now, after the exile, "the days to come" have arrived, and the prophet draws attention to the foreigners who, although outside the community of Israel, are showing their desire to become part of it. They express their faith in the Lord by observing the Sabbath and by fidelity to the covenant, and so they are to be welcomed into the community of worship in the Jerusalem Temple. Their prayer and sacrifice will be as acceptable to God as that of the people of Israel. Isaiah's vision of the Temple is that of a house of prayer that is no longer exclusively reserved to Israel but open and hospitable to all peoples, a place of unity in diversity. Yet the history of Israel (see Neh 13:1-3) would show that this vision would not be easily realized.

Given how persistent our own cultural and religious prejudices can be, we need to pray the responsorial Psalm 67, originally a harvest song, with open hearts and awareness of those whom we exclude from our communities, or at least be aware that we have felt more comfortable when those who are "different" are not present at our worship. We have received God's blessing, but are we living this by being a blessing to those whom God wishes to harvest into the kingdom? Or are we an obstacle to the inclusiveness that is God's vision?

The blessings that the Jewish people received have become the blessings to the Gentiles through Jesus Christ, a Jew according to the flesh. So Paul also struggles with the realities of inclusion and exclusion, although his is the reverse situation: not the exclusion of the Gentiles by Jews but the reluctance of Christians to accept the Jews as a privileged people called by God. The "gifts and calling of God are irrevocable," is one of the most significant of Paul's professions of love for his own people, and is a truth that, if observed by Christians, would have saved the Jewish people from the horrors of prejudice, pogroms, and persecutions which culminated in the twentieth century Holocaust, the catastrophic whirlwind (*shoah*) which ripped six million branches off the olive tree (Rom 11:17). It is onto this olive tree that Christians have been grafted. If God has shown mercy to the Gentiles, says Paul, how much more will he show mercy to the Jewish people who first received the gifts that we heard proclaimed in last week's reading? Israel has stumbled in their relationship with God by their rejection of Christ, but this is not the same as a fall from which they cannot rise. In his apostolic mission, Paul was sharing with the Gentiles the good news that Israel's God, Abraham's God, was gathering them into a community around Jesus, the Messiah for whom Israel was waiting. His hope is that the Jews will see the results of this and become "jealous," in the sense of longing for a share in such blessing. When this happens, it will be like a "resurrection." There is no place for arrogance or superiority among Christians, because they, like all humanity, need the salvation won for them by Christ, the most faithful Israelite. At the heart of the Letter to the Romans lies Paul's humility, his conviction that all we have to boast about is the mercy of God which will be shown to Jew and Gentile in God's own way and God's own time.

Twenty-first Sunday in Ordinary Time

• Isa 22:19-23 • Ps 138:1-3, 6, 8 • Rom 11:33-36 • Matt 16:13-20

In northern Galilee, a few miles from the present border between Lebanon and Syria, is a place of majestic beauty. It is at the base of the southern slope of Mount Hermon, the source of the Jordan River, and the site of a towering rock cave which was devoted to the worship of the god Pan, from which its name, Banias, was taken. After the emperor Nero's death, Banias passed to his son, Philip, who renamed the place Caesarea Philippi in honor of Caesar Augustus and himself. This is Matthew's setting for "the Sunday of the keys," with its focus on ecclesial authority and leadership that is so different from pagan beauty and Roman imperial power. Dwarfed by the huge rock cavern and temples is the little huddle of disciples, one of whom is about to be named "Rock."

The disciples are quick with their answer to Jesus' query: "Who do people say that the Son of Man is?" This is a safe question requiring no personal involvement. The haunting memory of John the Baptist, the passionate preaching of Jeremiah, the legendary expectation of Elijah hang in the air. Then comes Jesus' direct question: "But who do *you* say that I am?" In the boat after the storm the disciples had paid homage to him and confessed him as the Son of God. Here all the confessional attention is fixed on Peter. He confesses more than he himself understands about the identity of Jesus, but now Jesus is going to tell him how the identity and mission of both of them are linked together. Jesus pronounces a blessing over Peter because of God's revelation to him, gives him a new name and a new mission. The renaming of Simon Peter as the "rock" on which Jesus' church would be built is a wordplay between the Greek name *Petros* (Peter) and *petra* (rock). It is almost a biblical and ambivalent "nickname" for this "rocky" man who was to be both the foundation stone of the community of disciples and ironically, some time later, the unstable one who on the night of Jesus' passion would crumble into shifting sand. But as a leader for his church Jesus surely wants someone with whom we can identify in our own weaknesses. In Matthew's Gospel it is only Peter who receives a personal beatitude, a blessing of God pronounced over him by Jesus. The assurance is given that no matter what destructive powers are hurled at the church, and not withstanding Peter's role in it, the church will stand firm because, as Jesus says, it is "*my* church."

It will be Peter's privilege, and the privilege of his successors in the Petrine ministry, to be given the "keys," the authority which will enable him to unlock the riches of the revelation of Jesus Christ that has been entrusted to the church. In contrast, the scribes and Pharisees who oppose Jesus will later be accused by him of locking people out of the kingdom by their teaching and example (Matt 23:13). "To bind" and "to loose" were rabbinic terms for "to permit" and "to forgive," and Peter is assured that Jesus will always be present in the authority which Jesus delegates to him to interpret the law, to make exceptions, to forgive, or to demand obedience. Peter is to be a good steward of the church's treasure house of grace. However, until Peter and the other disciples have learned fully what it means for Jesus to be the Messiah, until he has suffered, died, and risen, and until they have been drawn into this mystery, they are not to tell people about what has been revealed here at Caesarea Philippi, for it would be only the partial truth.

The first reading from Isaiah is about stewardship and the "power of the keys." Isaiah prophesies about Shebna, the steward of King Hezekiah (ca. 701 B.C.E.), that he will be stripped of the power of the keys that give him literal and figurative authority over the royal household. In the verses immediately preceding today's reading we learn that it was the ostentation of Shebna's chariots and the elaborate rock tomb that he had built for himself, in addition to an unexplained "shame," that would warrant his dismissal. The clear suggestion is that Shebna has misappropriated the royal household's funds for his own use. In another rock scenario, in the place where Shebna has cut out his tomb, Isaiah confronts him, and tells him that he is to be stripped of his stewardship. This office will be given to Eliakim who will exercise his authority with fatherly concern for the inhabitants of Jerusalem and Judah, watching over all who come in and go out. Metaphorically, Eliakim's stewardship will be like a peg that God drives securely into a wall to hold the structure together, and he will be honored for his fidelity and the stability he brings. Humility, integrity, and service that is concerned for others rather than oneself are expected of stewards, be they Eliakim, Peter, or those who hold the Petrine office in the household of the church today. Such a ministry is not easy; the peg may become detached and the rock crumble, so with the psalmist we pray with great sincerity and trust that God will not forsake the work of his hands. "On the day I called, you answered; you increased the strength of my soul," is surely both the experience of the psalmist and God's stewards.

After the dense and demanding theology of the last few weeks' readings from the Letter to the Romans, after Paul's (and our) wrestling with complex relationships between God and the chosen people of both Jews and Gentiles, everything converges into a hymn of praise to the "depths of the riches and wisdom and knowledge of God," depths which are so infinitely unfathomable and inscrutable that all we can do is to offer thanks. Quoting from the comforting Isaiah (Isa 40:13) and the wrestling Job who finally surrenders to the wisdom of God (Job 41:11), Paul draws on his rich biblical heritage to remind us that God is God, and is never in debt to us. All we can give to God is glory and praise for creation, redemption, and final salvation, and rest trustingly in God's graciousness.

Twenty-second Sunday in Ordinary Time

• Jer 20:7-9 • Ps 63:2-6, 8-9 • Rom 12:1-2 • Matt 16:21-27

Last Sunday we heard Jesus pronounce a beatitude, a personal blessing over Peter when he acclaimed his master as the Messiah, the anointed One of God. Jesus responds by naming Peter as the "Rock" on which Jesus will found not Peter's but his own church. It all sounds positive for Peter—until the next, immediate exchange in today's gospel. For the first time Jesus predicts his passion and tells his disciples that he is heading for Jerusalem. Then Peter shows, ironically, how "rocky" he is in his misinterpretation of what being the Messiah is all about. Largehearted and passionate, reasons why Jesus no doubt chose him as leader, Peter wants the best for Jesus from a human point of view. And this is the trouble. Peter will have to be schooled in discipleship that recognizes the different point of view that Jesus has just tried to communicate. Peter has been so overwhelmed by the talk of suffering and killing that he seems not to have heard the mention of rising on the third day; and what could he make of that, anyway! So Peter, flush with his new name and intimation of his new responsibility, starts to exercise this straightaway—on Jesus. He not only takes Jesus aside, but he *rebukes* him. For this action of rebuke Matthew uses the same word as he does to describe Jesus exorcising demons. In the original Greek text, what Peter says is, "May God be gracious to you, Lord"—which is exactly what resurrection will mean—"this will never happen to you!" with the implication that he, Peter, will be the one who will take the initiative to do all he can to put a stop to such a future. Involvement in emerging problems is a good quality of leadership (see Matt 17:24-27; 18:21-22), but Peter has to learn more holy discernment.

In strong language that does not exclude love, Jesus puts Peter in his place: behind him, following him, which is the right place for every disciple. He addresses Peter as "Satan." When the Rock puts himself in front of Jesus, he becomes a stumbling stone or a "scandal" (Greek *skándalon*). Peter's good-hearted but false interpretation of Jesus' mission is a temptation like that of Satan in the wilderness, a temptation for Jesus to follow an easier path, to have life on his own terms rather those of his Father. Peter has a long journey to make with Jesus, with much blundering along the way, before he realizes how costly the discipleship of a crucified and risen Messiah will be. So Jesus explains not only to Peter, but to all disciples, that those who follow him will have to share his cross. This is not a call to self-destruction, but a challenge to find life by living with all our energies centered on God rather than on the false idol of the autonomous self which can be so dear to us, especially in circumstances of affluence and upward mobility. Jesus promises that there will be a reward for those who have done what the unselfish orientation of their lives to him and their sisters and brothers demands. This reward will be revealed at the end time when Jesus, as the Son of Man, comes for the final judgment (see Matt 25:31-46).

There is a wonderful and ecumenical tribute in stone to suffering discipleship in the very familiar West Front of Westminster Abbey. When the twenty-five-year-long restoration program of the Abbey's exterior was completed in 1995, there remained a row of ten niches above the front door that had been empty for five hundred years. It was decided not to fill these with saintly or worthy figures of the past, but to proclaim the message of the costly Christian witness of those who had been willing to take up their cross and die for Christ in the twentieth century. These ten statues are of individual martyrs, some well known, others not, but the intention was to represent those who have died, and continue to die, in circumstances of oppression and persecution throughout the world. They include victims of the struggle for human rights in North and South America, those who confessed Christ and died in the Nazi and Soviet persecutions in Europe, martyrs of religious prejudice and dictatorial rule in Africa, of fanaticism on the Indian subcontinent, of brutalities during the Second World War in Asia and the Cultural Revolution in China. The statues were unveiled in 1998.[39]

One of the responses the disciples make to the question that Jesus asked them in last Sunday's gospel was that some thought he might be the prophet Jeremiah, and today the first reading is from that prophet. Of all the Old Testament prophets, he suffered the most. He speaks painfully to his own people about impending disaster and exile because of, among other sins, their idol worship and their offering of their children as burned sacrifices to Baal (Jer 19:4-5). Nor is Jeremiah afraid to denounce the corrupt religious powers. He is considered a troublesome alarmist, and we hear today how the Temple authorities punish him by keeping him overnight in the stocks. When he is freed, we hear Jeremiah describe himself as someone whom God has "seduced." Jeremiah accuses God of attracting him like a man who attracts a woman and then dominates her, forcing him to accept his prophetic role although he didn't understand what this would entail. But his lament, which sounds almost blasphemous, rises from Jeremiah's passionate and familiar love of God, for only a great lover could dare to speak so honestly to God. No matter what, Jeremiah cannot stop talking to his God. Elie Wiesel reflects about his Jewish ancestor:

> Jeremiah does not stop talking, dictating, writing down every dream, every command, every whisper, every anecdote, every episode, every moan and

outcry. He knows his voice will not carry, and yet he yells, shouts, warns, pleads, prays. He has no choice: he must do something with his life. If he survives it must be for a reason; he must do something with every minute— for every minute is a minute of grace.[40]

Jeremiah cannot stop speaking the prophetic word that burns like a fire in his bones (Jer 20:9). In the night of suffering, Jesus will be consumed by such a holy fire and rise from it; Peter will be deeply scarred by it and eventually branded for Jesus by it; sometimes even we ourselves may be touched by a spark from its flame in a moment of wild recognition of what suffering is all about.

The dry heat of such love causes the psalmist to cry out to God for the water of salvation that will quench his thirst in the struggle to remain faithful in what seems the absence of God. The faith of every martyr or great sufferer can confess to God in the words of the psalm that "your love is better than life," and so the threatening darkness is transformed by faith into what is imaged as the protective presence of God's overshadowing wings.

Paul appeals to the Christians at Rome to offer their bodies not in martyrdom but as a living and holy sacrifice. For "body" Paul uses the word *sōma* that refers not only to the individual corporeality of a person, but also to concrete relationships in time and space, the ability to be in touch with people and the world because of our bodies. Such relationships will be a sacrifice of obedience if we offer our lived experience to the will of God as revealed in Christ. Paul reminds his Christian community that their "minds," their inner selves, have been made new by their sharing in the new life of the risen Christ, and so they must never allow the inner freedom of his Spirit to be captivated by externals that will lead them away from the good and perfect will of God. This is not easy; often it will be sacrificial if Christians are not to let themselves be squeezed into the world's mold but be constantly conformed to the image of Christ.

Twenty-third Sunday in Ordinary Time

• Ezek 33:7-9 • Ps 95:1-2, 6-9 • Rom 13:8-10 • Matt 18:15-20

We all have the responsibility for the pastoral care that requires us to deal with one another's sinfulness, especially when this threatens the cohesion of the community of disciples. The offering of forgiveness to a sister or brother is one of the painful ways that we take up our cross and follow Jesus, whether in the first century Matthean community or in today's church.

Jesus tells his disciples how this painful but healing process of forgiveness is to be conducted. The authority of "binding and loosing" that we heard given to Peter to exercise in a particular way is here extended to the whole church because it is not only the leaders who must accept responsibility for reconciliation within the community. The model that Jesus presents to the disciples is one of "gospel subsidiarity," not a "pyramid" model. Subsidiarity means that we do not do something at a higher level when it can be done at a lower, in contrast to starting at the top of the pyramid with the highest authority. So the first approach in reconciliation is to be the one-to-one between the offended and the offender. It is the former who is to seek out the latter, in courage and loving humility, and with no intention of a judgmental confrontation, hard as this may be. For Matthew's Jewish Christians, this would be no surprising advice if they remembered the Torah tradition (Lev 19:17-18) about reproving someone with love and loving one's neighbor as oneself.

If the person who has done wrong is deaf to the words of this initial and personal encounter, the next step to be taken is not an exasperated resignation to the misconduct: "Too bad! Now it's up to you." Rather, pastoral zeal requires that one or two other members of the community accompany the wronged one to witness the effort being made and confirm that there is a just attempt to win back the sinner without misconceptions, arbitrariness, or personal prejudice on either side. If this fails, then the matter is to be brought before the "church." Only twice in all the gospels is this word (*ekklesía*) used—in Matt 16:18 (the building of Jesus' church on Peter) and in this narrative. The decision about membership in the community, the church, is also entrusted to the local assembly. They are to be accountable and responsible because of the abiding presence of the risen Jesus in the community.

If the community cannot bring the offending member to repentance, that person is to be to them "as a Gentile and a tax collector." This is, however, not the harsh and permanent severance of relationships that it might at first sound to be. In the gospel context, it is a reminder that it was Gentiles and tax collectors, people on the religious and social margins, whom Jesus befriended, never giving up on his efforts with the "hundredth lost sheep." (This parable in Matt 18:12-14 comes immediately before today's reading.) The mention of the "two or three gathered" in the name of Jesus would have reminded Jewish Christians of what was said of the study of Torah, traditionally and still done together by two companions (*chaverim*): "If two or three sit together and the words of the Torah pass between them, the Divine Presence (*shekhinah*) abides between them" (tractate *'Abot* 3:2 in the Jewish *Mishnah*). Now, in the Spirit, the words of Jesus which are his gospel teaching must be continuously studied and prayed by the church, especially at such times of serious decision making about the exclusion of the unrepentant sinner and the church's continuing responsibility for the care of the excluded one. The risen Christ will intercede for both his community and the sinner. In the context of the faith community, such prayer makes reconciliation much more than conflict management or legal mediation. For both their own sake and that of the Christian community, troublesome people cannot just be ignored, yet this is sometimes a very real temptation for those in authority.

The prophet Ezekiel is not one to ignore dangers to the community. He is called by God in the sixth century B.C.E. to be an alert, watchful "sentry" for the exiled household of God, someone who sees approaching dangers and threats to the people's existence, so vulnerable in exile because of the wicked among them. Ezekiel is not to be an alarmist or an undercover policeman, but as a prophet he is charged with the responsibility of the "forth telling" that will enable the conversion of the offender. Such a kind of "biblical whistle-blower" will often be unpopular, but that is both the price and privilege of being a prophet. If Ezekiel fails to speak out and warn the offender, both Ezekiel and the offender will pay for this with their lives, but if the prophet does his best and the offender is still not converted, God will not hold Ezekiel accountable. Community leaders are, to a great extent, the watchers, the discerning "eyes" of a community: those who can look to wide horizons, think with loving concern for the future of both the individual and the whole community, and speak out when necessary. Such was the wisdom of John XXIII's saying: "See everything, overlook a great deal, correct a little."

In his Letter to the Romans, Paul has a beautiful phrase that echoes the gospel concern for love and respect in the community when he writes that the only debt that we should owe one another is "the debt of mutual love" (Jerusalem Bible). We are all debtors to Christ because of the inexhaustible love of God that he has shown us by dying for us, even when we are sinners. How can we, therefore, withhold love from anyone else? Paul quotes the commandments that prohibit actions that would do harm to one's neighbor, and then emphasizes the positive and transformative power of love. As in the gospel, the love command of Lev 19:18 is quoted by Paul; but now that Spirit of Christ dwells within them (Rom 8:9-11), Christians have an interior law which commands love—even beyond the Christian community.

In a lighter and different genre, the temptation and folly of repaying evil with evil is spoken by another Jew in the closing scene of the musical, *The Fiddler on the Roof.* Dismayed at the prospect of their immediate banishment from their village, one of the villagers shouts: "We should defend ourselves! An eye for an eye and a tooth for a tooth!" The wise old Tevye replies with kindly and sad irony: "That's very good. And that way, the whole world will be blind and toothless." If, as we pray in the responsorial Psalm 95, we listen to God's voice speaking to us in the Scriptures and in the events of daily life, and do not harden our hearts, then forgiving love will make us people of gospel vision and gospel bite.

Twenty-fourth Sunday in Ordinary Time

• Sir 27:30–28:7 • Ps 103:1-4, 9-12 • Rom 14:7-9 • Matt 18:21-35

We are usually quite good at counting. It is convenient, objective, and calculating, whether of birthday candles or bills. Sometimes it may be alarming (especially with our bills), but at least it alerts us to what we have to manage, and allows us a certain degree of control over our small world. In today's gospel, Peter indulges in what he thinks is a very generous calculation in response to Jesus' call to forgiveness of a sister or brother, and he answers his own question about how many times he should do this with "Seven times?" But Jesus replies with a disconcerting, "Not seven times but, I tell you, seventy-seven (or seventy times seven)." Such a multiple of seven, the Hebrew number symbolic of perfection or fullness, implies that forgiveness is to be "infinite" because it is to reflect God's unconditional and enduring forgiveness of us. As the response to Psalm 103, we profess our faith that: "The Lord is compassion and love, slow to anger and rich in mercy," a compassion which is as intimate as the womb-love of a parent for a child and a mercy which is expansive as the heavens.

To help a no doubt deflated Peter understand more about the quality rather than the quantity of forgiveness, Jesus tells a "shocking" parable which, by its conclusion, is intended for all his followers and not only Peter. The parable is a dramatic and imaginative expansion of Jesus' words in the Sermon on the Mount: "And forgive us our debts, as we also have forgiven our debtors" (Matt 6:12). Given the contemporary trials of highfliers for insider trading or the arrests of executives for mismanagement of corporate funds, it may not be too difficult to appreciate the scenario of the parable. It is a drama in three acts: the dealing of the king with his high ranking, bureaucratic slave, the dealing of that slave with his fellow slave, and the second encounter of the king and the slave in the light of what happened between the two slaves. Jesus likens membership in the kingdom of heaven to the expectation that is at the heart of the parable; namely, that forgiveness received from a loving and compassionate God, as God is named in the responsorial Psalm 103, is the basis for forgiveness offered in return to others. There can be dire consequences when such an expectation is not met.

The slave has abused his position of trust by fiddling with his master's accounts, and the first shock is the extent of the defrauding that the king discovers when he calls in his accounts. In today's reckoning 10,000 talents would amount to about a billion dollars! According to the historian Josephus, the Romans extracted the same amount from the Jews after Pompey's conquest of Palestine during the decade of the 60s B.C.E.[41] That such an astronomical amount would be siphoned off in the much smaller context of *one* king's property makes the parable memorable for Jesus' audience. In response to his lord's pronouncement of punishment, the slave falls down before him and begs to be given time and he will he pay off the debt. But to do this he would need about 200,000 lifetimes, which makes his plea as fantastic as the amount of the debt. The parable is not without its humor—that Peter may or may not have appreciated. Then comes the second shock. Out of compassion, the servant's lord not only grants him the time he begs for, but also forgives him and cancels the whole debt, as if to say: "Get going! Forget the money!"

But what the slave does forget is the mercy he has been shown. Before his lord he had the right words, the right humble posture of sorrow, but in his heart he was unrepentant. The third shock comes when, immediately after his own experience of such large forgiveness, the slave meets a fellow slave who owes him a hundred denarii, on calculation about 1/600,000 of his own debt to the king. The first slave acts toward him in a way that is a pitiless parody of the mercy he has received. Confronted with a minor debtor, the first slave barges his way into a legalistic ethic of rights and duties, attacks his debtor physically, and throws him into the prison he himself has just mercifully escaped.

There is a ministry of "bringing to attention" the injustice suffered by others that today we call "advocacy." The other slaves in the service of their same lord become advocates for their brother slave who has been so unjustly treated and, in response, the lord joins justice to mercy. The lord now imposes the punishment that he had previously waived on the first slave because of his lack of forgiveness. So it will be, says Jesus, with those who do not forgive as they have been forgiven. The great Forgiver is God (Matt 6:14). The first slave has been forgiven for mishandling his lord's money, but not for mishandling his lord's mercy.

"Pray you now, forget and forgive. I am old and foolish," says the deranged King Lear to his daughter Cordelia,[42] yet this injunction can be an obstacle to forgiveness, an attempt at some kind of psychological contortion that is not humanly possible. The real challenge is to remember and forgive. Forgiveness is a personal demand of discipleship of Jesus, but in a world where we have experienced so much destructive bitterness between peoples, often bred from generation to generation, there is also a need for forgiveness among nations. Do we believe that the forgiveness the disciples offer to one another can help create a healing milieu for our world whose time we share? In Eastern Europe, Africa, Ireland, the Middle East—and where tomorrow?—memory has so often caused hatred, not forgiveness. Jonathan Sacks, Chief Rabbi of Britain and the Commonwealth, writes of the pain of generations of exile, persecution, and pogroms, culminating with the Holocaust, that is written into the Jewish soul and so into their identity. It cannot be forgotten, and so he struggles:

> How can I let go of that pain, when it is written into my very soul. And yet I must. For the sake of my children and theirs (the enemy's), not yet born. I cannot build their future on the hatred of the past, nor can I teach them to love God more by loving people less. Asking God to forgive me, I hear, in the very process of making that request, His demand of me that I love others. I forgive because I have a duty to my children as well as my ancestors . . . I honour the past not by repeating it but by learning from it—by refusing to add pain to pain, grief to grief. That is why we must answer hatred with love, violence with peace, resentment with generosity of spirit and conflict with reconciliation.[43]

And the Dalai Lama recounted a meeting with a Tibetan monk who had served eighteen years in a Chinese prison. When he asked the monk what he felt to be the greatest threat or danger during his imprisonment, the monk replied, "Losing my compassion for the Chinese."

The reading from the Book of Sirach (Ecclesiaticus) is also a call to the wisdom of forgiveness. Our first response when we are wronged will probably be anger and outrage, but what we do with this response is the important challenge. Forgiveness always means letting something go. By cherishing resentment rather than letting it go, we imprison ourselves in a cycle of negative emotions; we allow ourselves to be fixated in the role of victim. Life is too short to be wasted and our energies exhausted in this way. "Remember . . . Remember . . . Remember . . ." says Sirach, not the wrong done to you, but the need to forgive because we have been forgiven by God; remember the certainty of our death when we will have to face the judgment of God—which reflects the judgment we have already made in life: either to offer forgiveness or withhold it; remember the covenant promises of God which embrace us in love, and do not struggle out of that embrace because of relentless anger against another person.

What Christians let go of, says Paul to the Romans, is belonging "to ourselves." We have been baptized into Christ who, by his death and resurrection, is now the "lord" over life and death, the living and the dead. This lordship is not domineering, but was established by the love of Christ who did not live for himself alone but poured himself out in total, personal, and cosmic love for us. Everyone and everything is now caught up in this love, so that the whole of our existence, and even our death, belongs to Christ. Like the slave in the gospel, we are accountable for the way we handle—or mishandle—Christ's mercy.

Twenty-fifth Sunday in Ordinary Time

• Isa 55:6-9 • Ps 145:2-3, 8-9, 17-18 • Phil 1:20c-24, 27a • Matt 20:1-16a

With only ten weeks to go, we are moving toward the end of the liturgical year, and the Liturgy of the Word starts to nudge us gently toward larger thoughts about "ends": the end of Jesus' life, our own personal time which will end with our death, and the cosmic end of all things when human history has run its course. Because these are often daunting, even fearful thoughts, especially since no one can tell us about their personal experience of these events, Jesus invites us into the world of story, into parables. Megan McKenna calls parables "the arrows of God" because:

> they pierce us and make us painfully aware of our need to change the way we relate to ourselves, others, and God. We look—and we see. This is how we must live in God's kingdom. We are called, and we know ourselves called.[44]

Jesus addresses this Sunday's parable to his "called ones," his disciples. What we do not hear is the previous encounter of Jesus with the rich young man who went away grieving because he could not bring himself to give away all that he possessed and follow Jesus. The disciples are interested observers of the encounter, and Peter, typically, has a question for Jesus that amounts to: "What's in it for us who have left everything and followed you?" With the parable usually called "The Laborers in the Vineyard," Jesus reinforces his answer about the hundredfold reward, eternal life, and the paradox of the first being last and the last first in the kingdom. A more appropriate title for this parable might be "The Generous Landowner."

Perhaps many of us can remember what it was like to be "picked last." As children, perhaps, it was for the playground teams; as adults, it may have been an issue of promotion or missing out being on the short list after a job application. This parable is about the landowner's generosity toward the last picked people. The scenario would be familiar to first century Palestinian society: the hopeful gathering of the unemployed in the market place, anxious for the subsistent but average daily wage of one denarius, and then the process of hiring. The one unfamiliar note, hinting that there may be more in this than a simple vignette of village life, is the fact that, contrary to normal procedure, it is the landowner himself and not his lesser estate manager or steward who comes out to look for and hire the workers. Everything is done justly; the wage is offered, which is neither overgenerous nor miserly, and is accepted by the laborers. As the demands of the day's work unroll, more laborers are hired in the morning and early afternoon. At the "eleventh hour" (about 5 p.m.), the landowner comes out for the last time and finds some men still hanging around hopefully. With the patient hope of the poor, the "not chosen" have stood there all day, worried that they would have to go home empty-handed to their families. We need to refrain from social analysis of the parable, or treating it like a case study in industrial relations (why leave it so late in the day to hire more men?), or asking questions that spoil a good story. The "arrows" are about to be shot and targeted at our lack of generosity and superficial judgments.

Now comes the time for payment of the wages. The last to be hired are the first paid, because the parable requires an audience for what is coming next. There are probably some raised eyebrows and delighted nudging among those hired earlier when they do their comparative mathematical calculations. After more hours in the vineyard there will surely be more of a payoff for them. Then the parable arrow hits the target, and there is painful grumbling from the other workers that the "eleventh hour" workers have been paid the same as them for less work and for working in less grueling conditions than the heat of the day. The landowner replies to one of the workers with the reminder that he has been given the just wage agreed on when they were hired; the denarius is the laborer's right; generosity is the landowner's right, "because I am good." But what earns an even stronger rebuke is the complaint that "you have made them equal to us." This is an arrogant attack on the personal worth of the latecomers that is more than economic. It is an expression of envy, literally (in the Greek) looking at someone with an "evil eye," a vision that distorts and darkens all our perceptions (see Matt 6:22).

The parable ends with a reversal of expectations: "The last will be first and the first will be last." We are in the territory of God's kingdom where we realize that the generosity of the Landowner God reaches out to the last called as equally as to the first; that, in Jesus, God is present to the people who are poor, sick, disabled; that the tax collectors and the prostitutes all have equal access if they answer the call into the "vineyard," a symbol of God's holy people (cf. Ezek 17:6, 8; Hos 10:1; 14:7). As this parable is found only in Matthew's Gospel, it obviously had relevance for his community into which the "latecomer" Gentiles were entering, with consequent tensions between them and the Jewish Christians with their well established traditions. The Gentiles were to be accepted as equals, just as today the First World church must welcome the new Christians of the developing countries, even to the extent of accepting that the future of the church may rest with them. As we listen to this parable as a eucharistic community, we are powerfully reminded of the equality and solidarity of all God's laboring disciples who receive the same food at the same table. Yet are there people about whose presence we are judgmental? And outside Eucharist, is our vision of our brothers and sisters darkened by envy, and even by an unexpressed suspicion of or open grumbling about God who seems to be unfair with his generosity—especially to me? Does making comparisons override being in communion?

We need a clear, discerning eye to seek and see God's ways. The first reading is part of the concluding chapter of Second Isaiah, a call to repentance and worship for the exiles who are returning to Jerusalem. Turning and returning to God in their hearts must accompany their physical return to Jerusalem. God is always ready to forgive and full of abundant compassion, never giving up on his people. Lest there be any doubt about this, Isaiah is quite explicit: "For my thoughts (dreams) are not your thoughts, nor are your ways my ways, says the Lord." Metaphorically, the distance between God's mercy and the sinner is as impossible to calculate as the distance between the earth and the heavens. With the responsorial Psalm 145 we sing our faith in God who is both near to all who call upon him and beyond what we can imagine in mercy and compassion. Only God's generous love can span the distance with forgiveness and pardon. We have the privilege of knowing what the psalmist did not know: that the most embodied mercy, the fulfilled messianic dream of Israel, the clearest way of God that bridges this distance, comes to us in Jesus.

This Sunday we begin the reading of Paul's Letter to the Philippians, the first church to be founded by Paul in Europe (ca. 50 C.E.) on his second missionary journey (Acts 16:11-15). Joy, gentleness, and bonds of friendship between Paul and the Philippians characterize this Letter, even though Paul writes it from prison, and life was not perfect in the Philippian church. In today's reading we hear Paul torn between two very real possibilities, both of which so express his total commitment to Christ that he can say that for him either to live or die is for the glory of Christ. So he looks at the possibilities: his death by execution—which would mean for him the great advantage of sharing in Christ's resurrection; or on the other hand, if he continues to live this will mean he can continue his ministry of proclaiming Christ—which seems more necessary for the Philippians. In his struggle of discernment, the decisive factor, as always with Paul, is not his personal preference but the needs of others, in this case his dear community at Philippi.

Like the disgruntled laborers in the parable, we are often inclined to look at life from our own limited perspective, so that "What's in it for me?" may be our uppermost concern, sometimes followed by envy when there seems to be more in a situation for other people than for me. Paul's confidence in God and his faith in the expansive generosity of God in Christ witness to us the truth that God's ways and dreams for us surpass the limits of our human reason and understanding. And that is payment enough.

Twenty-sixth Sunday in Ordinary Time

• Ezek 18:25-28 • Ps 25:4-9 • Phil 2:1-11 • Matt 21:28-32

In Matthew's Gospel, Jesus has already entered for the last time into Jerusalem (Matt 21:1-11), cleansed the Temple, recognized its withered liturgy for which the chief priests and elders are responsible, wrestled verbally with these religious opponents over the role of John the Baptist, and now returns us to a "parable place" that, after last Sunday's parable, is not hard for us to recognize: the vineyard of the kingdom, in the company of the vineyard father and his two sons who are his potential laborers. Jesus tells this parable in the unreceptive company of the chief priests and elders who are questioning his authority, and for whom he primarily intends it to act as a mirror for their consciences. But it also has significance for the wider Christian family. From our own experience we know that we can respond to a request for assistance by professing the best of intentions—but then waver and never carry it out; or, after an initial refusal, we have second thoughts which cause us to change our minds (or hearts). This parable dramatizes the earlier verse from Jesus' Sermon on the Mount: "Not every one who says to me, 'Lord, Lord,' will enter the kingdom of heaven, but only the one who does the will of my Father in heaven" (Matt 7:21), and is followed by a comment on how astonished the people were at the way Jesus taught with authority, not like their scribes.

Because of our own cultural contexts we often imagine parables such as this one to be set in an intimate, private scenario, but first century Palestinian life was essentially communal. Honor was a highly prized virtue, just as shame was considered a despicable vice, and the significance of both the virtue and vice was that they were obvious to the community, as in this parable. The first son offers an honest "No," and this is a shameful insult to a father to whom he should be obedient. Later he feels remorse, regrets his response, and goes obediently into the vineyard. The second son gets an honorable approval rating when he readily agrees to his father's request, but this turns out to be only the lip service of a suavely public "Yes" man who does nothing. Then Jesus puts in the parable hooks and drags the chief priests and elders into answering his question as to which of the sons did his father's will. They cannot escape the reply in which Jesus has netted them: "The first." Jesus then makes an application of the parable so that it reflects the shameful action of the religious leaders and the honorable response of those whom they despised and ostracized. The former adhered to the Torah, which might suggest that they were ready to recognize John the Baptist, whose preaching they had heard and who had even baptized some of them. But a mere ritual acceptance of the good news, like words mouthed but not lived, is worthless unless it bears fruit (Matt 3:7-8). They had seen tax collectors and prostitutes say their "yes" to the Baptist's call to repentance. Both of these groups were considered shameful, especially by the Jewish religious and civil leaders, because they collaborated with the Romans, one through employment in the imperial tax system, the other by providing sexual services to their clients, many of whom were Roman soldiers. The tax collectors and prostitutes who repented would go into the kingdom before the chief priests and elders, says Jesus. It is important to note that the marginalized people whose hearts were changed will *precede* the chief priests and elders; Jesus does not exclude them definitively. The door will always be left open for anyone who repents. The kingdom is to be inclusive, and the early history of the church shows that many of the priests became "obedient to the faith" and entered the Christian community (Acts 6:7).

So often it is easy to say an initial "yes" when fervor is high, failure seems impossible, and the future looks golden. But time passes, the enthusiasms cool, the relationships that have to endure through the long haul of married love, the promises of friendship or vocation, have to be truthfully discerned and embraced every day, and the original "yes" is repeated—not with an initial blaze but with the burning embers that are daily fanned by our fidelity, in good times and bad. We may have been disillusioned in recent years by those in the church who have failed in integrity and whose "honor" has been shamed by revelations of abuse and mismanagement, but no matter how personally and ecclesially tragic these revelations have been for both the victims and the perpetrators, we need to remember what today's parable tells us: that the kingdom door is never closed; that we are all an imperfect "yes and no" community of disciples no matter what our role in the church, and that we are people for whom not only one but many changes of heart and conversion to the Father's will are possible and necessary.

Paul challenges the Philippians to become an obedient community of supportive and compassionate love, not selfishly centered on individual ambition and rivalry, but on the needs of their brothers and sisters. This will require the recognition by each member of the Philippian church that there are other people who are better than themselves. Because such conversion is never humanly easy, there is only one way to achieve it: by having the mind and attitude of Christ. Paul then bursts into his magnificent hymn to Christ, the most radically obedient Son, whose life, death and resurrection were always a "Yes" to God (2 Cor 1:19-20). This Christ is not only an example for but also the foundation of Christian life. The Philippians are to reflect on what they have truly become in Christ, and live these attitudes with one another. Christ did not hang onto his equality with God but abandoned its privileges, emptying himself into our humanity in order to make the clearest possible, fully human and fully divine statement about what God is like, the God in whose image humanity is created. Christ's identification with our human condition and his servant obedience took him to death, "even death on a cross," the most humiliating death that the Romans could mete out to a criminal. God's response to his servant son's obedience and self-giving love is to raise Christ to glory. This is what God is like: a compassionate lover who is glorified in the obedience of the humble, the apparent failures, the ones who empty themselves out for their sisters and brothers. Because they live now in Christ, the Philippian community and every Christian community must discern the practical expression of such obedient love that they, like Christ, must show toward God and one another.

The developmental psychologists tell us what every parent knows: that one of the distinctive and normal characteristics of children in middle childhood is their conviction that many things are: "Not fair!" When this becomes a chronic and pervasive adult attitude, there is trouble; and when the charge of unfairness is directed at God, there is a real spiritual malaise. This is at the heart of the problem that the prophet Ezekiel sometimes had to face with the exiled house of Israel. The people charge God with injustice, with being unfair to them. Ezekiel replies by describing two situations where people change their behavior. Like the two sons in the parable, one of whom changed from an apparent right and obedient attitude to disobedience, and the other from disobedience to obedience, God's justice or "fairness" with his people is a response to either their repentance for their sins or their abandonment of integrity in order to walk in the ways of sinfulness.

We respond to the first reading with Psalm 25, a prayer that God may show us steadfast loving kindness, reach out to us with forgiveness, and teach us how to walk in the path of salvation. It is the humble and obedient ones, those who do not go their own arrogant way, whose prayer God will hear. The way we walk is our own free and personal choice, but it is made within the community of disciples who should be united in conviction and love, and so support one another in their commitment. As Paul has reminded us, from birth to death Christ walked the servant way of humble obedience, and for this he was raised as cosmic Lord over all creation, "to the glory of God the Father."

Twenty-seventh Sunday in Ordinary Time

• Isa 5:1-7 • Ps 80:9, 12-16, 19-20 • Phil 4:6-9 • Matt 21:33-44

Listen to the top song hits in any country, and you can be guaranteed to hear about spurned love. Eighth century Judah was no different. Once again the Liturgy of the Word takes us into a vineyard where the prophet Isaiah sings a love song—and tells a parable. The movement from one to the other is part of the surprise that focuses our attention. At the beginning of the reading we listen to what seems to be the prophet's song about an actual friend who loved his vineyard and lavished on it his tender care: digging its soil, clearing it of stones, planting in it the choicest vines, even building a tower in the middle of the vineyard from which he could keep watch over his precious vineyard. There is no hint that this is anything but what it sounds and seems to be, but then the song transposes into a discordant key. The efforts and hopes of the friend for his beloved vineyard are bitterly disappointed, for when the vintage season comes, the yield is only bad fruit.

The song is over. Now it is the friend who turns to his audience, the inhabitants of Jerusalem and Judah, and invites them to make a judgment: was there anything more that could have been done for the vineyard so that it would yield sweet and not sour grapes? We are reminded of the parable that the prophet Nathan told to King David (2 Sam 12:1-15) after his adultery with Bathsheba and his planned "front line" killing of her soldier husband, Uriah the Hittite. In response to the story/parable about the rich man who stole and slaughtered the poor man's one beloved little ewe lamb rather than take one of his plentiful flock to feed a guest, David protests in horror that such a man deserves to die. "You are the man!" replies Nathan. David has pronounced judgment on himself, but is saved by his own repentance and God's forgiveness. Jerusalem and Judah are asked by the owner of the vineyard to pass judgment on the relationship between himself and his beloved vineyard. He argues the case that he has done all he could to ensure a good harvest, but even if it has turned out to be paltry, how can the unnatural yield of sour grapes be explained? It is surely not the vineyard owner's fault but the fault of the vineyard itself, which now takes on a parabolic, "personal" life of its own treacherous self. It has rejected all the loving care of the vineyard owner and gone its own willful and wild way.

The unnatural vineyard has brought punishment on itself, and so the protection that the owner put in place will be removed. Hedges and walls will be demolished, and the vineyard will be made vulnerable to marauding plants, animals, and people. The vineyard owner will command a drought—and at this point the barb of the parable sinks deeply and painfully into the listening houses of Israel and Judah, for who can command the clouds and rain except God? It is God who is the owner of the vineyard, and it is his "pleasant planting," his own people who are expected to be rooted in justice and righteousness, in right relationships between themselves and God and other men and women. But the vineyard is overgrown by the aristocratic rich who exploit the poor, and by the powerful who take advantage of the weak (Isa 1:10-17, 21-22). Bloodshed and lamentation water the vineyard. Yet God will not destroy the vineyard which has spurned his love, so great is the divine *pathos*. God is not "anesthetized," indifferent to humanity, with nothing to say to the mortals he created. God takes us seriously. As Abraham Heschel writes: "The God of the prophets continues to be involved in human history and to be affected by human acts. It is a paradox beyond compare that the Eternal God is concerned with what is happening in time."[45] What God longs for, then and now, is social justice and integrity. Bad grapes may look like good fruit until we bite into them. Just as in the eighth century B.C.E., we need prophets who will sharpen our taste to discern any flavor of hypocrisy or violence, and offer us instead a taste of righteousness. In such discernment we are also challenged to pass judgment on ourselves.

We respond to this reading with verses from Psalm 80 and the refrain from the Isaian reading: "The vineyard of the Lord is the House of Israel." We, too, hope for another chance after our rebellions against God. Like pillaged Israel, like people confronted with atrocities in our own time, we struggle to profess our faith that we are safe in God's hands. The psalmist blames God for the misfortune, and seeks to find a source of the trouble outside of Israel. We are all inclined to take this attitude to our own personal, communal, or national wrongdoing, but the fact that such a lament finds its place in the prayer book of Israel is a recognition that we show our faith in God when we bring such honest reactions before God, when we struggle to go on believing. Then God will turn his face to us with healing, even though our struggle may be long and difficult.

Today's gospel is the third of a trilogy of vineyard parables (the first two were in the 25th and 26th Sunday gospels). It is told in the presence of the chief priests and elders of the people (Matt 21:23), and is obviously patterned on the Isaian reading (as is Mark 12:1-12), but Matthew weaves the threads of the first reading into a new design, into an allegory of Jesus' imminent death and his disciples' reactions.

Absentee landowners were well known to Galilean peasants. Sometimes they would rent out their land to tenant farmers who worked the land and were recompensed by a certain meager percentage of the crop's return. At harvest time the owner's agents would be sent to collect his dues. The parable vineyard has been created by the landowner God who planted it, protected it, built a winepress in it for the crushing of the grapes, and a watchtower from which to guard it. With our biblical antennae well-tuned after three weeks, we recognize the vineyard as Israel and the landowner's servants that are sent to collect the fruit of the harvest as the prophets who were mistreated and abused (see 2 Chr 24:21-22). Finally, after the repeated sending of servants, the landowner's son is sent with the full authority of his Father, only to be killed by the tenant farmers. Jesus is the last and greatest of the line of servant prophets who are resisted by the chief priests and elders who attempt to usurp control over the people of God. But the vineyard is not destroyed, only those who failed in their stewardship of God's precious possession are punished. Homilists, especially, must guard against any supersessionist view of salvation history, the false belief that the history of Israel as God's people reached its end with the Christ event, and that the church has replaced and excluded Israel from salvation. Salvation is not taken away from Israel but from its failed leadership, and given to new leaders of the community of disciples, Jews and Gentiles, who are challenged to produce the righteousness that God demands. The contemporary situation of Matthew's community, made up of Jewish and Gentile Christians, the destruction of the Temple in 70 C.E., and the consequent growing hostility between church and synagogue, are also considerations for Matthew as he shapes this parable. The Pontifical Biblical Commission drew particular attention to this parable in its 2002 document:

> It should be noted that Matthew's polemic does not include Jews in general
> . . . . Although in Isaiah's message the whole vine is reprimanded (Is 5:1-7),
> in Matthew's parable it is only the tenants who are accused (Mt 21:33-41).
> The invectives and accusations hurled at the scribes and Pharisees are similar
> to those found in the prophets, and correspond to a contemporary literary

genre which was common in Judaism (for example, Qumran) and also in Hellenism. Moreover, they put Christians on guard against attitudes incompatible with the gospel (23:8-12).[46]

The parable stresses the need to bear fruit. In Matthew this is a metaphor for productive, life-giving conduct which results from repentance and the conversion to kingdom living. This conversion was preached by John the Baptist (Matt 3:8, 10) and Jesus (Matt 7:16, 20). Jesus asks the chief priests and elders two boomerang-type questions: one that comes back to hit them with their role as failing tenants of God's vineyard; the other, a quotation from Psalm 118:22-23, and a returning challenge to accept Jesus as the authoritative interpreter of the Hebrew scriptures. Heard in Matthew's and our post-resurrection communities, these words affirm that Jesus, the rejected stone, has become the cornerstone which holds together the walls of the building of living stones (Acts 4:11; 1 Pet 2:7).

This parable offers a warning to those who are unproductive and bear no fruit, especially at vintage time when the Son of Man will come to claim the harvest of our lives. Do we believe that suffering and rejection can be a following of the way of the Servant Son who is the beloved of the Vineyard God, and whose rising to new life is the Lord's own doing which we will share if we share his sufferings? Are we possessive rebels who want people and possessions to serve our own ambitions, with no thought of offering service or dispossessing ourselves for the sake of others? Can we honestly recognize that by our hypocrisy or lack of integrity, our deafness to the prophets in our own times, we run the risk of becoming self-condemned tenants of God's vineyard? And in a post-Holocaust age when interfaith dialogue is so important, are we making any attempts to be involved in, or at least supportive of such rapprochement?

When Paul writes to the Philippians he is in prison, and it might be expected that he would have plenty to worry about, not only because of his own suffering, but also because of pastoral problems in the Philippian church such as the internal dissension between some of his coworkers, Euodia and Syntyche, two women who were apparently in disagreement and to whom Paul referred only a few verses before today' reading (Phil 4:2-3). Most of those to whom Paul addresses these words were poor, many of them were slaves, yet despite this Paul encourages the Philippians and tells them not to worry but to turn to God in prayerful thanksgiving that is much more than a recital of personal needs. Their confidence should be in God, not in financial or social security. This does not mean that Paul is encouraging his people to live unengaged lives nor trust in a convenient remedial God, but rather in a God who will help them to bear difficult circumstances.

Anxiety can cripple and cause one to turn in on oneself rather than outward toward the welfare of others in the way Paul's companion, Timothy, was concerned about the Philippians (Phil 2:20). Gratitude to God will allow God's peace to guard our hearts and minds with the attitude of Christ, and not with the anxiety that attacks and disturbs our confidence in God. The peace of Christ was the fruit of his all-encompassing trust in his Father. Paul then encourages the Philippians to take account of qualities that were not specifically Christian, as they were also admired in the pagan world. Anything that is honorable, just, pure, beautiful, or commendable is divine in origin. It was in this tradition that Vatican II endorsed literature and the arts as of great importance in the life of the Church:

> In their own way literature and art are very important in the life of the church. They seek to penetrate our nature, our problems and experience as we endeavour to discover and perfect ourselves and the world in which we live; they try to discover our place in history and in the universe, to throw light on our suffering and joy, our needs and potentialities, and to outline a happier destiny in store for us. Hence they can elevate human life, which they express under many forms according to various times and places.[47]

Twenty-eighth Sunday in Ordinary Time

• Isa 25:6-10a • Ps 23:1-6 • Phil 4:12-14, 19-20 • Matt 22:1-14

Announce a wedding, and life changes for all those involved. Decisions have to be made about dates, places, guest lists and, of course, what to wear! The invitations go out from the parents who delight in (or worry about) the wedding of their children, or from the couple themselves, and the RSVPs are awaited as a prelude to more planning. Along the way to the great event there will be joys and sorrows, hurdles to be overcome, imminent catastrophes, frayed nerves as well as eager expectation, and the final joyous resolution so beloved of script writers and film producers. In this Sunday's gospel we are still in the Temple precincts in the same company as the last two Sundays: with the chief priests and elders of the people (Matt 21:23, 45). In this context, Jesus tells a parable about a wedding and the crises that result from the refusal of those invited to it. It is obviously an allegory, a story that speaks of one thing yet signifies something else. As in the previous parables of the Two Sons and the Wicked Tenants, in the parable of the Wedding Feast Jesus is speaking of salvation history into which people are invited yet may refuse to participate. Guest lists consequently have to be drastically revised to the comfort or discomfort of those who eventually do turn up, and the appropriateness of one's clothing for the wedding and feasting needs to be considered.

The kingdom of heaven may be compared to all this. A king (a metaphor for God) has summoned people to a wedding banquet (the messianic feast and rejoicing of the end time of the kingdom) in honor of his bridegroom son, Jesus (see Matt 9:15; 25:1-13; Rev 19:7, 9). To the king's servants who issue the invitations, the response of those first invited ranges from careless dismissal by those satisfied with their status quo, through excuses about more pressing business by those with other priorities, to exasperated violence against the messenger servants and even killing of some of them by the powerful. Such an unusual response to what would normally be considered a good opportunity to curry favor with the king, and the mayhem of the king's response by sending his troops to murder and destroy those who shamed him by their refusal and burn their city, serves to emphasize the allegorical genre of the parable. The dramatic impact on the audience is also heightened. Unless these actions signified something else, one wonders how there would be anyone left, or willing, to answer the second wave of invitations! The first invitees are those who might have been expected to accept: the religious and lay leaders of Israel who should have heard the call of God through the prophets who were sent to them and through the Hebrew Scriptures. But they reject God's invitation. The invitation is now offered to the street people: the beggars, the prostitutes, the socially outcast and vulnerable. There are echoes here of the Wisdom Woman of Prov 9:1-6 who sent her servant girls to call out a similar invitation to the simple. The servants bring both good and bad into the wedding feast, without any sorting or discrimination ahead of time. Allegorically, the invitation passes to the Gentiles.

There will be a judgment about the worthiness of the guests because participation in the wedding feast of the Son means more than just showing up. Such judgment, however, belongs to the king. Just as in the parable of the Weeds and Wheat (Matt 13:24-30) when the sorting out was left until the final harvest at the end of time, so now it is the king who comes into the assembly of guests and finds there someone "not wearing a wedding robe." Again, the allegorical nature of the parable is obvious, for taken literally how could any of the street people in a devastated city fit themselves out with wedding apparel? "Clothing" is often a metaphor for good works and faithful discipleship. The baptized "put on the Lord Jesus Christ" (Rom 13:14) and "have clothed themselves with Christ" (Gal 3:27); the Colossians are encouraged to clothe themselves with virtues, and above all "with love, which binds everything together in perfect harmony" (Col 3:12-14). This is the answer to "What shall I wear?" to the wedding feast of the kingdom that, in the long run of salvation history, is the only wedding that really matters. Those who wish to share the Son's wedding feast must always be clothed and ready in this way of love.

Like Matthew's community, as a church we are also servants sent out to invite others to the wedding feast, to proclaim that God's door is always open and welcoming. Our mission is not to judge, but to carry the message to our streets and workplaces, and suffer unconcern, ridicule, and sometimes even persecution for the sake of the King and his Son. But we are also the invited guests. Do we reject the invitation because of priorities that disregard the Gospel: addiction to personal success, selfishness, materialism, fear of judgment of others rather than mercy for them? At the feast of the Eucharist, do we just show up, not caring much about the guests around us, not caring if we are clothed in love for God and our sisters and brothers, just partaking of the bread and wine but not offering ourselves to others, both present and absent, as broken bread and drained wine for their nourishment? And does all this make our baptismal clothing tattered and grubby, unfit for a holy feast?

The prophet Isaiah describes another abundant feast on a mountainside that is, presumably, the mountain of the Lord, Mount Zion, to which Isaiah had a vision of all the nations flowing (Isa 2:1-5). This will be a messianic banquet for all people of all nations who will sit together and share God's table hospitality that is, for Semites, a pledge of friendship and peace. The rich foods and the flowing wine that are served are symbols of the fullness of life. God will remove the veil of ignorance that has shrouded the nations and blinded them to one another and to God, and death will be no more. There is no reference here to resurrection but to the end of the mourning and pain of those who are still alive, the banishment of anything that diminishes life. Like a tender mother comforting a weeping child, God will wipe away all tears from the eyes of mourners. And because it is God who performs this gentle act, "on that day" of eschatological fulfillment there will be no more tears (see Rev 21:4). As so often in the psalms, Isaiah speaks of "waiting" for God as an expression of faith (see Pss 25:3, 5, 21; 40:1; Isa 8:17). Even the natural world will be touched and transformed, not because of ancient Canaanite myths that celebrated the swallowing up of winter's death by spring, but because God's "hand," his saving presence and power, will rest on the holy mountain.

In both the gospel and the first reading, it is God who prepares the banquet, who calls, who longs for all peoples and nations to sit down and feast in friendship. But as nations, communities, individuals, we can be so deaf, so preoccupied with other concerns, so wrapped in shrouds of death-dealing ignorance or bitterness, that we miss the blessings for which we must be always ready. The Australian poet, Judith Wright, speaks of:

> . . . a wine
> a drunkenness that can't be spoken or sung
> without betraying it. Far past Yours or Mine,
> even past Ours, it has nothing at all to say;
> it slants a sudden laser through common day . . . .
>
>   . . . It plunges a sword from a dark star.
> Maybe there was once a word for it. Call it grace.
> I have seen it, once or twice, on a human face.[48]

That is where God's grace comes, that is where God's call is heard. We have to be ready to recognize it in our "common day" among our sisters and brothers, in preparation for the Great Day of the Lord.

Paul has known what it is to be both poor and rich, well fed and hungry. In his ministry he adapted to the circumstances in which he found himself (1 Cor 9:20-23), but he is not self-sufficient. He relies always on God in Christ to give him strength. He is grateful also to his beloved Philippians who have been a grace to him by their love and concern and which he values more than the material gifts with which they have supported him in his "defense and confirmation of the gospel" (Phil 1:7), even when in prison. Paul assures the Philippians that God will be the lavish provider for them, as he is for Paul himself. So there is no more fitting conclusion to this final reading from this letter of Paul than the doxology to *our* God and Father, for ever and ever.

This is the God whom we praise in the responsorial Psalm 23, probably the best known and most loved psalm in the Psalter. God is described metaphorically as both shepherd and host. The shepherd has the responsibility of finding rich pasture that will provide his flock with lush grass for grazing and abundant water for drinking. There is a tender intimacy in the psalm; for the psalmist, the shepherd is "my" shepherd, who also nourishes the spirit and guides along the way of righteousness. Even in darkness and danger, the shepherd creates an environment of trust. Then the shepherd turns host to the banquet of the kingdom, and we remember that we are a community gathered in the house of the Lord, about to partake now of the eucharistic feast that is not yet the eternal banquet into which the shepherd Lamb will guide us (Rev 7:16-17) to share in the unending hospitality of heaven.

Twenty-ninth Sunday in Ordinary Time

• Isa 45:1, 4-6 • Ps 96:1, 3-5, 7-10 • 1 Thess 1:1-5b • Matt 22:15-21

The controversies with Jesus' opponents that he has tackled through the parables of the last three Sundays now become a challenging confrontation and a battle of wits. The Pharisees take counsel with one another about how to trap and discredit Jesus, and enlist the help of the Herodians. Determination to destroy Jesus unites these two groups as they seize on the issue of the collection of the poll or "head" tax as their common cause. This was a tax that had been imposed on Judea in 6 C.E. when Judea became a Roman province. It was a one denarius tax (equal to the day's wage of a laborer) imposed on every man, woman, and slave between the ages of twelve and sixty-five—the price for living in and enjoying the dubious rights of a subject of the Roman Empire. It was bitterly resented by the poor and the nationalistic Zealots, tolerated by those who, like the Herodians, tried to ingratiate themselves with the powerful, and resented by the Pharisees because of their opposition to the occupation of the Land by the Roman Gentiles.

But integrity is now eroded by expediency. Disciples of the Pharisees and the Herodians join forces and go to Jesus to spring their trap, well-oiled with insincere flattery. When Jesus is tackled about the tax issue, if he speaks out against it he can be charged with sedition and arrest; if he speaks for the tax, he will discredit himself as a prophet in the eyes of the oppressed. Ironically, what they say to him is true: Jesus does sincerely, truthfully teach the ways of God; he has no regard for social status. But in the mouths of his opponents these honeyed words are bitterly insincere, no more than a lure into their trap as they ask him whether he considers it lawful or not to pay taxes to the emperor ("Caesar"). Jesus reads the malice of their hearts, lets them know that he is not deceived by their collusion that makes it obvious that it is not really the tax issue which is at stake, and calls them hypocrites to their faces. Then Jesus springs his own trap. He asks them to show him the coin used for the poll tax. He does not have one himself, but before his opponents have time to think, someone in the group readily produces a coin. What they have in their possession, what they are handling in the Temple precincts, is a coin that most Jews considered blasphemous. Not only did it bear the image of the emperor, but it was also inscribed on one side with the words: *Tiberius Caesar Divi Augusti Filius Augustus* (Tiberius Caesar, august son of the divine Augustus), and on the other, *Pontifex Maximus* (High Priest). Such accordance to the emperor of both political honor and divine status should have been abhorrent to Jews. In fact, in Roman deference to such sensibilities, some copper coins without the image were available for ordinary commercial exchange and, because of such an image and inscription, the Temple tax could not be paid in Roman or Greek coinage but had to be changed into the acceptable currency (see Matt 21:12). The Pharisees had even devised ways of avoiding the handling of the coins by using foreign moneychangers to exchange Roman for Judean coins. In one swift move, Jesus has changed the whole issue from that of paying the tax to one of accepting images, a highly sensitive issue in Judaism based on the Decalogue (Exod 20:4). In Jesus' hand, the coin becomes a kind of parable. Like the Pharisees, Jesus probably is not opposed to paying taxes if this is necessary for peaceful coexistence (see Matt 17:24-27), but such an obligation is worthless when compared to the ultimate loyalty that is owed to God. Jesus' response of "Give therefore to the emperor the things that are the emperor's, and to God the things that are God's" is not to be read as an explanation for the contemporary separation of church and state. Jesus does not "compartmentalize" life, and such a dualistic interpretation would have been completely contrary to his worldview. Real wisdom recognizes the legitimate function of human authority in relation to God's authority. Vatican II reminded Christians, "as citizens of two cities, to strive to discharge their earthly duties conscientiously and in response to the gospel spirit."[49] What is demanded is that we engage in the difficult discernment of how to live in history and society and also, and above all, be aware of our commitment to the reign of God. As with most of his parables, Jesus does not elaborate on the "how" to do this. This gospel is for all times and places and so, as Brendan Byrne comments:

> Members of God's people are summoned to constant discernment as to how, within the overall claim of God, they are to discharge civic obligations. In the matter of relations between Church and state, Jesus bequeaths an ethical task rather than a detailed prescription.[50]

Such an ethical task demands the action that Jesus exemplified: truthfulness rather than hypocrisy, honesty rather than flattery, justice rather than opportunism. This is still a challenge to leadership—both political and ecclesial—as well as to every Christian disciple. We might ask where is God's impression in the "coinage" of our daily life? The answer is: on everything that God has made, and especially on other women and men.

The reading stops before v. 22 that tells us how the Pharisees and Herodians went away amazed. The way in which Jesus has escaped the trap and deflected the discussion from talk about Caesar to discussion of God stuns them. We might pray for some of this same "slippery" wisdom in difficult situations (Matt 10:16).

Isaiah professes that the secular and political can be the arena of the holy and ethical. The pagan ruler, Cyrus the Persian, is the only non-Israelite to be named in the scriptures as God's anointed or "messiah." Cyrus is unaware that in the liberation of the Babylonian exiles he is acting as God's servant. Isaiah twice repeats that it is God who names and empowers Cyrus as a servant of the divine will, "though you (Cyrus) do not know me." Isaiah's audience is primarily the sixth century B.C.E. exiles, and the prophet wants to give them hope by convincing them that God can work in unexpected people, people that they may consider "outsiders" but who have a privileged "insider" role to play in their salvation, according to their surprising God. This will witness to the truth that from the rising to the setting of the sun, across all the boundaries of the earth, from nation to nation, God can work in all and through all as the one true God.

In a moving passage of Albert Camus' *The Plague*, the atheist physician Dr. Rieux and the isolated priest Fr. Paneloux are desperately tending a child who is dying in agony. Rieux is unconvinced by the priest's plea that he try to love what he cannot understand, but he recognizes that both of them are united in the fight against death and evil. Grasping the priest's hand, he admits that "even God cannot separate us now."[51] The presence and work of God's Spirit is not restricted to the Catholic Church. To encourage the world to walk in the ways of peace and justice, three times during his pontificate John Paul II gathered leaders of the great world religions to pray with him at Assisi—against the advice of some members of the Roman Curia who were worried about syncretism. In doing this, the Pope was endorsing the truth of today's prophetic reading and the most solemn and authoritative teaching of the church announced by Vatican II in the *Declaration on the Relationship of the Church to Non-Christian Religions.* In that document we are reminded that there is often reflected "a ray of that Truth which enlightens all people" (art. 2) in those who in their conduct, way of life and belief differ from the Catholic Church.

The responsorial Psalm 96, an enthronement psalm, calls us to sing a new song in praise of the God who does new things, as he did in Cyrus and continues to do in so many people and places throughout the world. As Isaiah has proclaimed, true power belongs only to God, and human power that is just is a sharing in the divine power over the cosmos. We might also sing this psalm for the nations of the world who are still struggling for the rule of justice, praying that God may raise up other "Cyruses" to be instruments of God's liberation.

Each of today's readings has some concern with power. Cyrus is unknowingly the human instrument of God's divine power; the Pharisees and Herodians plot against Jesus because they know that his powerful authority is attracting the people and distracting them from their own power. And in his First Letter to the Thessalonians, the earliest writing in the New Testament, Paul warmly praises this church for their fidelity to the good news which has come among them "in the power of the Holy Spirit and with full conviction" through the ministry of Paul, Silvanus, and Timothy. For the first time, Christians are called by Paul an *ekklesia*, a "gathering," which is a special and privileged gathering in God the Father and the Lord Jesus Christ.

In the absence of Paul and his missionary companions, the Thessalonians have continued to believe, to work in love, and to endure in hope—just as many contemporary local churches continue as vibrant communities with limited presence of ordained ministers. This is a far cry from the distressing words of a parish priest newly arrived in a parish of very disadvantaged people who had, nonetheless, been loved and empowered by their previous pastor. During a radio interview he announced: "The people with the priest can do everything. The people without the priest can do nothing." Paul would beg to differ!

Thirtieth Sunday in Ordinary Time

• Exod 22:20-26 • Ps 18:2-4, 47, 51 • 1 Thess 1:5c-10 • Matt 22:34-40

Those antagonistic to Jesus do not give up. The Sadducees have just been silenced by Jesus' interpretation of scripture (Matt 22:23-33), but now the Pharisees return to confront him. As in last Sunday's gospel, Jesus sees through what seems to be an acceptable question put to him by one of them who is a lawyer, a "professional theologian," primed up to question Jesus about the greatest commandment of the 613 precepts of the Mosaic Torah (Law/Teaching). The word Matthew uses for the word to "test" or "disconcert" Jesus by the question is the same word that the evangelist uses when Jesus is led into the wilderness to be "tempted" by the devil (Matt 4:1). This encounter, therefore, is another bedeviling attempt to involve Jesus in a hairsplitting debate, not a typical discussion as was held in rabbinic circles for the sake of clarification.

As an observant Jew, Jesus responds to his tempter by saying that the first and greatest commandment is the fifth verse of the great Jewish profession of faith, the *Shema* ("Listen") of Deut 6:4-9. Jews have recited this ancient love song every day down through the generations, even when attempts have been made to smother it on the funeral pyres of history. These holy words have drifted over the world in the tragic smoke of Auschwitz and other death camps; they have also risen as the incense of joyful prayer: "Hear, O Israel, . . . you shall love the Lord your God with all your heart, and with all your soul, and with all your mind." Love is to bind together our interiority ("heart"), our life force ("soul"), and our rationality ("mind") into a dynamic and total engagement that integrates and directs the whole person toward God.

Although asked for one commandment, Jesus responds with two, quoting a verse from the Jewish Code of Holiness—a practical summary of the

Jewish way of life—because, he says, the "second is *like*" the first (see Lev 19:8). It is equal in importance and inseparable from the first. Everything, Jesus says, hangs on these. A door hangs on two hinges, but if one is out of alignment it will not swing properly or open easily. If love of God and neighbor are out of balance, our lives will be badly aligned. Jesus is not discounting the other commandments, not talking about "heavier" or "lighter" commandments, but emphasizing that their weight, and the tradition of the prophets, is borne by these two commandments that balance one another. Jesus defines for us in his own person what this love of God and neighbor is. Unconditionally and without limit, Jesus loves his Father and humanity from birth to death and into his risen life.

Perhaps our greatest temptation is to separate our love of God and love of people. We may go out of today's Eucharist only to show how little we really are "in communion" with our brothers and sisters when we omit to love them in the small but demanding ways of everyday neighborliness, or commit loveless deeds against them. In the Old Testament, "neighbor" was another Israelite, or resident alien without rights of citizenship. In Matthew's Gospel we have seen how Jesus has already extended this to love of enemies (Matt 5:43), and on the last Sunday, the Solemnity of Our Lord Jesus Christ the King, in the parable of the Last Judgment, the challenge to practical love will reach out to those of all nations.

To emphasize that biblical love is neither a matter of soft, fuzzy contentment, nor compulsive obsession with minutiae of our human devising, the Lectionary twins the gospel with the robustly practical first reading from Exodus. Out of the Hebrews' lived experience of being strangers in Egypt emerges the image of a God who, like a fiercely protective parent, watches compassionately over the most vulnerable. In situations of social oppression and war, the cost is usually paid by the widows and orphans whose cries God will hear and be moved to action on their behalf (Exod 2:23-25; 3:7-8). Israelites are to have ethical standards different from those whose aim is to take advantage of the poor by charging them excessive interest or demanding collateral that they cannot offer, and so imprisoning them in indebtedness and dependence. The social fabric of marginalized groups and nations is still being ripped apart by political disregard, and our action and advocacy for them is still an urgent religious challenge.

Only the beginning and end of Psalm 18 are used as today's responsorial psalm, and these are verses that resound with the praise of God who, after the Exodus reading, is fittingly described with strong images of protection: as rock, fortress, savior for those who are being threatened with some disaster. The cries of the widow, the orphans, the dispossessed, have been heard by God who acts through his anointed king. In the Christ event of which the psalmist knew nothing, God's saving love for the poor will be most fully revealed.

Love is contagious. Carried on the inspired breath of the Holy Spirit, the Gospel had spread from Paul and his companions to the church at Thessalonika, and from them throughout the neighboring regions. What is most effective for the acceptance of the Gospel is the witness of people's lifestyle, and the Thessalonians' commitment to the word of the Lord was not just a passing enthusiasm for fads and the latest spiritual "idols." It was a steadfast faith in and abiding hope for the promised salvation through Jesus Christ, in spite of opposition and suffering. For them, he is the rock and fortress of their faith, and they had become his servants who build their lives on Jesus until he comes again.

What is the example that is being asked of us today? In our own culture and society, who do we recognize as the ones whose cries rise up to God for love and freedom from oppression: the women and children who are trafficked, the frail aged who are disregarded, the people with disabilities of body and mind, the refugees from new pharaohs? And how good are we at responding to those cries and hearing in our commitment or omission the thanks or tears of God?

Thirty-first Sunday in Ordinary Time

• Mal 1:14b–2:2b, 8-10 • Ps 131 • 1 Thess 2:7b-9, 13 • Matt 23:1-12

Jesus is no longer confronting his opponents in this Sunday's gospel; he is speaking to his disciples, the potential Matthean community leaders, and the crowds who are following him. As history has sadly demonstrated, this is a gospel that runs the risk of much misunderstanding. It has been wrongly used by Nazi sympathizers and "revisionist" historians to brand all the Jewish people as hypocrites and has created in too many Christian minds an image of the Jewish religious tradition as a religion of external observances only. Nor should we read it as a total condemnation of all Pharisees. No doubt some of them deserved such criticism and, indeed, were criticized from within Pharisaic Judaism itself, especially when faced with the mammoth task of rebuilding Judaism and preserving traumatized Jewish identity after 70 C.E. and the destruction of the Temple. Anyone or anything, including Christianity, which seemed a threat to this identity was condemned. Matthew is writing one or two decades after 70 C.E., and so much of the contemporary tension appears in his gospel. Sustained polemical opposition was also recognized at that time as a biblical and secular convention. Perhaps tuning in to current parliamentary or congressional debates may give us some appreciation of this convention of polemic! Jesus is using the artifice of denunciation as a foil against which the qualities demanded of *Christian* leadership will show forth. These are also words for us about temptation to petty power plays and lust for recognition and advancement, especially at the level of leadership in the community of disciples.

Jesus' first criticism is of those who "do not practice what they teach." They are like play actors (the original meaning of the Greek word *hupócrites*) who wore stylized masks to denote their roles. Their public and performing faces do not match their inner and personal truth. Some religious leaders, says Jesus, exercise control by teaching interpretations that are excessively legalistic and burdensome. After the destruction of the Temple and the consequent cessation of the active Jewish priesthood, the priestly purity laws were progressively transferred to the whole people in an attempt to fortify a vulnerable Judaism from external attack and internal laxity. For many Jews, such laws became a heavy burden. What Jesus offers is burden-lifting mercy and rest to those who come to him (Matt 11:28).

Clinging to nomenclature that indicates importance and power, thrusting oneself into the public limelight, and attachment to ostentatious religious regalia, are signs of exaltation rather than humility, says Jesus. He criticizes the Jewish leaders who wear showy phylacteries (Heb. *tefillin*), the small leather cubes containing biblical texts that a Jewish man straps to his forehead (symbolizing his mind) and left biceps (nearest to his heart) during morning prayer in order to dramatize the command in Deuteronomy (Deut 6:6-8). Likewise, Jesus also criticizes the wearing of excessively long tassels on the Jewish man's (then) outer garment which were fringed and knotted symbolically as a reminder of the 613 precepts of the Mosaic Law, and the honorific titles which are also a flamboyant effort to impress others with one's holy status.

If we are inclined to dismiss these criticisms as rather quaint and irrelevant, we might consider the appropriateness of the titles of "Eminence," "Excellency" or "my Lord," or expensive ecclesial dwellings and insignia. In contrast, we have prophetic bishops like the late Hélder Câmara who died in 1999, at the age of ninety, in his simple house at Olinda in the parched, impoverished northeast of Brazil. As one of the younger bishops at Vatican II and wearing his wooden cross over a simple black cassock, Dom Hélder had urged his fellow bishops to sell their silver and gold pectoral crosses and give the money to the poor. Together with Cardinals Pierre Gerlier and Giacomo Lecaro he created a small think tank of about forty bishops, "the church of the poor group," which met regularly during the Council. Just before its close, they made a public declaration of "Thirteen Commitments."[52]

Having recognized, they said, the deficiencies of their life of poverty in accordance with the Gospel, the members of the group proclaimed the thirteen commitments, each of which was based on and referenced by gospel texts. Two of the commitments read:

> We henceforth renounce the appearance and reality of riches, especially in clothing (fine cloth, striking colors), insignia in precious materials, for these signs should be evangelical.
>
> We shall refuse to be addressed orally or in writing by names indicating importance and power (Eminence, Excellency, Monsignor). We prefer to be addressed by the evangelical title Father.

With regard to the last mentioned, and in the context of the disappearance from Christian use of the title "Rabbi" because of its centrality within Judaism, Daniel Harrington remarks that: "The struggle between the sociological necessity for institutionalization and the mandate for community fellowship affected the Matthean community as it does many Christian communities today."[53]

The Book of Malachi is sometimes called the "seal of the prophets," as it is the last and closing book of the prophetic writings. His words in the first reading are a searing denunciation of unfaithful priests. No real clues are given about dating, but it is presumably after the reestablishment of the Temple in 515 B.C.E. The lack of precise dating may help us to appreciate that the issues with which Malachi is concerned are generic to most periods of biblical or ecclesial history. The choice of today's portion in the Liturgy of the Word is obvious, given the gospel reading.

Through the words of the prophet, God castigates the priests for their failures. God's name is honored among the nations but, in contrast, is tragically dishonored by the irreverent worship of Israel's priests. They have also failed in being custodians of the holy traditions and the teachers of these to the people (Lev 10:11). They are not called to suffocate and restrict the people with the old but to share with them the accumulated wisdom that enables them to discern their present and future according to God's will. The corrupt priests have ignored integrity and uprightness and indulged in favoritism; what is implied by this with regard to the relationship of worship and justice will later be made explicit by Malachi (Mal 3:5). The final reminder is that both priests and people belong to the same Creator, and so are called to keep faith with their God and with one another. This is a timely admonition for all times and communities.

Today's responsorial Psalm 131 most gently and confidently expresses God's loving care of the people and contrasts this with the lack of care of their priests. The reading from Malachi ends with the question, "Have we not all one father?" and the psalmist answers with the image of God as Mother. In the relationship of mother and child there is no ambition, no climbing the social ladder; there is only the climb into the mother's lap. The child is described as "weaned," something that did not happen in Israel (as in many cultures today) until the child was about three years of age and running around actively. Weaning is an early "No" of the mother to what the child wants and expects, yet here is the image of the child who returns to the mother after the refusal of her breast, and enters into a new stage of maturity in their relationship, experiencing in the mother's tender and continuous nurture the blessings of peace and confidence. This is the image of our God who embraces us in love that will mature and deepen as we return again and again to her.

The responsorial psalm also leads us into the reading from Paul's First Letter to the Thessalonians, and Paul's description of himself as a leader who is like a nursing mother who suckles and cares for her child with the very substance of her body. Paul has given to the Thessalonians both the substance of God's good news that sustains his own life, and also his daily work that has relieved the church of any burden of providing financially for the upkeep of himself and his fellow workers. They have generously foregone such hospitality and support, and no doubt this added to the solidarity and mutual love between the church leaders and the Thessalonian community. This reading is a wonderful "case study" for the strong yet gentle leadership that we are entitled to hope for today.

Thirty-second Sunday in Ordinary Time

• Wis 6:12-16 • Ps 63:2-8 • 1 Thess 4:13-18 • Matt 25:1-13

As we enter into the last three weeks of the church year, the Liturgy of the Word draws our attention to the end time, the end of human history, and the Second Coming of Christ to hand over all creation to the Father as the new heaven and new earth. The early Church had gradually come to terms with the delay of this event that they had thought was imminent after the resurrection and return of Jesus to heaven. This expectation is probably in the far background of our Christian vision, but every year the Church reminds us of its significance. Although its date is God's secret, there are unhelpful and recurring fundamentalist calculations of this coming followed by recalculations when an announced occurrence fails to eventuate. More proximate, though we may avoid thinking about it, is the end time of our own biological life, and we may be much more apprehensive about the latter than the former.

At the end of the liturgy of baptism, a candle is lit from the paschal candle and handed to the parents of the child with these words:

> Parents and godparents, this light is entrusted to you to be kept burning brightly. This child of yours has been enlightened by Christ. He/she is to walk always as a child of the light. May he/she always keep this flame of faith alive in the heart. When the Lord comes, may he/she go out to meet him with all the saints in the heavenly kingdom.

Behind this prayer stands the parable we hear today, "The Ten Wise and Ten Foolish Young Women."

Unique to Matthew, this is the only parable of watching and waiting where discipleship is portrayed in a feminine context. In the parable, the kingdom of heaven "will be like" a gathering of young women, unmarried but of marriageable age—at twelve years in first century Palestine—who according to cultural norms are waiting at the bride's parental home so that they can meet the bridegroom as he approaches the house to claim his bride for the consummation of their marriage. Jesus has earlier referred to himself in Matthew's Gospel as the "bridegroom" (Matt 9:15), and God as "husband" is a recurring Old Testament metaphor (see Isa 54:5; Jer 31:32; Hos 2:16). The parable presents us with both a positive and negative model of how disciples are to wait for the return of Jesus the Bridegroom at the end of human history. The emphasis is on the oil and the burning lamps, not on the falling asleep, which all ten girls do when the arrival of the bridegroom is delayed. In baptism, we are chosen to illumine the passage of Christ the Bridegroom through our world by lives that are fueled with the oil of good works (Matt 5:14-16). For Matthew, "oil" and "lamplight" are symbolic of good works and Christian witness that gives glory to God. Given Matthew's mainly Jewish Christian community, it is perhaps significant to remember that in Judaism, lamp-lighting from Sabbath eve to wedding vigils, was predominantly women's work. Perhaps the parable also hints at a symbolic challenge to women, especially, to light the flame of expectation for the coming of the Bridegroom Christ, and set a course in the midst of the darkness for his coming home to our world.

What will gain entry to the wedding feast is the young women's ready ability to greet the arrival of the Bridegroom. It is not just a matter of the foolish young women crying out "Lord, Lord, open to us!" This has echoes of the cry of the believer who calls out to the Lord and drops names but has no good works to merit Jesus' attention (Matt 7:21-23). In gospel terms, readiness to greet the Bridegroom and go in with him to the eternal wedding banquet means a life lived in constant vigilance for and obedience to the reign of God that Jesus proclaims. The baptized neophyte, the newly married, the newly professed or ordained, the beginner in a longed-for job, are all excited and determined about the life to which they have committed themselves; all have their "lamps" burning brightly. Deeper into the night, into the demands of decades of oil refilling and wick tending, some flames may have flickered out while others continue to burn steadily and brightly, even though some may light up paths that differ from the original way the lamp carriers thought they would walk.

Although the parable is primarily concerned with what lies behind the as yet closed doors of the end of cosmic history and Christ's Second Coming, the Bridegroom will also come to us in our own death. One Eucharist will be the last from which we take the oil from the two tables of Word and sacrament that help us to keep our lamps burning and light our way to open the doors of our hearts to the Bridegroom.

The "midnight cry" is shouted in the tradition of the decisive moment of divine manifestation: the sparing of the Israelites and the slaying of the firstborn of the Egyptians (Exod 11:4; 12:29); the hour of the angel's liberation of Paul and Silas from prison (Acts 16:25); the sighting of land after Paul's and his companions' shipwreck (Acts 27:27); the time of praise and petition (Ps 119:62). Once the shout, "Look! Here is the bridegroom! Come out to meet him!" is heard, the time for preparation is over. The good intentions that remain only intentions, the visits not made, the reconciliation not offered: there is something of the foolish young women in us all. But there is also something of the wise and their lamps of kindness: friendship offered, compassion shown, forgiveness asked. There is in us, too, the deep longing that the responsorial Psalm 63 expresses: our thirst for God that we at times ignore or try to satisfy by what is not of God until, by divine blessing, we realize how parched our lives have become and we cry out for God from our inner depths and in the watches of the dark night.

God's wisdom, personified in the first reading as a Woman, is the constant, intimate, and enlightening companion who first seeks out and then guides with her radiance those who seek her. Lady Wisdom places herself where she can be found most obviously—metaphorically, in the dawn hours and at the city gates—by those who desire her. She is imaged as in the midst of the flow of daily life and human activity. Matthew refers to Jesus as wisdom personified (Matt 11:19), and those who seek him can do so only because of his initiative.

In the second reading, Paul is also concerned with the delay of the Second Coming (*parousía*) of Christ. Some of the Thessalonians are worried about those who have already died, struggling with the question of whether

Jesus' resurrection meant their exemption from death in this world. Paul assures them that they must not grieve over the death of members of the community because the death and resurrection of Jesus are their assurance that the new age has begun and, whether we are alive or dead at the *parousía*, those who believe in Christ will be united with him. His enduring presence is with both the living and the dead, and at Christ's return his disciples will be swept into eternal union with him and with one another. Not to predict the details of this final revelation and homecoming to God, but to help him to communicate its wonder, Paul uses apocalyptic images of clouds, angels, and trumpet blasts from Israel's tradition.

Very appropriately, this Sunday usually falls close to the Feasts of All Saints and All Souls. The interconnectedness of the living and the dead with Christ—which can often worry us as it worried the Thessalonians—is beautifully expressed in the words of Bede Jarrett:

> We give back to you, O God, those whom you gave to us. You did not lose them when you gave them to us and we do not lose them by their return to you. Your dear Son has taught us that life is eternal and love cannot die. So death is only a horizon, and a horizon is only the limit of our sight. Open our eyes to see more clearly, and draw us closer to you that we may know that so we are closer to our loved one who is with you.[54]

Thirty-third Sunday in Ordinary Time

• Prov 31:10-13, 19-20, 30-31 • Ps 128:1-5 • 1 Thess 5:1-6 • Matt 25:14-30

The Parable of the Talents continues the eschatological discourse in which Jesus teaches about the last days. As with the parables of the last two Sundays, the crowds have gone and Jesus is with his disciples who have come to him "privately" on the Mount of Olives (Matt 24:3). The opening words of the parable cue us in to the fact that Jesus is again using allegory to teach about the kingdom of heaven. We are not in the world of high financial investment, but investment in gospel living. Shares will come to maturity when Jesus returns at the end of human history on the cosmic Day of the Lord. Jesus is not talking about theories of capitalism, but using situations of first century Palestine life to illustrate, not model, appropriate behavior for his disciples. Likewise, the master's concluding harsh words and actions that we may find disturbing are dictated by the logic of the story and not by a theological imaging of God as revealed in Jesus.

For Matthew and his community, and the first intended readers of his gospel, Jesus has gone on the journey back to his Father, but he has told them that he will come again. That this would be a "long time," but just how long, was a reality that the early church wrestled with—as we still do two millennia later. Every disciple, like the master's slaves in the parable, has the responsibility of using the gifts we have been given by God for the sake of the kingdom. There is to be no "playing safe" in such an investment.

To each of the three slaves the master gives an enormous amount of money in the currency of "talents." At a conservative estimate, a talent was worth more than fifteen years of wages for a laborer, and this is the lowest amount given to the third slave! The amount for the five and two talent recipients soars correspondingly, and again the literary device of exaggeration comes into play for the sake of impressive and attention-catching storytelling. The slaves are given no instructions about what they are to do with the money; they are simply entrusted with it, each according to his own ability. Each must decide how to exercise his stewardship during the master's absence; there is no question of the slaves being in competition with one another. The master has taken a risk with both his money and his slaves, and the first two slaves respond by taking risks and trading with the money in order to make more, not for themselves, but for their master. The third slave "plays it safe." Cautious, unimaginative and fearful, he buries the one talent. In the ancient world this was considered a safe way of hiding money, especially in time of war (see Matt 13:44), but safety is not the issue here.

God's risk-taking in the life and death of his Son has "paid off" in Jesus' resurrection. But Matthew sets this parable on the Mount of Olives where, in the flow of this gospel, Jesus will soon fall agonizingly into its dust as he struggles with the risks and responsibilities to which he must commit himself as a good and faithful Servant entrusted with the incomparable treasure of the world's salvation. Every disciple of Jesus is called to share in the risk-taking of salvation. It is not the quantity of the gifts with which we have been entrusted, but the quality of how we use them that will earn the Master's approval or disapproval when he returns. And so, the parable continues, when the master does return he calls the three slaves to an account of their stewardship. The first two had doubled their trust and they receive proportionately the same reward for their adventurous 100 percent trading. These slaves are then empowered with more authority and a greater share in the master's possessions. Then the one-talent slave comes forward. He tries to justify his action, or inaction, by arguing from his judgment of his master as a harsh and exploitative man—a great insult! This slave has imprisoned himself in misconceived fear of both his master and his own personal failure that paralyzes his activity and imagination in favor of a policy of noninvolvement. It is this that earns him his punishment, for the investment of the one talent had meant as much to the master as that of the five or two.

Discipleship is not just a comfortable holding on to the gifts that God has given us. It challenges us to action, to risk-taking, to increasing the yield of good works and sharing these with others, and to refraining from excuses for our failures. As the fifth century Desert Father, John the Dwarf, once reprimanded his community: "We have put the light burden on one side, that is to say, self-accusation, and we have loaded ourselves with a heavy one, that is to say, self-justification."[55] We cannot take refuge in our own preconceived and often sterile images of God, nor revel in what we regard as a "victim" relationship with God. The risks that earn us affirmation as "good and trustworthy" servants are the ordinary kingdom exchanges of daily life: forgiving rather than burying a grudge in our hearts; standing by another in times of sorrow, failure, or misunderstanding; giving someone the benefit of the doubt; associating with those whom many consider the "wrong kind" of unacceptable people; laying down one's life for another—perhaps a misunderstood friend, rebellious child, a terminally ill spouse, aged parents. All this "now" effort is preparing us for the "not yet" entry into the kingdom.

Some members of Matthew's community may have struggled to accept that being a Jewish Christian meant that they could not just dig a hole and keep their Jewish inheritance safe without any new investment in the new interpretations of the Law that Jesus taught. Some Catholics today would like to bury Vatican II and keep the church (especially its younger generation) safe from or ignorant about the risky business of that new Pentecost.

In the reading from the Book of Proverbs, in the portrait of what is variously translated as "a valiant woman" or "a capable/noble wife," we are given a wonderful foil to the passive, unproductive, and fearful slave-disciple. The wisdom of God, described in exalted poetry in the early chapters of this book (see Prov 8), has come down to be "at home" in all the aspects of daily domestic life which are presided over by a woman of feminine strength, dignity and creativity, and one who reverences the Lord. This woman is not a stereotype of what in contemporary terms we might describe as either a housebound wife or an ambitious career woman. She is energetic, discerning, and respectful of the inner reality of people, be it her husband "whose heart trusts in her," the members of her household, including the servants, or the poor beyond her household. Her hands not only use the spindle to provide for her household, but also are open wide to provide for the needy. Praise of her extends to the center of local community life, "the city gates," where she is also known and active. The qualities with which this wife is clothed are strength and dignity, attributes which elsewhere refer to God and men (see Pss 21:5; 93:1). The reading concludes with a profound corrective to the erotic praise of women who are valued only for their physical beauty and sex appeal, qualities that can be deceitful and insubstantial. Such praise for a woman and wife is all the more impressive because of the accepted patriarchal dominance in the management of a Jewish household of the period (probably after the return from the Babylonian exile in 538 B.C.E. for this section of Proverbs). However, when we see a number of verses omitted, a little subversive reading around the text is also in order. We discover that these omissions are connected with her business acumen beyond the home as well as her domestic management and teaching (vv. 14-18, 21-27). Also omitted are the verses of praise that her children and husband offer her. At every Jewish Sabbath Eve meal in our own day, the whole of this portion (Prov 31:10-31) is often read or sung by a woman's husband and/or children. We could learn much from this loving ritual wisdom that every week tells a wife and mother how much she is loved and valued.

The responsorial Psalm 128 affirms that God's blessings are to be found in the ordinary joys of family relationships and work. Although this is a "song of ascents," a pilgrimage psalm for the journey up to Jerusalem and the Temple, the pilgrims bring with them to the holy place their daily joys and needs and hopes, for in these, and not only on pilgrimage, they are called to walk in God's ways. As we pray this psalm we might hold before God those families, known and unknown, for whom home and family is not a holy place but a place of violence and disunity, and ask for God's blessing on them.

Paul compares the Second Coming of Christ, the ultimate manifestation of God's justice to all creation, with two very different images that nevertheless emphasize the same truth about this future event, namely, that it will be unexpected—as unexpected as a thief in the night or the birth pangs that seize a woman. Just as we have no control over the timing of burglary or birth, the Day of the Lord will be according to God's *kairós*, his privileged decision-making time. Like the Thessalonians, like the slaves in the gospel parable, we have to be vigilant and alert to the signs of the times of the true prophets, not false prophets who can lull us into a complacency that is disastrous for our readiness for Christ's coming. Birth pangs come upon a woman suddenly; they are unexpected and painful, but they cannot be escaped if new life and joy is to come into the world. Just so, the birth pangs of the messianic age will be painful but will usher in the joy of the new age of the kingdom's fulfillment. Disciples are not to be skulking nighttime people but sons and daughters of the light that is already shining on us from the radiance of Christ's resurrection. One day this will blaze forth to burnish and transfigure all human and cosmic reality as the new heaven and new earth.

Thirty-fourth Sunday in Ordinary Time

The Solemnity of Our Lord Jesus Christ, Universal King

• Ezek 34:11-12, 15-17 • Ps 23:1-3, 5-6 • 1 Cor 15:20-26, 28 • Matt 25:31-46

Since its institution by Pius XI in 1925 until our own time, the liturgy of this feast has gradually shed its triumphalism and militarism. We do not march into the celebration of Christ the King with blasts of trumpets and drumbeats, but with the Son of Man's words about his identification with the poor and needy echoing in the ears of our heart. The pilgrimage of the church year that we have made in company with Matthew's Gospel leads us to this last and defining gospel about entrance into the kingdom of God where those who have been a blessing to others now receive the definitive blessing of the inheritance of the kingdom. Here is the arrival of Jesus, about whose coming the parables of the last few weeks have warned, challenged, and comforted us. And the images of the gospel flow together today when we hear of his coming as Son of Man, Shepherd, King, and Judge of humanity. The parable is often called "The Last Judgment," but in fact the judgment has already been made—determined by the way in which those who now stand before the Shepherd King have responded, or failed to respond, with mercy and hospitality, to those in need during their lives. What we hear is the sentencing, and the message is at its clearest: what we do *now* is a judgment that will be passed at the *not yet* time of Christ's final coming.

It is pointless to try to find any intrinsic reason for the imagery of "sheep" and "goats" except that it serves the theme and fact of end-time separation which Matthew has emphasized in his other parables of weeds and wheat (Matt 13:24-30), edible and inedible fish in the dragnet (Matt 13:47-50), and the five wise and five foolish maidens (Matt 25:1-13). Before the king is gathered humanity. It is for humankind that Jesus came, and Matthew has expanded our insight into the saving mission of Jesus from "the lost sheep of the house of Israel" (Matt 10:6) to hope for the Gentiles (Matt 12:21) and his response to the saving faith of the Canaanite woman (Matt 15:22-28) up to this parable of the last time. Jesus will appoint his disciples to carry on his mission in the great commissioning of the final verses of Matthew's Gospel when he sends them to "all the nations, baptizing them in the name of the Father and of the Son and of the Holy Spirit" (Matt 28:19).

For whom have the blessings of the kingdom been prepared by the Father "from the foundation of the world"? They are the people who have responded with merciful love and hospitality to the needs of others, just as Jesus did. We often see some of them on our TV screens or read about them in our newspapers in situations of disaster. But such people are also walking our streets in less spectacular and tragic circumstances. The needs they meet are listed: hunger, thirst, nakedness, sickness, imprisonment: these are needs that are representative, although not exhaustive, of universal pain and poverty. The surprise of the parable is the surprise of the ones on Christ's right hand, the place of honor, and their emphasis on "when was it that we *saw*" the Lord in others. Jesus' face is obscured by the faces of the suffering and vulnerable ones of the world, but he *is* there as the "Emmanuel," God-with-us, with whom Matthew begins (Matt 1:23) and ends (Matt 28:20) his Good News. He identifies himself with "the least of *my* brothers and sisters." The way to serve Christ is to serve one's neighbor—for the neighbor's sake. As Arland Hultgren comments:

> Gone is the view that the only way we can serve Christ (or God) is a prior commitment to him. The old argument that one must be religious in order to be moral—and so religious faith becomes only instrumental to ethics—goes by the board. The down-to-earth service of the person in need—without any sense of religious obligation or motivation—*that* is service to Christ![56]

This is the great surprise of the parable.

We might be tempted to ask: Why then be a Christian or worry about the Christian mission? Knowing the human tendency toward selfishness and exploitation of others, our compassion, self-sacrifice, and recognition of the precious dignity of every person should be more enabled by knowledge of Christ's saving servanthood and the values of his gospel. That this may happen is the reason why the gospel is preached (Matt 20:28).

With those on the left hand of the king, their response has been a reverse image of those on the right. Again there is the emphasis on *seeing*. They respond that they have *never seen* Jesus in any of the human suffering described. The sentencing goes beyond the issue of whether one is a believer or nonbeliever: if one has not responded to human suffering, one has not responded to Christ. The commandment to love God and its "like" command to love one's neighbor (Matt 22:34-40) converge here in their Christological significance. For those who failed in seeing the needs of those who suffer, there is separation and exclusion from the kingdom that Matthew describes in apocalyptic imagery. But Christ does not say that this was prepared for them by the Father "from the foundation of the world" as were the blessings of the kingdom. They have prepared the punishment for themselves. What this will actually mean at the end of the ages, we leave to God.

At the end of the church's year of grace, it may be helpful to take some longer reflection time to judge ourselves about our *now* in our preparation for the *not yet*.

How have we fed the hungry? Have we responded not only through our financial appeals and projects, especially in times of disaster, or to service calls in our parishes, but also to offering ourselves as food for those who hunger for friendship, for a listening ear and heart? Are we ready to be eucharistic people, broken and consumed by our service of and sacrifice for others?

Do we recognize how arid the lives of our sisters and brothers can be when they are dried up by a sense of failure and worthlessness? Can we offer them a drink of compassion and affirmation of their personal worth?

The homeless are on our streets in the thousands, and refugees and asylum seekers are seeking hospitality from oppression and injustice. If we can do nothing directly, do we support those in face-to-face ministry to them, become more informed about their plight, advocate for them by the ballot box, and pray for them? Can we see them as icons of our own inner homelessness, our sense of not-belonging, of searching for something or Someone "more"?

Exposure and nakedness are cruel human indignities. Life can be cold, not only when exposed to climatic conditions or social impoverishment. Have we stripped others naked by malicious gossip or failures in confidentiality? Do we leave our relationships in bitter cold through overt or subtle humiliation, rather than clothing them with the warmth of forgiving love?

We are all prisoners, each in our own way, to the reality that is sin. Some of us may minister with great compassion to those who are physically imprisoned, but in everyday life do we try to lead each other into freedom or lock one another out?

The sick are always with us: in our families, in our parishes, in hospitals and nursing homes. Do we care for them and visit them, or do they embarrass us, frighten us, seem to be a waste of our time? Do we fail to recognize them as "sacraments" of our own mortality?

When Jesus finishes this parable, he has nothing more to do than to show himself for the last time as Messiah of both the word and deed. Immediately after the parable the Shepherd King goes forth to his passion, for the love and salvation of humanity.

The prophet Ezekiel also speaks of the Day of the Lord with shepherd imagery. God is the true Shepherd King of his people, sensitive to their weariness and weakness, in contrast to the irresponsible and exploitative treatment of Judah's rulers (see Ezek 34:4-6). Under the care of the unfaithful shepherds, the people were scattered into many lands, but God, "I, myself" says God, will lead the flock back to their own land as if in a new exodus. Just as the Shepherd King of the gospel contrasts the *not doing* of the "goats" in contrast to the *doing* of the "sheep," so God will act for his sheep. God will seek out the lost, bring back the strays, bind up the wounds of the injured, care for the sick, and strengthen the weak—and all this without neglecting the strong and healthy, for all are subject to God's compassion and justice. But he will call to account those who have taken advantage of the vulnerability of others.

Our response to this reading is Psalm 23 which gathers together the themes of the Liturgy of the Word: the loving and intimate shepherding of God and the hospitality of the kingdom banquet offered to those who allow themselves to be guided along the Lord's way. All fear has gone; there remains only the confidence of eternal abiding with the Good Shepherd. One day this Shepherd came humbly and vulnerably among us as Emmanuel; on another day which neither we nor the psalmist have yet seen, the Shepherd King of the parable will come again in glory.

On this last Sunday of the liturgical year, Paul's vision embraces all human history: from the beginning of our human solidarity in Adam to our end in the glory of the Second Adam who will hand over all created reality to God the Father. On that day, says Paul, God will be "all in all." It is a huge and human hope—but when we remember today's gospel, we realize that this hope will be achieved by what may not seem so large: by the daily deeds of loving service of our sisters and brothers. These will transform the world and make it ready and able to be handed back as kingdom. Vatican II beautifully expressed this mystery in terms of the nurturing on earth of *human* values, quoting also from the Preface of today's feast:

> For after we have obeyed the Lord, and in his Spirit have nurtured on earth the values of human dignity, community and freedom, and indeed all the good fruits of our nature and enterprise, we will find them again, but freed of stain, burnished and transfigured. This will be so when Christ hands back to his Father a kingdom eternal and universal: "a kingdom of truth and life, of holiness and grace, of justice, love, and peace." On this earth that kingdom is already present in mystery. When the Lord returns, it will be brought to full flower.[57]

At what more wonderful point could we finish the Church's year of grace?

Notes

1. Eugene Peterson, *Christ Plays in Ten Thousand Places: A Conversation in Biblical Theology* (Sydney: Hodder & Stoughton, 2005) 113.

2. George Herbert, "Ungratefulness," *The Complete English Works* (New York: Everyman's Library, 1995) 79.

3. Catherine Mowry LaCugna, *God for Us: The Trinity and Christian Life* (San Francisco: HarperSanFrancisco, 1991) 272.

4. See Alice Walker, *The Color Purple* (London: The Women's Press, 1983) 167–68.

5. *De Trinitate*, VIII, 8, 12. Quoted by Benedict XVI in the Encyclical Letter, *Deus Caritas Est*, art. 19.

6. Vatican II, *Constitution on the Sacred Liturgy*, art. 14.

7. Anecdote recounted to the author.

8. Gerard W. Hughes s.j., Foreword to the New Edition of Donald Nicholl, *Holiness* (London: Darton, Longman and Todd Ltd., 2004) n.p.

9. Donald Senior, *The Gospel of Matthew* (Nashville: Abingdon Press, 1997) 36.

10. See Dietrich Bonhoeffer, *The Cost of Discipleship*, 6th edition (London: SCM Press Ltd, 1959) 95–102.

11. Gerard Manley Hopkins, "The Wreck of the Deutschland," *Poems and Prose of Gerard Manley Hopkins*, edited by W. H. Gardner and N. H. MacKenzie (Oxford: Oxford University Press, 1970) 22.

12. Etty Hillesum, *Etty: A Diary 1941–1943* (London: Triad Grafton Books, 1985) 113.

13. John J. Pilch, *The Cultural World of Jesus: Sunday by Sunday Cycle A* (Collegeville: Liturgical Press, 1995) 31–32.

14. Pontifical Biblical Commission, *The Jewish People and Their Sacred Scriptures in the Christian Bible*, 2002, art. 19.

15. Ibid., articles 19, 21.

16. Harold S. Kushner, *When Bad Things Happen to Good People* (London: Pan Books, 1982) 81.

17. M. Eugene Boring, "Matthew," *The New Interpreter's Bible*, vol. 8 (Nashville: Abingdon Press, 1995) 195.

18. Julian of Norwich, *Showings*, trans. Edmund Colledge, o.s.a., and James Walsh, s.j., The Classics of Western Spirituality (New York: Paulist Press, 1978) 293.

19. Ibid., 298.

20. See Elizabeth Johnson, *She Who Is: The Mystery of God in Feminist Theological Discourse* (New York: Crossroad, 1992) or Edwina Gateley, *A Warm, Moist, Salty God* (New York: Source Books, 1993).

21. Johnson, *She Who Is*, 4.

22. Mechtilde of Magdeburg, quoted in Marchienne Vroon Rienstra, *Swallow's Nest* (Grand Rapids, Michigan: William B. Eerdmans Publishing Company, 1992) 247.

23. Vatican II, *Dogmatic Constitution on the Church*, art. 8.

24. Brendan Byrne, s.j., *Lifting the Burden: Reading Matthew's Gospel in the Church Today* (Strathfield, NSW: St. Paul's Publication, 2004) 80.

25. Homily of Pope Benedict XVI at the Inauguration of his Pontificate, St. Peter's Square, April 24, 2005.

26. Brendan Byrne, s.j., *Romans*, Sacra Pagina Series, vol. 6 (Collegeville: Liturgical Press, 1996) 168.

27. Mary Catherine Hilkert, *Naming Grace: Preaching and the Sacramental Imagination* (New York: Continuum, 1998) 52.

28. Timothy Radcliffe, o.p., "Preaching to the Perplexed," *Priests & People* (December 2002) 444.

29. See "Passion of St. Perpetua," quoted in A. G. Hamman, "Les premiers martyrs de l'Eglise," *Les Pères dans la foi* (Paris: Desclée de Brouwer, 1979) 75.

30. William Shakespeare, *The Tragedy of Hamlet, Prince of Denmark*, in *The Complete Works*, second edition, General Editors Stanley Wells and Gary Taylor (Oxford: Clarendon Press, 2005) 345.

31. Hopkins, "God's Grandeur," *Gerard Manley Hopkins: Poems and Prose*, 27.

32. Based on a story from Martin Buber, *Tales of the Hasidim: Later Masters* (New York: Schocken Books, 1970) 245–46.

33. The statement of the Pontifical Biblical Commission, *The Jewish People and Their Sacred Scriptures in the Christian Bible* is a rich source that helps such discernment.

34. Senior, *The Gospel of Matthew*, 127–28.

35. Pedro Arrupe, s.j., "The Eucharist and Hunger," *Justice With Faith Today* (St. Louis: Jesuit Resources, 1980) 176–77.

36. Walter Brueggemann, *Cadences of Home: Preaching Among Exiles* (Louisville, KY: Westminster John Knox Press, 1997) 130.

37. Hopkins, "The Wreck of the Deutschland," *Gerard Manley Hopkins: Poems and Prose*, 33.

38. Francis Thompson, "The Kingdom of God," quoted in *Sound of Heaven: A Treasury of Catholic Verse*, ed. Russell Sparkes (London: St Paul's Publishing, 2001) 216.

39. The statues and dates of their victims' martyrdoms are: Grand Duchess Elizabeth of Russia, saint in the Orthodox Church, killed by the Bolsheviks, 1918; Manche Masemola, South African catechist aged 16, killed by his mother, 1928; Lucian Tapiedi, Papua, New Guinea, one of 12 Anglicans killed by Japanese invaders, 1942; Maximilian Kolbe, o.f.m., saint of the Roman Catholic Church, killed by the Nazis, 1943; Dietrich Bonhoeffer, German Lutheran pastor and theologian, executed by the Nazis, 1945; Esther John, Presbyterian evangelist in Pakistan, killed by her brothers, 1960; Martin Luther King, Jr., American Baptist pastor and campaigner for civil rights, assassinated, 1968; Wang Zhiming, Chinese Protestant pastor, killed in the Cultural Revolution, 1972; Janani Luwum, Ugandan Anglican Archbishop, assassinated during the rule of Idi Amin, 1977; Oscar Romero, Roman Catholic Archbishop of San Salvador, assassinated, 1980.

40. Elie Wiesel, *Five Biblical Portraits* (Notre Dame: University of Notre Dame Press, 1981) 124.

41. Josephus, *The Antiquities of the Jews*, Book XIV, V. 5.

42. William Shakespeare, *King Lear*, Act 4, sc. 5, 1179. Folio Text.

43. Jonathan Sacks, *The Dignity of Difference: How to Avoid the Clash of Civilizations* (London: Continuum, 2003) 190.

44. Megan McKenna, *Parables: The Arrows of God* (Maryknoll, New York: Orbis Books, 1994) 2.

45. Abraham Heschel, *Between God and Man: An Interpretation of Judaism* (New York: The Free Press, 1959) 122.

46. Pontifical Biblical Commission, *The Jewish People and Their Sacred Scriptures in the Christian Bible*, art. 175.

47. Vatican II, *The Church in the Modern World*, art. 62.

48. Judith Wright, "Grace," *Collected Poems 1942–1985* (Sydney, NSW: Angus & Robertson, 1994) 331–32.

49. Vatican II, *The Church in the Modern World*, art. 43.

50. Byrne, *Lifting the Burden*, 166.

51. Albert Camus, *The Plague*, trans. Robin Buss (London: Penguin Classics, 2002) 170.

52. "Thirteen Commitments: A Group of Bishops," *Concilium* 4 (1977): 109–11.

53. Daniel Harrington, *The Gospel of Matthew*, Sacra Pagina Series, vol. 1 (Collegeville: The Liturgical Press, 1991) 324.

54. Bede Jarrett, o.p., quoted in Flor McCarthy s.d.b., *Funeral Liturgies* (Dublin: Dominican Publications, 1999) 10.

55. *The Sayings of the Desert Fathers: The Alphabetical Collection*, trans. Benedicta Ward, s.l.g., rev. ed. (Kalamazoo: Cistercian Publications, 1984) 90.

56. Arland J. Hultgren, *The Parables of Jesus: A Commentary* (Michigan: William B. Eerdmans Publishing Company, 2002) 326–27.

57. Vatican II, *The Church in the Modern World*, art. 39.

6

"With the Gospel as our guide"

Short conversations between the Sunday Lectionary for Year A and the Rule of Benedict[1]

At the beginning of his Rule, St. Benedict encourages his followers to "set out on his path with the Gospel as our guide" (RB Prol 21), and in the last chapter he expresses his conviction of its worth by asking "what page or even what word of the divinely inspired Old and New Testaments is not a completely reliable guidepost for human life?" (RB 73.3). The placement of these two significant references to the importance of Scripture, the good news or "gospel" of both Testaments, makes them the bookends that hold the Rule in place as a particular interpretation of Christian discipleship. It is also a reminder of what Benedict knew well and demonstrated in his Rule: that all our words are under obedience to the Word of God.

The first Prologue reference is in the context of "faith that leads us to the performance of good works," the practical living out of the biblical good news that is applicable to all the people of God, not only those who follow the monastic way of life. In his last chapter, Benedict refers to scripture as the guidepost for *human* life, and so again universalizes the relevance of his Rule.

The following reflections, therefore, are offered as a kind of liturgical and biblical "chat room" into which those who are interested can enter for a conversation between themselves, the Lectionary readings, and the Rule of Benedict. In his Rule, Benedict frequently places the biblical word in the context of a direct address to the monk; for example, "If you hear this and respond 'I do!' God says to you" (Prol 16); "the Holy Scripture cries out to us" (RB 7.1); "for Scripture says to us" (RB 7.19). As we listen to the Sunday readings, or reflect on them before or after the liturgy as *lectio divina*, it is hoped that inviting Benedict to join us will add another dimension to our personal, practical, and human responses to the Word of God, no matter what our life situations. Like our conversations, there will be variations in length and intensity. There will be no attempt to talk through the three readings with Benedict, but usually to focus on one or two points. Inevitably, over the fifty-two weeks of the year, there will be some repeated conversations, just as with friends we often return to memories and issues that are more important than others, but these will be in different contexts and can serve to emphasize what Benedict considered most significant.

Benedict was convinced that the biblical word cannot be locked in the past. In his own fifth and sixth century life, he hears it speaking to his concerns for a new vision of community at the heart of a decadent society and in the midst of great social change. In such times there can be a temptation to withdraw nostalgically behind the barriers of the past, or to storm ahead into the future. Benedict was seduced by neither option. He chose a middle way, a lifestyle in which he tried to hold in dynamic balance both respect for individual differences and commitment to community, work and prayer, nature and grace.

Originally written for men and for monastic life in the Roman church, its wisdom has also been inclusive of women who for centuries have lived and adapted the Rule to the feminine. Beyond the monastery, this Rule that comes from the time of the undivided church has proved to have ecumenical appeal today for those longing for an often undefined, but strongly felt "something more" that could be shared among those of different Christian traditions. It is hoped, therefore, that there will be no gender, lifestyle, or faith barriers that prevent anyone's entry into this biblical, liturgical, and Benedictine chat room. Given its original genesis, and out of respect for this, references to and direct quotations from the Rule are left in the masculine.

First Sunday of Advent

To urge his community to watchfulness for God and attentive listening to God, Benedict quotes the opening words of today's second reading in the Prologue to his Rule (RB Prol 8). It is Benedict's first direct biblical quotation, and has an urgency that reflects the Church's call to expend new effort on our discipleship at the beginning of this new church year. Paul is also explicit about the "arms" that Christians should take up, and Benedict encourages his followers to take up the "powerful and shining weapons of obedience" in order to do peaceful battle for the Lord Christ (RB Prol 3), and also prayer which is an essential part of the Christian armory (RB Prol 4; Eph 6:18).

At the beginning of this new liturgical year the church calls us into the ways of peace with the words of the prophet Isaiah, so Benedict urges his communities at the beginning of his Rule to "seek peace and pursue it" (RB Prol 17). His double imperative is a reminder that we do not amble mindlessly into peace, but come to it by way of constant and often painful perseverance. The desire for "true and lasting life" which demands such a search requires practical action that is easily transplanted outside the monastery, namely, good and honest speech, and the discernment and commitment to good rather than evil (RB Prol 17).

The gospel warns us of the "unattended moment" when our discipleship is vulnerable to destructive forces because of mindless immersion in the ordinary and everyday that can lull us into forgetfulness of God, our beginning and end. God is present in the ordinary stuff of life: the people around us, our successes and failures, the beauty and terror of creation. As we grow in this awareness of God in our lives, our sense of our own self-importance decreases, and for this reason the first rung on Benedict's ladder of humility is "to utterly flee forgetfulness" by keeping the "fear of God always before one's eyes" (RB 7.10). The biblical meaning of "fear," "the root of wisdom" (Sir 1:20), is not a response to divine policing, but an expression of God's loving regard for us and our reverent yearning for God (RB 4.46-49). Even when life seems a dull and monotonous grind, there can be an inner excitement in this yearning that Michael Casey describes as "creative monotony."[2]

Second Sunday of Advent

Benedict was realistic about his communities. Then as now, and beyond the monastery, in our families, workplaces, parishes, or leisure activities, there may be "wolves" and "leopards," "lions" and "bears" with whom we have no wish to "lie down" in close association (Isa 11:6-9). It is our fidelity to the love of God present in our sisters and brothers, says Benedict, that tames our natural antipathies and urges us to "bear each other's weaknesses of both body and character with the utmost patience" (RB 72.5) and create peace and mutual acceptance.

Paul believes that the prayerful reflection on and study of the Scriptures will encourage the Roman disciples to hope in God who never gives up on them. Benedict, too, believed in holy and intent listening to or reading of the Scriptures. This would hand his monks a tool that would help them shape their lives after the example of Christ (RB 4.55; 48.4, 14, 18, 22). Paul writing to his first century Roman communities, and Benedict writing five centuries later for his communities, both urge their followers to treat one another with respect so that they can live together in harmony out of love of Christ (RB 72.4-11). Without this love, we are still in the desert wilderness out of which the Baptist calls us to repentance and conversion.

Third Sunday of Advent

For Benedict, as for James, patience is an important virtue. It is because of patient endurance in the request to join the monastery that a candidate is finally allowed to step over the threshold at the beginning of religious life (RB 58.3); it is by patience that one can persevere in this life through suffering and even injustice (RB 7.35, 42). Patience helps us to put up with the demands of the sick (RB 36.5), and with what is unattractive about those with whom we live (RB 72.5). And all this is not a gloomy stoicism, says Benedict, but a sharing in the sufferings (*passio*) of Christ with joy that expands our hearts so that we can run strongly toward the death that opens out onto the eternal life of the kingdom (Prol 49-50). Patience helps us not to lose heart and to keep running so that in death the Lord will come to meet us and welcome us into a share of his glory. This advent is the goal not only of the monastic life but also of every Christian life. It is one significant focus of this season, named for the coming of the Lord.

Fourth Sunday of Advent

Nowhere is Joseph or Mary mentioned specifically in the Rule of Benedict, presumably because their significance needed no mention. But Benedict praises qualities which today's gospel attributes to Joseph. He is described as a "righteous" man, and this is the kind of person that Benedict assures us will find a straight way to the tent of God's kingdom. Surely Joseph fits the profile that Benedict draws in the Prologue, quoting the words of Ps 15:2-3: "The person who walks blamelessly and acts justly; who speaks the truth candidly and has not committed fraud with his tongue; who does the neighbors no ill, nor listens to slander against him" (RB Prol 23-27). Because of his young wife, Joseph had to agonize over doing justice with love and close his ears to the slander and evil gossip that would have circulated if and when Mary was found to be with child before they came to live together. It can be interesting to read Benedict's gentle chapter on the election of an abbot and the qualities that the steward of the monastic household needs, and then reflect on God's election of Joseph to be the steward of the holy household of Mary and Jesus (see RB 64.5, 7, 21).

Christmas Day

Benedict does not refer specifically to the season of Christmas, but central to his spirituality are humanity and humility, two words deriving from the Latin *humus*—earth, soil. In the Incarnation, the Word of God takes on our human clay, earths himself in our humanity with a humility that is so radical that it can be grasped only by faith. Christ's humanity is the new "Jacob's ladder" that is stretched between heaven and earth (John 1:51; RB 7.6). It is out of deep and humble love of Christ, says Benedict, that one can be true to one's humanity. What so often makes us miss a rung on the ladder of humility are the difficulties that arise in our relationships with other people when we fail to affirm the human dignity which they have in the eyes of God. From birth to death, the vulnerable Child humbled himself most radically to take on our humanity and affirmed it in all those whom he met: poor and rich, friend and enemy. They are gathered there already at the Christmas crib. To read RB 7, "On Humility" through the Christmas prism may give it a new significance.

Feast of the Holy Family

Benedict names the abbot as "father" (cf. RB 2.24; 33.5), usage that may have grown out of Egyptian reflection on the biblical use of *abba*. Jesus uses this to express his intimate, loving relationship with his Father. We do this relationship a disservice when we translate *abba* as "daddy," for it was not childish terminology but an expression of adult endearment between a son/daughter and father, something closer to our "dad." Benedict does not want an infantile relationship between the abbot and the members of his community. Moreover, nowhere does Benedict use the word "family" in his Rule, and the model of the human family for a monastery or religious community of adults united by very different bonds has inbuilt difficulties. This is not to discount the truth that parents, both *abba* and *amma* (mother), can be seen reflected in RB 2, "The Qualifications of an Abbot." The interpersonal relationships that are so important for today's families who are called to holiness as communities of love are suggested: the need for wise teachers—more by example than by word (RB 2.11-15); equal love for all members, but accommodating to individual differences; the avoidance of favoritism; respect for different personalities (RB 2:22, 31-32).

The Epiphany of the Lord

In his commentary on Gregory the Great's *Life of Saint Benedict*, Adalbert de Vogüé remarks that through the discovery of the young Benedict in his cave at Subiaco by a priest and by shepherds, Gregory is evoking the memory of the seeking and discovery of the Christ Child by the shepherds and the Magi.[3] We can imagine that Benedict would have been very fond of the Magi, those persistent and wise seekers of the Child to whom they wished to offer their homage. Benedict believed that one of the most important signs of the genuineness of a monastic vocation was that he/she "really seeks God" (RB 58.7). This seeking is, of course, a response to God's seeking, without which the search could not begin (RB Prol 14–15). It is a journey of a lifetime, a journey of love (RB Prol 37-50), which makes daily demands of fidelity (RB 7.27-29) to the one who was born King of the Jews.

It may have been surprising that it was strangers from the East who were among the first to come seeking Christ. It may be just as wonderfully surprising today that those who seek Christ in religious life, or in Christianity, are often "strangers": the unexpected and even unchurched who somehow, somewhere, glimpse and follow the leading of a God-given star shining in the dark night of alienation or rising over thick clouds of often inarticulate longing for deeper meaning in life. In 2005, the BBC three-part TV feature, *The Monastery*, which invited five very modern men to live the monastic life for forty days and nights at the Benedictine abbey of Worth, UK, while TV cameras tracked their progress, attracted an audience of three million viewers. In the month following, the Worth website received 400,000 hits, and hundreds of people signed up to come on retreats at the abbey.[4]

The Baptism of the Lord

Benedict quotes from Isaiah's first Servant Song, today's first reading, in his chapter on "The Installation of the Abbot" (RB 64.13). The Servant refrains from resorting to power play when dealing with people. What is given to the Servant by God is a spirit of God's own merciful love for his people. It is a spirit of the divine gentleness that, as Isaiah says, does not break the bent reed of those who are weak and struggling, yet also does justice. The abbot is to act with this same strong love for the weak members of his community (RB 64.13).

Matthew describes the spirit given to the servant as descending in the symbolic form of a dove when it comes upon Jesus after his baptism by John the Baptist. Jesus is the gentle Servant par excellence and so, as Terrence Kardong comments, "Benedict compares the abbot to the Servant, which also connects him to the nonviolent Jesus, who preferred to be crucified rather than return evil for evil."[5] If only political power and the ecclesial and individual authority of all the baptized could be exercised with this same gentle strength.

First Sunday of Lent

Much of Benedict's chapter on "The Observance of Lent" (RB 49) was inspired by the fifth-century pope St. Leo the Great's pastoral Lenten sermons, rather than by a strict legislative tone. Benedict transplanted the spirit of Leo's exhortation to the wider church into his monastic community, and Christ's faithful in today's wider church can find much to replant in their own lives.

Only in this chapter and nowhere else in the Rule, does Benedict mention "joy." In these weeks, each monk is to offer to God "with the joy of the Holy Spirit" (RB 49.6) something beyond his usual spiritual endeavors. This offering is not to be undertaken with grim determination, but as positive, spontaneous, and liberating effort that will prepare for Holy Easter "with the joy of spiritual desire" (RB 49.7). Such longing is a gift of the Holy Spirit who holds in our hearts the memory that Christ has conquered sin and death, and who enlivens our human clay with the Breath of God. Lent, therefore, is the paradoxical season that reminds us that, for Christian disciples, joy is born out of sorrow. Tears and joy, passion and resurrection, Lent and Easter are necessarily and intimately related. This is why Benedict says that at all times the lifestyle of a monk should have a Lenten character (RB 49.1). Lent is "sacramental," a privileged time of focus and fidelity that reminds us of what all our life should be. Benedict strikes a delicate balance between the individual and communal effort to live with greater fidelity during Lent. He speaks of the Lenten efforts of "each one" in the community, but then urges "all" to support one another by their witness of single-minded commitment to their way of life (RB 49.2-3). He is realistic and humane in his expectations. The monk should deny himself only "some" sleep, food, chatter, and joking. A dour community was not to Benedict's liking, just as a dour church should not be to ours. Too much fasting, too much keeping vigil, too much frosty silence, can end up the same as too little—in revolt—and then back to overeating, oversleeping, over-gossiping!

Second Sunday of Lent

On the mountain of transfiguration the Father's voice is heard: "listen to him." Listening to the Beloved Son could be a summary of Benedict's teaching. Aquinata Böckmann comments that the whole Rule lies between two words: *obsculta* ("listen") in RB Prol 1 and *pervenies* ("you will reach") in its last verse (RB 73.9).[6] Like the disciples on the mountain of transfiguration, Benedict calls his disciples to listen: to obedient, loving attention to and action for Christ, with the gospel as their guide (RB Prol 1-3, 21).

After the brief transformative brilliance of Jesus, after his taking counsel with his ancestors, after the voice and the cloud and the fear, there is "no one except Jesus"—un-transfigured—to touch the fearful Peter, James, and John and raise them up to follow him down to the plain. For Benedict, the following and love of Jesus was to hold first place (RB 4.10, 20-21) in both the high and low points of our lives. No one except Jesus can bring us to the transfiguration of everlasting life (RB 72.11-12).

Third Sunday of Lent

Benedict asks us to open our eyes and listen "with astonished ears" to God's voice in the words that Benedict quotes from Psalm 95, the responsorial psalm of today's liturgy: "Today, if you hear his voice, do not harden your hearts" (RB Prol 9-10). The Samaritan woman at the well certainly opened her eyes and listened with astonished ears, the ears of her heart, to Jesus. He recognizes this woman as one whom Benedict would describe as desiring life and longing to see good days (RB Prol 15), and she searches, quests, and questions in Jesus' presence, responding to him as another un-expected seeker of God.

In contrast to the Samaritan woman are the grumbling Israelites—and grumbling monks. Grumblers exasperated both God and Benedict! In his Rule, Benedict is very explicit about the fact that he regards grumbling as an evil (RB 34.6-7), as a kind of pervasive and almost compulsive negativity about most aspects of life: about obedience (RB 5.14), the distribution of goods that respects individual differences (RB 34.6), the amount of drink provided (RB 40.9). Despite outward compliance, the heart can still be grumbling and negating the worth of one's actions before God who sees to our personal depths (RB 5.17-19). Out of a grumbling heart come harmful words that run down the reputation of others (RB 4.39-40), and Benedict seems to suggest that those who loaf around the monastery may be the ones most susceptible to this evil. Constant grumbling can be corrosive to the monk's commitment and eventually contribute to exclusion from the community, at least for some time, until he becomes repentant and reconciled. For Christians who are grumblers in any life situation, the call is that of the responsorial psalm: "Harden not your hearts" (Ps 95:8).

Fourth Sunday of Lent

God looks to the heart and not to outward appearances, God tells the prophet Samuel, and so it is the youngest of Jesse's eight sons that is surprisingly anointed for kingship. Benedict impressed on his communities this importance of the heart, of entering into and living from one's interiority that is the root and source of all one's inner truth, and is grounded in God. Monastic formation might be described as education of the heart, the ongoing conversion that changes it and directs it away from superficialities towards God. Progress in this way of life makes the monk's heart swell "with the unspeakable sweetness of love" and, like a good marathon runner, enables him "to race along the ways of God's commandments" (RB Prol 49). As with the monk, so with all Christians: our hearts should be open to love and truth, not concealing malice or deceit in the heart (RB 4.24). From the heart we should speak what we think, without any hypocrisy (RB Prol 26). God will raise up those who are humble of heart (RB 7.8), and even though we may not always be mindful of God, God is always mindful of us, searching our hearts out of longing for their love (RB 7.14).

Fifth Sunday of Lent

After Jesus has raised Lazarus from the dead he calls on those who witnessed this great sign to unbind him and let him go free. It is another powerful and poignant sign: others are to be involved in freeing Lazarus for the life that Jesus has given him again. In RB 72, Benedict speaks of "The Good Zeal That Monks Ought To Have," the zeal that leads to God and eternal life, contrasting it with evil and bitter zeal. He implies that everyone in the monastery (and we might also say in a family, in a community) has both strengths and weaknesses of body and character, some good zeal and some evil zeal. Each one of us depends on others for our "unbinding" through the patient, self-sacrificing love that enables us to walk freely together toward the promise of everlasting life in him who is "the resurrection and the life." Without this unbinding for free and joyful life, we are bound, and can bind others, in a restricting and sad existence that can become a "hellish" alienation from God and our sisters and brothers (RB 72.1).

Palm Sunday of the Lord's Passion

Isaiah's call to listen daily like a disciple with the open ears of our heart is echoed by Benedict as the first obedience to which he calls his followers (RB Prol 1), and is repeated throughout the Rule as an obedience not only to God (e.g., RB Prol 9, 16, 24, 39), but also to the abbot (RB 6.6), to one another (RB 3.2; 71), to holy reading (RB 4.55). During this Holy Week, more than during any week in the church year, we are reminded that our listening and our obedience is to the paschal mystery which Paul sings to us in the great Christological hymn (Phil 2:6-11). In each year of the three-year cycle, this is the second reading for Palm Sunday. In his chapter "On Humility," Benedict quotes directly from Phil 2:7 (RB 7.34). The Christ who became the obedient self-emptying Servant, even unto death, is the model for the monk's humble obedience. Love for Christ, and trust in him who was raised from death on a cross to reign as the cosmic Christ over all creation, will progressively form the monk to hear the will of God in the words of his superior, even when hard and difficult obedience is asked. Dialogue with the one in authority, discernment which is devoid of self-interest—these are acceptable, but the final and radical response is to trust oneself to the God of the humbled and exalted Servant (RB 68).

Easter Sunday

The celebration of Holy Easter, the joyful goal of our spiritual desire, is here (RB 49.7). A charming story recounted by Gregory in the Dialogues[7] witnesses to the truth that we can also meet the Easter Jesus and his joyful grace in our human encounters.

The young hermit Benedict, says Gregory, had lost track of the date of Easter as he was so distanced from other Christians. Our Lord appeared to a priest who had just prepared a meal for his Easter festivities, and told him that while he had a fine feast, Benedict was suffering from hunger. Immediately the priest set out to search for Benedict, a long and difficult journey (and presumably with some of his Easter feast!), "among the steep hills and the low valleys and the hollow pits." Eventually finding him in his cave at Subiaco, the two of them prayed, blessed God, and then sat down together for some pleasant conversation. The priest said to Benedict: "Get up. Let us take some food. For today is Easter." The man of God replied, "I know that it is Easter because I have the honor of seeing you." How wonderful it would be if we could all recognize the Easter mystery in our sisters and brothers, in their companionship and conversation, and in simple shared meals—and if they could have the same joyful experience with us.

Second Sunday of Easter

When Benedict first speaks of faith in the Prologue (RB Prol 21), he uses a Jewish Passover image. On the Exodus night the Hebrews were to eat their meal with "your loins girded, your sandals on your feet, and your staff in your hand" (Exod 12:11), in urgent readiness to obey their God who was calling them forth from slavery into freedom. Benedict tells his community: ". . . let us belt our waists with faith that leads to the performance of good works," in readiness for their new exodus of obedience "with the Gospel as our guide."

At the end of her chapter on the Prologue, Esther de Waal comments that what the Prologue teaches us is the paschal Christ:

> . . . the Christ risen in fullness from the grave, the risen Christ who has come through death-embracing love into his fullness which is our liberation from the dark powers within and without. In Benedict's school we shall learn Christ, not in any intellectual or cerebral way but in heart and mind and feeling.[8]

This is the Christ who came to Thomas to free him from his doubts. What Thomas learned in his heart at that moment is summarized in his deep cry of faith: "My Lord and my God!"

After all his protestations, the gospel does not record Thomas as touching Christ's wounds, but as the Iona community sings, "Christ makes of his own a touching place." Benedict knew that in the wounded and vulnerable ones in our midst Christ can be touched in faith, and so his special concern was for the sick (RB 36), the frail aged and young children (RB 37), the poor and the travelers who are searching not only for a lodging but also for somewhere for their spirits to be at home (RB 53.15). Blessed are we who see this and believe; blessed are those who can recognize resurrection in nail holes.

Third Sunday of Easter

Hospitality is central to Benedictine community life. It is, as Kathleen Norris says, "a tool that keeps us focused, not on ourselves, but on the divine presence [that] is everywhere" (RB 19.1).[9] In RB 19, Benedict is speaking of our being mindful of our ever-mindful God when we are praying the psalms at the Work of God (the Prayer of the Church or Divine Office), but the radical hospitality that Benedict demands of his communities should prolong this mindfulness because "All guests who arrive should be received as Christ," for he himself will say, 'I was a stranger and you took me in'" (RB 53.1). Guests are to be greeted eagerly with "every mark of love" (RB 1980 53.3), with prayer, with symbolic gestures, with the reading of scripture, and with a meal.

Every Benedictine community is something of an Emmaus. The Incarnation is God's most amazing hospitality to us, and on the way to Emmaus the risen Christ, who has welcomed death and overcome it, continues to both offer and receive hospitality. He is hospitable to the disillusionment of the two disciples on the road who have turned their backs on Jerusalem and the mystery of salvation that has been enacted there. He greets them, shares the Scriptures with them, but does not impose himself on them, acting as if to go on when they reach the village to which they were going. He gives them the opportunity to offer him hospitality. A shared meal, revelatory gestures, a departure—all this involves the kind of disciples which Benedict wants his monks to be: hospitable people with burning hearts and eagerness to run back to, not away from life and salvation (RB Prol 49). The hospitality of Emmaus was an event of conversion, and Joan Chittister believes that "Hospitality is the way we turn a prejudiced world around, one heart at a time."[10] Our contemporary world has need of such hospitality.

Fourth Sunday of Easter

Benedict often compares his community to a flock, with the abbot as shepherd. The pastoral role of the abbot is exercised in imitation of Christ's shepherding and compassionate care, especially for the wounded and straying members of the community (RB 27.8-9). Just as in today's parable John emphasizes that the sheep follow their shepherd because he knows them individually, calling them "by name," so Benedict expects his abbot to know his "sheep" personally, with their individual strengths and weaknesses. He can then call the strong to a more challenging following of Christ, and gently encourage the weak (RB 2.32; 64.19). The abbot's wise discernment of the character and understanding of each member of the community will establish mutual trust. He is not to use his authority to play power politics with the members of the community, but he must act with justice towards them and before God (RB 63.2).

Fifth Sunday of Easter

Although the monastic life is unthinkable and unlivable without the Scriptures, new methods and approaches to biblical interpretation have developed in our own day.[11] To Benedict can be applied what this document says in regard to patristic methodology: "Their chief concern being to live from the Bible in communion with their brothers and sisters, the fathers were usually content to use the text of the bible current in their own context."[12] Allegory and typology were woven together ". . . always for a pastoral and pedagogical purpose, convinced that 'everything that has been written has been written for our instruction'" (see 1 Cor 10:11).[13] In today's second reading, Christ is described as "a living stone." In his Prologue and later (RB Prol 28; RB 4.50), Benedict reflects the patristic approach by combining this verse with Psalm 137:9 and the vengeful bashing of the heads of the Babylonian babies against the rocks. For our comfort, rather than discomfort, this verse is accepted as inspired Scripture—not to encourage baby bashing, but as an example of the abrasive honesty of psalmic prayer. Although we may not dare to say it, except to God, what parent or teacher or religious superior has not felt like this at some time! To put this reaction into prayer before God is to offer it for healing in our helplessness. Benedict sees Christ as a "spiritual rock" against which the wrongful thoughts of the heart should be dashed in the battle against temptation.[14] We cannot avoid such thoughts, but we are responsible for what we do about them. To help with such temptation, Benedict also advises the monk to seek the help of one of the spiritual counselors (wise elders) as well as his abbot (RB 4.50; 46.5-6), just as today we might seek the guidance of a spiritual director or wise friend.

Sixth Sunday of Easter

Jesus' love for us is unconditional, and Benedict emphasizes that this is the kind of love that we should return to him. Early in his Rule, one of the tools of good works that Benedict hands the monk is to "Prefer nothing to the love of Christ" (RB4.21). In RB 72, regarded as the climax, and indeed the foundation of the whole Rule, he says, "Let them prefer *absolutely* nothing to Christ" (RB 72.11). Aquinata Böckmann sees this as Benedict's hope that the monk's love of Christ will become increasingly more ardent. In words that have application to the life journey of every disciple, not only monastics, she writes:

> Initial enthusiasm must grow deeper, become stronger through difficulties and discouragement (Prol 48), become more radical and permeate the entire person. The monastic is ever in danger of preferring something else to Christ: persons, his own honor, comfort, self-interest. But there is also the grace of a second or third conversion, chances for a fresh decision.[15]

Seventh Sunday of Easter

The Ascension of the Lord

Psalm 47 praises God as king over all the earth, and its use in today's Liturgy of the Word declares the theme of this feast: that the reign of God is the transcendent reality that Christ inaugurated. So the first title that Benedict gives Christ is that of "King." To do spiritual battle for Christ, one takes up "the powerful and shining weapons of obedience" (RB Prol 3). In contemporary culture, both kingship and military terminology is not much favored, and we have to search for relevant contemporary language to express spiritual realities. In Benedict's time, however, the power struggles between great and lesser kings were a social reality, and he uses this language symbolically to encourage his monks to fight for the King whose authority and service will be rewarded with a share in the heavenly kingdom (RB Prol 50).

The Ascension celebrates the return of Christ to his kingdom, his own "homeland," and at the end of the last chapter of his Rule (RB 73.8), just as he had at the end of the Prologue (RB Prol 49-50), Benedict speaks directly to everyone who is "hastening to the heavenly home" with energy and commitment. Benedict has no time for lazy and negligent monks who stand around the monastery, gazing into the heavens, but doing little to help themselves or anyone else to arrive at our heavenly home (RB 73.7-9).

Pentecost Sunday

Early in his Rule, and quoting Rev 2:7, Benedict reminds his followers that "Whoever has ears for hearing should listen to what the Spirit is saying to the churches" (RB Prol 11). He follows this with words from and references to Psalm 34, a psalm that was much used in baptismal catechesis in the early church, given its emphasis on the call and presence of God and the enlightenment of those seeking the One who is a refuge especially for the weak and brokenhearted (see RB Prol 12-18). Benedict saw his monasteries as ecclesial communities, sensitively attuned to the Spirit together with all the local churches. Pentecost is the celebration not so much of the birth of the church, but of its members—in and beyond the monastery—who are church.

Benedict ends his chapter "On Humility" with an acclamation of the Holy Spirit as the one who works within us, healing us, making us passionate lovers of God rather than fearful slave drivers of ourselves (RB 7.67-70). Life is to be seen in the positive terms of the love of God and the daily disposition to do what is good, and delight in it.

As Pentecost ends the Easter season, we might well reflect again on what Benedict says about the Holy Spirit in RB 49.6. Even though he is speaking about the observance of Lent, it is the joy of the Holy Spirit that urges a monk to be generous and self-disciplined in preparation for holy Easter. At Pentecost, the fruits of this are harvested.

The Most Holy Trinity

The way in which the Persons of the Trinity are in dynamic communion, the way in which Paul encourages his Corinthians to relate to one another, the way in which Benedict describes the good zeal of a community in RB 72, all flow from love.

As Benedict describes a monk's profession, after he has pronounced his promises he casts himself on the love of the Triune God and the love of his many brethren (RB 58.19-23). The newly professed has placed his promises on the altar, and he then sings the "Suscipe" ("Receive me, Lord") three times. The whole community repeats this verse of Psalm 119:116, adding after the third repetition the "Glory be . . . ." With this praise of the Trinity, the icon of every community, ringing in his ears and heart, the newly professed then prostrates himself at the feet of the very human community in which he is committing himself to God. These are the brothers who, individually or communally, will show him the love of God that will encourage him along the way of life to which he has just committed himself—or they will disappoint and hinder him.

When the Work of God (the Liturgy of the Hours) is prayed, Benedict writes that the doxology is to be added at the end of each psalm, and as it is said the monks are to bow their bodies as a sign of reverence for the Triune God (RB 9.7; 11.3). The body has always been considered important in liturgy, for we worship as whole persons, not just as talking heads.

The Body and Blood of Christ

Every year on this solemnity it is probably worth reminding ourselves of the comment in *RB 1980* that: "To the modern reader the scarcity of references to the Eucharist in RB may seem scandalous."[16] The term *eucharistía* is not found in RB, but in RB 63.4 Benedict speaks of *communio* when the brothers approach "for the kiss of peace and communion" during what would probably have been a Communion service outside of Mass.

In RB 38, "The Weekly Reader," Benedict mentions that the weekly reader during meals should begin his service on Sunday, and after Mass and Communion. In relation to this, de Vogüé comments that: "Communion was received at the end of Mass on Sundays and feast days and outside Mass on ordinary days."[17] Whatever may have been the eucharistic practice in Benedict's time, and its adaptation according to liturgical renewal down the centuries, there is one necessary constant: the love which brothers and sisters must have for one another, the communion which is taken to and flows from the liturgy of the Eucharist. Without this love, the bread that is broken and the cup that is shared is an empty ritual.

Second Sunday in Ordinary Time

What the Isaian Servant, John the Baptist, and Paul offered to God were lives of obedient and humble praise in response to the divine call. In their own times and places they could each cry out: "Here I am . . . I delight to do your will" (Ps 40:8). This was also Benedict's hope for his monks (RB 5.1). Although (perhaps surprisingly) he does not quote from today's responsorial Psalm 40, we could pray this psalm as both a thanksgiving hymn in gratitude for God's attentive listening to our cries, and as a pledge of our obedience to God. "Here I am" (RB Prol 18), conscious of God's presence, of his piercing the ears of our hearts so that we can "Listen" (RB Prol 1). This imagery reminds us of the ancient custom in which the ears of a servant/slave were pierced by the master as a sign of his ownership. The Christian disciple has a Master who does not enslave but liberates.

Third Sunday in Ordinary Time

Just as Jesus' first spoken words in Matthew's Gospel are about repentance and the kingdom, so at the beginning of his Rule Benedict describes the kingdom as the final goal of both monastic and Christian life (RB Prol 50). It is God who calls us to the kingdom, and the journey to it is by the response of faith that is translated into action, that witnesses to the reigning presence of God in our world, and that is guided by the gospel (RB Prol 21–22). For Benedict, "Gospel" was the good news of both Old and New Testaments (RB 73.3).

Following Jesus always demands some dispossession. For the first disciples it was boats and nets, a good work situation, and also their family ties. In RB 33, "Whether the Monks Should Consider Anything Their Own," the dispossession of material things is an outward and physical sign of the monk's gift of his whole person to God in the monastic context. The radical dispossession that is asked of the monk at his profession has the same significance (RB 58:24-26). And yet it is profitable to read the very next chapter after RB 33, and see how Benedict was concerned that the monks should receive whatever provisions they needed, with an emphasis on individual differences that must be respected by the abbot, without favoritism on his part, and without grumbling on the part of the community (RB 34). The same consideration is obvious in RB 55, "The Clothing and Footwear of the Brothers," and this is more important than our amused tolerance of archaic practices or unpleasant memories of the lack of privacy in boarding schools or some religious houses. Benedict does not encourage infantile reliance on the superior. He wants material needs to be met by those who wisely manage the house of God (and themselves) so that its members can seek the kingdom of God with greater freedom and commitment and less entanglement in material and economic concerns (RB 2.35-40; 31).

Fourth Sunday in Ordinary Time

"There was a man whose life was holy. His name was Benedict, and he was blessed by grace and by name," so Gregory the Great begins his life of St. Benedict,[18] and the gospel that is read on Benedict's feast day is the same as for this Sunday—the Beatitudes.

"Seek . . . Seek . . . Seek . . ." the prophet Zephaniah urges those who stand on the brink of disaster, and whose only hope is in God. It is God who is always the first seeker, says Benedict, taking the initiative in calling workers from the crowd (RB Prol 14). To seek God must be a priority for every member of a Benedictine community, from novice to abbot. The first concern in discerning a novice's vocation to the monastic life is "whether he really seeks God" (RB 58.7), and the main concern of the abbot is to safeguard spiritual priorities, not the material prosperity of the monastery. He will do this by seeking first the kingdom of God, and then he will be assured of no lack of pastoral resources (RB 2.35-36).

Zephaniah elaborates on two qualities that are important in the seeking of God: integrity and humility. Integrity is much dependent on an honest tongue, and Benedict is aware of the pain and disunity that we can inflict on one another by hollow greetings of peace or false protestations. What he asks is that all should "Seek the truth in both your heart and with your mouth" (RB 4.28). A rhythm of speech and silence is helpful to the development of serenity and wisdom, as is the avoidance of tasteless and harmful jokes.

"On Humility" (RB 7) is the second longest chapter of the Rule, and here is not the place for a detailed comment on such a complex chapter. Perhaps it is sufficient to say that Benedict sees humility as a grounding of one's humanity, an acceptance of our place in the universe, and a refusal to succumb to the primeval temptation: to be like God. It is, therefore, a chapter about right relationships with both God and one's brothers and sisters.

Fifth Sunday in Ordinary Time

Benedict challenges his monks to lifelong perseverance in their way of life. There is always the danger of allowing one's commitment to the monastic way—as with commitment to marriage—to become, in terms of today's gospel, "tasteless" and "unenlightened," without the savor or light of Christ. Such perseverance is the stability asked of the monastic candidate from the beginning of his arrival in the monastery (RB 58.9, 17) until his death (RB Prol 50). As Michael Casey remarks:

> Stability comes from the verb *stare*, to stand. We all know that it is very difficult to remain standing for a long period without moving. The best way to remain upright is not to stay still but to keep walking. We can walk for much longer periods than we can stand, because the various muscle systems are alternately worked and rested. Stability is not immobility. It is the knack of remaining constant in the midst of change.[19]

A great help to such stability is a community that assists the individual to pace him/herself consistently and energetically. Such companions encourage one another over the rough spots (RB 58.8), until their walk eventually breaks into a run and they reach death's finishing line with hearts that "swell with the unspeakable sweetness of love" and readiness for the kingdom (RB Prol 49-50).

Sixth Sunday in Ordinary Time

In today's gospel Jesus teaches that disciples are to live from the heart, the root and source of our inner truth. For Benedict, the essence of living from the heart, from the awareness of one's deepest and most intimate and true identity, meant conversion from the superficial self to a new person in Christ. To give examples from just two chapters of the Rule, the "Prologue" and "On Humility": listening, speaking, obeying, loving, must all be deeds of the heart understood in this way. (RB Prol 1, 26, 40, 49). And when he speaks of humility, Benedict frequently refers to the heart. Perhaps a profitable *lectio* for today might be to read RB 7, and give time to ponder those verses where we meet the "heart," and pray our "yes" to what God asks us in these words. As Thomas Merton writes: "Deep in our hearts is the most profound meaning of our personality, which is that we say 'yes' to God, and the spark is always there. All we need to do is to turn towards it and let it become a flame."[20]

Seventh Sunday in Ordinary Time

Benedict was well aware how destructive the lack of forgiveness and reconciliation in a community could be, and how easily "the thorns of quarreling" can spring up in a group that lives closely and constantly together. For this reason, the Lord's Prayer is to be recited at the end of every Morning (Lauds) or Evening Prayer (Vespers). In the morning the prayer is that during the coming day God may "Forgive as we forgive"; and in the evening, it is a significant examination of how this forgiveness has been offered and received (RB 13.12-

13). No day should end without the making of peace between those who have quarreled, lest the wounded relationship fester when the thorn is not removed quickly (RB 4.73). Each member of the community, therefore, makes a solemn and daily pledge to be a person of forgiveness and reconciliation. It may strike us as strange that in RB 13 Benedict says that the contemporary practice was for the superior only to recite the Lord's Prayer until the final petition: "But deliver us from evil." Terrence Kardong suggests that this may be explained by a comment of Augustine to the point that some people refrain from saying the prayer and so consider that they are not bound by it![21] Benedict emphasizes that he wants his community to listen to and speak from a forgiven and forgiving heart to this pattern of all Christian prayer.

It is not difficult to see the wider relevance that this prayer and practice could have for families or other close-knit communities.

Eighth Sunday in Ordinary Time

Many contemporary monasteries are discovering that one reason why comparatively well-off people are seeking hospitality for a short or longer time is because they are searching for refuge from the consumerist culture in which they live and which imposes so many pressures.[22] They seem to find sanctuary in a human environment where people have made a radical commitment to serve God, not wealth. This is the core value in RB 33.3-4. If monks have neither their own wills nor private possessions at their disposal, there is nothing to exercise consumerist tyranny over them—unless they decide in favor of some indulgence in private ownership which Benedict describes as a "vice" (RB 33.1). To prevent this, Benedict has a humane and balanced approach to the needs of his community: respect for what monks need for their work (RB 32), respect for individual differences (RB 34) and the pastoral attention that must be paid to these, especially by the abbot and the cellarer (RB 31). The latter is the one who reflects many of the abbatial qualities that make him a peacemaker and model of kindness in the minefield (even in a monastery!) of economics. Very expressively, Benedict warns both abbot and cellarer that they should not be *turbulentus* (RB 31.1; 64.16)—frenetic, excitable, restless—so that their brothers will not, in their turn, be *turbulenti*, but will be enabled to have faith in the provident God that today's gospel proclaims.

Ninth Sunday in Ordinary Time

"The ability to bring forth the right word from scripture for the occasion, or a saying derived from scripture, was the principal attitude that characterized an abba among early monks."[23] Mary Forman, o.s.b., makes the same point when she speaks of the desert mothers (ammas) as scripture scholars.[24] Benedict obviously followed in this tradition. He builds his Rule on the Word of God, and so this is also to be the foundation of the lives of his followers. In RB Prol 33-34, Benedict quotes directly from today's gospel. Christ, present in his Word, is the unshakable rock for the monk, but his stability depends on not only listening to the Word but also translating it into action (RB Prol 35).

One of the tools of good works is to "Listen intently to holy reading" (RB 4.55), and Benedict seems to suggest that this flows consequentially into frequent prayer (RB 4.56). The repeated mention of *lectio divina* (sacred reading) in RB 48, "The Daily Manual Labor" (in vv. 1, 4-5, 10, 13-15, 17-18, 22-23), underlines Benedict's concern for a balance between liturgy, *lectio*, labor and leisure. *Lectio divina* is not reading for information but for formation—by God—who widens our vision and our awareness of the human and the divine by conversation between the Word and our own lives. We need to be all the more discerning of formative reading today when, in contrast to Benedict's times, we are bombarded by so many printed, electronic, and "podcast" words, some of great value, but others of dubious and often enervating quality.

Tenth Sunday in Ordinary Time

Today's first and gospel readings are both passionate cries for mercy over sacrifice. That Benedict had heard these words with the ear of his heart is especially evident from his expectations of the abbot—and can be just as applicable to leaders in church, family, or government. In the middle of the chapters dealing with the penal code (RB 23-30) is the original and pastoral chapter, "The Abbot's Preoccupation with the Excommunicated" (RB 27). The very title alerts us to the fact that this is no secondary concern of the abbot, but is of high priority. Benedict is both realistic and compassionate about the failures of his monks. After the example of Jesus in today's gospel, and quoting directly from it, he writes: "it is not the healthy but the sick who need a physician" (RB 27.1; Matt 9:12), and so the troubled and troublesome monk was to be a central pastoral concern of the abbot's compassionate care, just as sinners were for Jesus. With delicate confidentiality, the abbot sends wise and experienced monks to the wavering monk with a mission of advice and consolation. (That he does not go himself may be because of his judgment that a less authoritative approach could be more successful.) If the temporary excommunication of a brother seems to be continuing because of his attitude, the whole community is to be called by the abbot to prayer, not judgment (RB 27.4; 28.4), in the hope that the spiritually sick brother may not have to incur the final punishment of banishment from the community. When discerning the qualities of an abbot, the community is advised in the gentle chapter, "The Installation of The Abbot," to look to a person who "should . . . always put mercy before judgment" (RB 64.10; Jas 2.13).

Eleventh Sunday in Ordinary Time

The twelve disciples are always named individually, as persons in their own right and with their individual differences. With regard to the abbot, the shepherd of the "flock" which is the monastic community, Benedict despises anyone who has a herd mentality. He expects the abbot to "tailor his approach to meet each one's character and understanding" (RB 2.32), lest any monk be lost to the community. If this does happen, an abbot must surely take great heart from the fact that even Jesus chose someone who would fail in discipleship. Justice without favoritism and without power play is how the abbot's shepherd role is to be exercised, because he must never be possessive of them, but remember that the flock is always God's, and has only been committed to him as an overseer (see RB 2.7). His wise discernment of individual differences in the community should hold him back from driving his flock too hard. "He should arrange everything so that the strong are challenged and the feeble are not overwhelmed" (RB 64.19).

Twelfth Sunday in Ordinary Time

It is in the celebration of the divine office (the Liturgy of the Hours) that the praying community is most aware of the presence of God (RB 19.1-2). This most focused time should make us mindful of the divine presence that embraces us everywhere and always, not as a policing presence that shackles us, but as a loving, constant care for our "sparrow" lives.

Proclamation of Jesus' good news "from the housetops" does not receive an explicit mention by Benedict, but the subsequent history of Benedictine men and women down to our own day shows them evangelizing on every continent. However and wherever this happens, their witness flows from and is partnered by their contemplative identity. Reflecting on the phrase *resonare Christum*, "to resonate Christ" (RB 73.4), Thomas Merton wrote:

> These words [*resonare Christum*] sum up the whole monastic life. Like a seashell, the monk, quiet and unobserved, possesses an unsuspected secret. He is all together silent, like a shell on the table. But when we approach him and know him well, we hear the sound of waves breaking on the shores of heaven.[25]

The sound that is heard is that of the God in whom the monk is immersed, as a shell is immersed in the sea, and like "an echo and carrier of the reality in which it is absorbed."[26] The monk is called to witness very obviously not only to what he is seeking to be, but also to what is the calling of every Christian immersed by baptism in the mystery of Christ, and to proclaim this from the housetops, to "resonate with Christ," so that our world may hear his Good News.

Thirteenth Sunday in Ordinary Time

In describing the tools of good works that are to be handled in and shape the life of his communities, Benedict says that monks are to "Prefer nothing to the love of Christ" (RB 4.21). When we read on to the end of the Rule we find that he adds an even stronger emphasis: "Let them prefer *absolutely* nothing to Christ" (RB 72.11). Just as Jesus instructed the Twelve on what must be their preferences, knowing that they had a long way to go in establishing these in their lives, so we often return to these two texts where Benedict voices his hope, and his experience, that the love of Christ might become more ardent, more urgent, more radical as one progresses through life. Like Jesus and Paul, Benedict knows that the temptation *not* to lose one's life for Christ will not disappear; it may even become stronger as time passes and some of the enthusiasm of the beginner has to be continually rekindled to burn with a steady flame rather than dramatic sparks.

One way in which the love of Christ is shown is by hospitality. In his chapter "On Welcoming the Guests," Benedict stresses three times that in the guest, any guest, Christ himself is welcomed (RB 53.1, 7, 15). Yet it is "most especially in the reception of the poor and of pilgrims" that attentive care is to be shown, because in them Christ is "all the more received" (RB 53.15). Kathleen Norris comments that in regard to Benedictine hospitality there is:

> No wriggle room, no way out, no chance to respond to a visitor's demands by saying, in an exasperated tone, "Can't you see that we're trying to run a monastery here?" The monk I know who did say that to a guest asking one too many questions about monastic life spent the next day apologizing to her, and the next ten years telling the story on himself.[27]

Fourteenth Sunday in Ordinary Time

"Grim and oppressive" organization was not to be characteristic of the monastery (RB Prol 46). In those who held authority in his communities Benedict wanted none of the "war horse" mentality that charged in and rode regardless over its members. Benedict's "school of the Lord's service" (RB Prol 45-47) is to be a place of gentle wisdom and easy yoke, with a discipline that is informed by love. The abbot is to fit "yokes" that respect individual differences (RB 64.14); he is not to try to rub off the rust of a monk's faults so harshly that he breaks his spirit. Sensitive to his own brittle weaknesses, the abbot must handle the "bruised reed" of the one who feels crushed by monastic life with prudence and charity (RB 64.12-14). Over and above the consideration that is given to children and the aged from a human point of view, Benedict adds the "authority of the Rule" to their care (RB 37.1), as he does with the sick when he stresses the special presence of Christ that should be recognized in them (RB 36.1).

Benedict is mindful of the "little ones" in whom wisdom may be found and who are a blessing to the community. In meetings convened by the abbot for taking counsel, it may often be to the younger members that the Lord reveals what is best (RB 3.3). The porter, a significant but unpretentious member of the community, welcomes the ones who come to the monastery, especially the poor person, as a gift of God to whom he responds with "Thanks be to God!" or the request that the visitor should bless *him*.

Fifteenth Sunday in Ordinary Time

Benedict wanted his monks to have listening ears (RB Prol 1) that would hear God's call, and open perceptive eyes (RB Prol 9) that would recognize how to receive the Word and walk "with the Gospel as our guide, so that we may be worthy to see him who called us into his kingdom" (RB Prol 21). Throughout the Rule, Benedict often begins a chapter with a quotation from Scripture, as if to place all his words under obedience to *the* Word (RB 4.1; 6.1; 7.1; 16.1; 19.1; 27.1; 34.1; 40.1; 53.1). This is the good soil in which a community must be planted if it is to yield a profitable harvest for the kingdom.

Sixteenth Sunday in Ordinary Time

Benedict wanted his communities to be full of good zeal and ardent love of Christ and one another (RB 72), but he did not want elitist, purist, and intolerant perfectionists. There would always be "wheat and weeds," human weaknesses, both moral and physical in oneself and others, mixed with even a strong commitment to the way of life. Benedict asks his monks to "bear" these weaknesses "with the utmost patience" (RB 72.5), in other words: ". . . to take them upon ourselves, to help carry them, to walk the way with others, and help them to overcome what is negative. This is a sign of the most ardent love (72.3 and 1 Cor 13:7) and a form of following Christ."[28]

The abbot's care for the brother who has been "excommunicated" shows the remarkable pastoral care that Benedict expected of the abbot. Patience is again required for what may be a long time for the brother to repent, and he is not to be uprooted and quickly cast out of the monastery. Even though the wayward brother is forbidden the oratory and the table, it is not to be a case of out-of-sight, out-of-mind. The abbot is to be humble and wise enough to use mediators and to keep the community in solidarity with the excommunicated brother through their prayer for him. His goal is to carry the brother with compassion back into participation in the full life of the community.

Seventeenth Sunday in Ordinary Time

To be seekers of God who is our richest treasure is what Benedict asks of his monks. But this is only possible because God has first sought them, and they have responded to this divine call, to the voice that offers the sweetest of invitations to the good days and life of the kingdom (RB Prol 14-20). Some commentators suggest that a baptismal catechesis may lie behind much of the Prologue, including these verses, for to respond to the call of God and continually seek God in whatever their lifestyle is obviously a vocation for all Christians.

Benedict applies the final verse of the gospel to the abbot (RB 64.9). He is to be formed by the Scriptures, not so much in the scholarly sense as in the wisdom tradition, so that he can apply this wisdom to contemporary issues. Today's responsorial psalm consists of verses from Psalm 119. This wisdom psalm, the longest psalm in the Psalter, is the most quoted by or has the most influence on Benedict, as seems appropriate in this "modest Rule for beginners" (RB 73.8) that contains so much wisdom.

Eighteenth Sunday in Ordinary Time

In his encouragement to hard and difficult obedience on the fourth step of humility, Benedict quotes directly from today's reading from Paul's letter to the Romans. For both Paul and Benedict, the paschal mystery of Christ's suffering, death, and resurrection is the foundation upon which the Christian life must be built. Things may happen to us that are unfair and unjust, both in and beyond the monastery, but rather than deafening ourselves with inner and outer cries of "victim," Benedict wants us to listen to Paul's words when he says: "In all these things we are more than conquerors through him who loved us" (Rom 8:37; RB 7.39).

Nineteenth Sunday in Ordinary Time

At the beginning of his Rule, Benedict emphasizes that, as with all Christians, the lives of monks are to be founded on faith—faith that is not static but dynamic, faith into which we are plunged at our baptism. Faith is a gift of God, and the response to it is to live in faithfulness. This is expressed by the performance of good works and by responding to God's call. Today's gospel describes the journey of faith in the rough lake crossing. Benedict describes the "crossing" from the time the monk sets out on the monastic journey to the kingdom (RB Prol 21) as a vigorous race in which the monk finally reaches the winning post of the kingdom because he is like a marathon runner, empowered by a strong heart which has been expanded "with the unspeakable sweetness of love" through the years of his faithfulness (RB Prol 49).

As Peter jumped into the water he was no doubt "belted up" with faith, ready for wind and waves, but then it all seemed impossibly dangerous, and with the tattered remnants of faith all he can do is call out for the saving help of his Lord. Benedict uses the exodus imagery of the monk being belted with faith (Exod 12:11; RB Prol 21), ready for action, and this will be tested painfully when he is assigned impossible things (RB 68). When all fails, even after respectful, humble dialogue with his superior, and he feels himself sinking and battered, the monk is to be confident in God's help, with faith that reaches farther than his imagination, and obey in love (RB 68.5).

Twentieth Sunday in Ordinary Time

This is a Sunday of inclusiveness and of boundary crossings, something that has always been expressed by Benedictine hospitality. Go to a contemporary monastery today, and in the guest house may well be found an interesting mix—perhaps an atheist, a religious sister, a priest, a bag lady, a married couple, young or aged people—all welcomed, received and cherished "as Christ" (RB 53.1). Joan Chittister, o.s.b., writes about Benedictine hospitality as "the unboundaried heart." She remarks (with an insight that has a much broader application than America) that in contemporary society:

> Hospitality has become very organized and very antiseptic in the United States today. We take into our lives only the friends we've made on the job, or the neighbors we know, or strangers that someone else can vouch for, but not the unknown other or the social outcast or the politically unacceptable foreigner. . . . So, is hospitality an impossible art for this time and this culture?[29]

When Benedict wrote his Rule it was a time of great social migration, with its accompanying dangers, but the monastery was to be a place of welcome and safety. Certainly there were rituals to be observed and monks with special responsibilities toward the guests, but the whole community was always involved in some way in "all the courtesy of love" (RB 53.3, *RB 1980* trans.) for the guests. Just as the newly professed was "received" by God and the community, and both he and his community sang the *"Suscipe"* ("Receive me") with the implicit promise of cherishing one another as God does (RB 58.21-22), so guests were also to be "received" and cherished as Christ (RB 53.1). The response of the disciples to the stranger Canaanite woman who intruded into their company could hardly be described as welcoming!

And yet she is a woman whom Matthew depicts as a catalyst in enlarging Jesus' missionary vision—and is praised by him for her great and persistent faith. In RB 61.4, Benedict tells his monks that a visitor (a monk in this case) should be listened to "calmly and with loving humility" if he points out some community shortcomings to the abbot. "Indeed, the Lord may have sent him for that very purpose," adds Benedict.

Twenty-first Sunday

Today's reading from Paul's Letter to the Romans is a hymn of praise of God. This praise is to rise up from the hearts and voices of Benedict's communities in a most significant way in the celebration of the hours of the Divine Office. Even though there may be contemporary variations in the number and time of hours and the arrangement of their psalms, in "How the Divine Office Should Be Performed During the Day" (RB 16) the enduring emphasis is on praise of God. Each of the quotations from Psalm 119 includes the word "praise," because as Paul wrote and Benedict repeats, all that exists—including humanity—comes from God, depends on God, and is meant to live for God. The prayer of the Liturgy of the Hours (the Work of God or *Opus Dei*) gives a voice of praise to the world around us, both to humanity and to inarticulate creation. Lamentation and gladness, gratitude and complaints, serenity and disturbances, are all subsumed into faithful praise. In the community gathered in Christ, praying as Christ's body, we are uttering what Holzherr calls "prophetic" speech[30] that tells forth the faith of its members and their experience of God as the center of their lives. Guests who share, even silently and with little familiarity in the Liturgy of the Hours, often comment about some intuitive feeling that God is very present.

Twenty-second Sunday in Ordinary Time

Resurrection is what Peter seems not to hear and not to understand, and we surely have sympathy for him. Suffering and death can loom so large that faith in the resurrection may retreat. Benedict never once uses the word "cross" in his Rule, yet its reality is certainly present and inescapable in the monastic way of life, as it is in every Christian life. Participation in the sufferings of Christ (RB Prol 50), obedience to the point of death in imitation of him (RB 7.34, 38-39), the renunciation that Jesus asks of his disciples in today's gospel (RB 4.10), the season of Lent (RB 49), are all mentioned—but under the overarching glory of the paschal mystery: the suffering, death, *and resurrection* of Jesus which bring the monk, and every Christian, to share in the reigning presence of God (RB Prol 50) and everlasting life (RB 73.8-9).

Twenty-third Sunday in Ordinary Time

Just as Paul asked the Roman Christians not to owe anyone anything except the debt of mutual love, so Benedict wants the members of his communities to be clear of all debts that would jeopardize their loving relationships. Respect and reverence for one another will ensure that destructive attitudes have no place in the monastery. Hatred, hankering after power, jealousy, and envy are obviously disruptive. Quarreling and the arrogant desire to impose one's ideas on everyone else put a monk in arrears of love. Mutual respect between the young and old, prayer for enemies (without expecting them to become friends!) because one has struggled to recognize Christ in them, and daily forgiveness of those with whom peace has been broken (RB 4.65-73): these are some of the "tools of good works" that Benedict hands to his monks as spiritual craftsmen who are committed to building a loving sanctuary in which all may peacefully find shelter. And lest all this might seem too daunting, as Benedict closes the lid on the toolbox he says these encouraging words: "And never despair of God's mercy" (RB 4.74).

Twenty-fourth Sunday in Ordinary Time

Again we come back to the need for forgiveness. Morning after morning, evening after evening, Benedict's communities stand in the presence of God and one another and pray "Forgive us as we forgive" (RB 13.12-13). As Thomas Merton reminds us with words of both consolation and challenge:

> As long as we are on earth the love that unites us will bring us suffering by our very contact with one another. Because of this, love is the resetting of the body of broken bones. Even saints cannot live with saints on this earth without some anguish, without some pain at the differences that come between them . . . Hatred recoils from the sacrifice and sorrow that are the price of the resetting of the body of broken bones.[31]

Twenty-fifth Sunday in Ordinary Time

Seekers and grumblers are again to the fore this Sunday. Isaiah's call to the exiles to seek God meant that they were to turn back to their richly forgiving God, not in the sense of a physical return from exile, but also in the return of their hearts. It is to such repentance and return that Benedict calls his monks (RB Prol 35-38). Fidelity to the monastic way of life and behavior in a community that is on the move, constantly turning and being turned to God through the gift of divine grace, is *conversatio morum*, conversion of life, the second of the Benedictine promises. Its reality is perhaps summed up in the answer of a wise old monk when asked what he and his community did all day. He replied, "We go on and fall down and get up; and go on and fall down and get up . . ."

As the landowner challenged the laborers about their envy of his generosity, so Benedict challenges the envious monk who thinks he is not fairly treated in the distribution of clothing and footwear. He seems to suggest that such a response in this practical, mundane situation is symptomatic of a deeper problem, and the abbot is to pay no attention to "the bad will of the envious" (RB 55.21). After all, he has to pay plenty of attention to other practicalities and individual needs in this chapter! As we reflected on the Third Sunday of Lent, God's "workers" are not to be grumblers like those in today's parable. Benedict's words are short and definite in RB 4.39; "not to be a grumbler" is sandwiched, perhaps significantly, between the condemnation of loafing and running down the reputation of others. Grumbling is, he says, an "evil" (RB 34.6). All the members of the community are to be satisfied with what is justly given to them (RB 34.6; 35.13; 40.8-9). The Latin, *murmuratio/murmuriosus*, certainly rolls off the tongue with sound-echoing sense and taste!

Twenty-sixth Sunday in Ordinary Time

Benedict wants his monks to be sincere, committed, and constant in their "Yes" that they say to Christ, not people who begin with apparent public fervor and then change their minds about their obedience. In RB 5.1-6, the response of obedience is described as listening to the call of God expressed through the superior. It is to be prompt and active; it is also to be a response to other expressions of God's call, not only to the superior. Mutual obedience also, the listening to what God reveals through one's brothers and sisters is a "blessing" that leads to God (RB 71.1-2), and the abbot is not exempt from this obedience. If he is to make an informed decision about serious matters, the abbot should take counsel with the whole community, listening to everyone, including the youngest (RB 3.1-4). Likewise, there is an obligation on the superior, and on the monk, to allow respectful dialogue over the problem of what seems to the monk an impossible assignment (RB 68.2-3) before a final obedience is asked.

Paul's canticle of praise to the obedient love of Christ is prefaced by the plea to his Philippians to be a community bound together in love, one in which others are considered better than oneself and so the interests of others take precedence. Benedict expresses the same hope for his communities (RB 7.51; 72.7). The whole of RB 72, "The Good Zeal that Monks Ought to Have," is an appeal of the heart to what both Paul and Benedict consider fundamental: the formation of a Christian community in Christ that lives in a Christ-like way. And this can only become a reality if nothing, absolutely nothing, is preferred to Christ and his love (RB 4.21; 72.11) that is then shown to others. This Christ is proclaimed by Paul as the humble and exalted one who "became obedient even to the point of death" (Phil 2:8), and the model of Christian obedience, in the monastery (RB 7.34)—and beyond.

Twenty-seventh Sunday in Ordinary Time

Prayer is to precede all work, says Benedict (RB Prol 4). It is a response to the first word of the Rule that Benedict proclaims so deliberately: "Listen . . ." to what is ultimately the word of God (RB Prol 10). His early reference to it in RB Prol 4 carries the same insistence as Paul expresses to the church at Philippi: pray with trust in God and so be at peace. Devotion to prayer is a tool of good works whose use is to be "frequent," says Benedict (RB 4.56). The communal prayer of the Hours punctuated the whole day with praise and thanksgiving, lamentation and petition, and Benedict ends the section of his Rule that deals with the communal Divine Office with the chapter that also speaks of private prayer (RB 8-20). This is prayer that is "pure," in the sense of being so fully and intensely focused on God that it is of its nature brief. Such prayer does not exclude petition (RB 20.2), as if this were a second-rate kind of prayer. It can become such only if it is self-centered petition. The "tears" of this chapter are what Karl Rahner describes as an attempt:

> . . . to bring our consciousness and commitment to God, to give articulation to the inarticulate groanings within our souls, to bring God's longings to speech.[32]

After all, it is "the Lord God of the universe," says Benedict, that we are petitioning with "great humility and total devotion" (RB 20.2).

Twenty-eighth Sunday in Ordinary Time

The monk who is received into the community at his profession is to be committed to receiving guests who come to the monastery, and Benedict's guest list was very much directed to a "street people" crowd rather than a royal gathering. The vulnerable poor and pilgrims were at the top of the list "because Christ is more especially received in them" (RB 53.15) rather than in the rich whose influence usually gives them easy access to most social circles. The reading of Scripture, the ritual prayer and blessings that are part of the reception of the guests enabled some discernment of the genuineness of each guest's presence (RB 53.4-9). Even the king in today's gospel parable had to check out individuals and evict the one who was judged disruptive and not ready to participate in the wedding banquet of the Son. Benedict wants to protect his community life—otherwise there would be nothing distinctive into which to welcome the guests—as well as share it with others. As Laura Swan comments:

> It is appropriate and valuable to protect what influences us. Yet we must be open to the God encounters that come to us in disguise. At the same time we are called to continually cultivate the attentiveness and self-awareness that guard us against hurtful or disruptive influences. As we anticipate Christ's return, so we welcome signs of Christ in our guests.[33]

Twenty-ninth Sunday in Ordinary Time

The counsel taken by the Pharisees and the Herodians is a debased plotting, a perversion of what the Scriptures encourage and which Benedict quotes at the end of RB 3: "Do all things with counsel, and afterward you will have nothing to regret" (Prov 21:3; Sir 32:4; RB 3.13). There is no place in Benedict's communities for the hypocritical and insincere flattery spoken by Jesus' enemies. "Speak the truth both in your heart and with your mouth," (RB 4.28) and "Close your mouth on evil and perverse talk" (RB 4.51), Benedict says. It is these sharp tools of good works, not sharp tongues, that belong in the spiritual workshop of the monastery (RB 4.78).

Thirtieth Sunday in Ordinary Time

Benedict places the two love commandments at the beginning of RB 4 and, as in other chapters of the Rule when he begins with a biblical quotation, all that follows is under obedience to the Word of God that we hear proclaimed in today's gospel. In the *Decree on the Appropriate Renewal of Religious Life*, Vatican II reminded religious communities that the gospel was to be their "supreme law" (art. 2a). In RB 4, Benedict does a very minor monastic "touch-up" to what is required of every Christian, and this chapter could well have been originally, at least in part, a catechetical instrument. Such catechetical listings existed in the church from the second century. As Terrence Kardong remarks, religious women and men are first of all Christians, and:

> . . . in its beginnings, the monastic movement was not all that distinct from Christianity itself. Many people became Christians at the same time as they took the habit . . . . By the time of Benedict no doubt most recruits were Christian, but it was apparently still necessary to educate them in basic Christian living.[34]

Many religious women and men today who are involved in the formation of new candidates are aware that we cannot assume that these newcomers are well-acquainted with the basics of Christian teaching. They have heard and answered the call of God, often in surprising situations, and we may marvel at the way in which God seeks his workers in the crowd (RB Prol 14), but they need human voices to speak to them of such basics, with the love commandments as the foundation of formation.

Thirty-first Sunday in Ordinary Time

All the readings today are concerned with leadership of faith communities: leadership that is strong yet gentle, that indulges in no hypocrisy or favoritism, that practices integrity and justice. These are some of the qualities that Benedict also looked for in the leaders of his communities, especially the abbot.

What the abbot teaches and orders is to be "kneaded into the minds of his disciples like the leaven of divine justice" (RB 2.5), and this language recalls the spread of the kingdom which Mathew describes with the image of a woman kneading leaven into her dough for its rising and transformation (Matt 13:33). In this sense, the abbot's teaching is to leaven his community, especially with the teaching that is based on the Scriptures. The abbot is to be a man of integrity, shunning hypocrisy, teaching both by his words and his actions, but more so by the latter than the former (RB 2.11-12). He, too, must be obedient to the Rule. Favoritism is to have no place in the monastery (RB 2.16). RB 64.7-22 is a beautiful passage of the Rule to read as a reverse image of today's gospel. Love is to rule over rigorous fanaticism and legalism, and knowing his own weaknesses should keep the abbot humble.

The cellarer, the economist of the monastery, is also and "above all" to be a humble person—often a challenge when one has authority, delegated though it may be, over material goods (RB 31.13). Benedict reminds the cellarer that the care of material goods comes second to the care of and respect for persons, and if there is honestly nothing material that he is able to give, he can offer a friendly word. In the cellarer's consideration for just and equitable relationships within the monastery and care for the most needy beyond its walls, he joins the abbot in the exercise of pastoral care whose neglect is the concern of both the Old and New Testament readings for this Sunday.

Thirty-second Sunday in Ordinary Time

Chapter 22 of the Rule, "How the Monks Should Sleep," hardly seems a very relevant chapter for contemporary disciples! However, Adalbert de Vogüé suggests that the mention of the constantly burning candles, the monks sleeping fully dressed and unencumbered by dangerous knives, calls to mind parables such as the "Ten Wise and Ten Foolish Young Women." Each signal for the night hour of Vigils is like the knocking at the door and the ringing cry of "Look! Here is the Bridegroom! Come out to meet him." Each awakening is a reminder of the *parousía*.[35] The hour of Vigils is a symbol of the truth that there is in all our lives a dark but grace-filled mystery to which we must be alert and awake, day after day. If we are "burned out," or our Christian ideals are flickering low, if we are drifting into the mindless sleep of apathy, Benedict urges us to rise and run and keep on racing energetically towards the kingdom (RB Prol 8, 13, 22, 49-50). For every monk, and for every Christian, the finishing line is death, and Benedict encourages his monks to "Keep your eye on death'" (RB 4.47), ready to meet it because it is a meeting with Christ beyond anything that our human imagination can envisage. Mindfulness of death adds a vigor and sense of immediacy to life that, even for the centenarian, is comparatively short. Having been present to the many good deaths of his brother monks, Abbot Christopher Jamison reflects:

> The ability to die well is a seriously underrated skill in western society; having watched it close up, I believe that it is one of the most encouraging things you can ever witness. Yes it is sad to lose a brother and we rightly mourn their loss, but in their dying well they leave us a great parting gift.[36]

Thirty-third Sunday in Ordinary Time

Benedict offers us a "glossary" of unprofitable inactivity throughout his Rule. In the second verse of the Prologue, lack of effort is to be overcome by working at obedience. If a monk obeys "fearfully, slowly, listlessly," such obedience is unprofitable to both the monk himself and the whole community (RB 5.14). A monk's spiritual energy is dissipated by apathetic idleness, gossiping, and wasting of the time that should be devoted to *lectio divina*, and such activities are also harmful to others (RB 48.18, 23). Too much eating, drinking, and sleeping seem to be related to laziness (RB 4.35-38). Lazy monks who invest little effort in their way of life are an embarrassment (RB 73.7)! The precious investments which will return dividends for the kingdom are the community's energetic engagement in the celebration of the liturgy (RB 18.25), in manual labor and *lectio* (RB 48.1), and in the good zeal that will be rewarded with the gift of everlasting life (RB 72).

Thirty-fourth Sunday in Ordinary Time

As we come to the end of the church's year with the celebration of the Solemnity of Our Lord Jesus Christ, Universal King, we recall that Benedict reminds the monk that Christ the King is the one whom he is called to serve and for whom he engages in spiritual battle (RB Prol 3; 61.10). This is a personal commitment, but a commitment in the context of a community. The compassion and hospitality which Christ is offered or denied in today's parable are works of justice that announce another's dignity and hurt are to be taken seriously, both within and beyond the monastery.

Twice Benedict quotes from the parable of the Last Judgment that is proclaimed today. He says, first and quite explicitly, that the sick are to be given priority in service. They are the first among the vulnerable "little ones" in whom Christ himself is served (RB 36.1-3), and it is the abbot's responsibility to see that there is no neglect of them. The care of the sick is to be both warmly personal and efficiently functional—what today we might term a "holistic" approach that is attentive to the sick monk's quality of life. Their physical needs, diet, privacy, and appropriate accommodation are important, as is patient concern for them when their morale is low. But the sick, too, are not exempt from their own particular challenges. Petulance, excessive demands on their caregivers or too much self-centeredness can be stumbling blocks for the sick.

Again we come back to hospitality and the welcome to guests about which Benedict quotes for the second time from today's gospel. "I was a stranger and you took me in" (RB 53.1). Such hospitality is not a social event but a holy event. The divine presence is everywhere, but when it arrives in Christ in the human presence of the hungry and thirsty, the poor and the homeless, it is an immediate and incarnate reality. Guests may be people who are materially disadvantaged; they may also be the spiritually starved in a world hungry for success; they are sometimes unanchored young people and wanderers seeking for that elusive "something more" that they cannot even name. Hopefully, their seeking and the Benedictine seeking of God will have much to say to each other.

Notes

1. Unless otherwise noted, direct quotations from the Rule of Benedict are from Terrence G. Kardong, *Benedict's Rule: A Translation and Commentary* (Collegeville: Liturgical Press, 1996) and are abbreviated to RB and RB Prol for the Prologue.

2. Michael Casey, *An Unexciting Life: Reflections on Benedictine Spirituality* (Petersham, MA: St. Bede's Publications, 2005) 13.

3. Gregory the Great, *The Life of St. Benedict*, trans. Hilary Costello and Eoin de Bhaldraithe, commentary by Adalbert de Vogüé, o.s.b. (Petersham, MA: St. Bede Publication, 1993) 23.

4. The book that grew out of this experience, written by the Abbot of Worth, Christopher Jamison, is *Finding Sanctuary: Monastic Steps for Everyday Life* (London: Weidenfeld & Nicholson, 2006).

5. Terrence Kardong, *Benedict's Rule: A Translation and Commentary* (Collegeville: Liturgical Press, 1996) 534.

6. Aquinata Böckmann, o.s.b., *Perspectives on the Rule of St. Benedict: Expanding Our Hearts in Christ*, trans. Matilda Handl, o.s.b., and Marianne Burkhard, o.s.b. (Collegeville: Liturgical Press, 2005) 12.

7. Gregory the Great, *The Life of Benedict*, 10–11.

8. Esther de Waal, *A Life-Giving Way: A Commentary on the Rule of St. Benedict* (London: Geoffrey Chapman, 1995) 10–11.

9. Kathleen Norris, "Hospitality," *The Benedictine Handbook* (Norwich: Canterbury Press, 2003) 125.

10. Joan Chittister, o.s.b., *Wisdom Distilled from the Daily: Living the Rule of Benedict Today* (San Francisco: Harper & Row Publishers, 1990) 131.

11. The document of the Pontifical Biblical Commission, *The Interpretation of the Bible in the Church* (Rome, 1993), gives an excellent summary of these in articles 11–116. Patristic exegesis is discussed in articles 166–72.

12. Ibid., art. 170.

13. Ibid., art. 171.

14. See "The Role and Interpretation of Scripture in RB," *RB 1980*, edited Timothy Fry o.s.b. (Collegeville: Liturgical Press, 1981) 475.

15. Böckmann, *Perspectives on the Rule of St Benedict*, 70.

16. Fry, o.s.b., ed., Appendix 3, "The Liturgical Code in the Rule of St. Benedict," *RB 1980*, 410.

17. Adalbert de Vogüé, *Reading Saint Benedict: Reflections on the Rule*, trans. Colette Friedlander, o.c.s.o., Cistercian Studies Series 151 (Kalamazoo, MI: Cistercian Publications Inc., 1994) 204.

18. Gregory the Great, *Life of St Benedict*, 3.

19. Michael Casey, o.c.s.o., *Strangers to the City: Reflections on the Beliefs and Values of the Rule of Saint Benedict* (Brewster, MA: Paraclete Press, 2005) 191.

20. Thomas Merton, *Thomas Merton in Alaska: The Alaskan Conferences, Journals, and Letters* (New York: New Directions, 1989) 153–54.

21. Kardong, *Benedict's Rule*, 187.

22. Jamison, *Finding Sanctuary*, 133.

23. Brendan Byrne, s.j., "To See with the Eyes of the Imagination," *The Way Supplement*, 72 (Autumn 1991): 4.

24. Mary Forman, o.s.b., *Praying with the Desert Mothers* (Collegeville: Liturgical Press, 2005) 20–25.

25. Quoted in Jean-Marie Howe, o.c.s.o., *Secret of the Heart: Spiritual Being*, Monastic Wisdom Series: Number 2, trans. Kathleen Waters, o.c.s.o. (Kalamazoo, MI: Cistercian Publications, 2005) 45.

26. Ibid., 46.

27. Norris, "Hospitality," *The Benedictine Handbook*, 126.

28. Böckmann, *Perspectives on the Rule of Saint Benedict*, 62.

29. Chittister, *Wisdom Distilled From the Daily*, 123–24.

30. George Holzherr, *The Rule of Benedict: A Guide to Christian Living*, trans. Monks of Glenstal Abbey (Dublin: Four Courts Press, 1994) 135.

31. Thomas Merton, *Seeds of Contemplation* (Norfolk, CT: New Directions Books, 1949) 55–56.

32. Karl Rahner, *Everyday Faith*, trans. W. J. O'Hara (New York: Herder and Herder, 1968) 81.

33. Laura Swan, *Engaging Benedict*, Christian Classics (Notre Dame, IN: Ave Maria Press, Inc., 2005) 126.

34. Kardong, *Benedict's Rule*, 95–96.

35. de Vogüé, *Reading St Benedict*, 151.

36. Jamison, *Finding Sanctuary*, 158.

Scripture Index

Genesis

1:1–2:2	Easter Vigil
2:7-9; 3:1-7	Lent 1
11:1-9	Pentecost Vigil
12:1-4a	Lent 2
22:1-18	Easter Vigil

Exodus

12:1-8, 11-14	Holy Thursday
14:15–15:1	Easter Vigil
17:3-7	Lent 3
19:2-6a	Ordinary 11
19:3-8	Pentecost Vigil
22:20-26	Ordinary 30

Leviticus

19:1-2, 17-18	Ordinary 7

Numbers

6:22-27	Octave of Christmas: Solemnity of Mary

Deuteronomy

8:2-3, 14-16	Body and Blood of Christ
11:18, 26-28, 32	Ordinary 9

1 Samuel

16:1b, 6-7, 10-13a	Lent 4

1 Kings

3:5, 7-12	Ordinary 17
19:9, 11-13	Ordinary 19

2 Kings

4:8-11, 14-16a	Ordinary 13

Psalms

16(15):1-2, 5, 7-11	Easter 3
18(17):2-4, 47, 51	Ordinary 30
22(21):8-9, 17-20, 23-24	Palm Sunday
23(22)	Lent 4, Easter 4, Ordinary 28, Ordinary 34: Christ the King
24(23):1-6	Advent 4
25(24):4-9	Ordinary 26
27(26):1, 4, 13-14	Ordinary 3
29(28):1-4, 9-10	Baptism of the Lord
31(30):2, 6, 12-13, 15-17, 25	Good Friday
31(30):2-4, 17, 25	Ordinary 9
33(32):1-2, 4-5, 18-19	Easter 5
33(32):4-5, 18-20, 22	Lent 2
40(39):2, 4, 7-10	Ordinary 2
47(46):2-3, 6-9	Ascension/ Easter 7
50(49):1, 8, 12-15	Ordinary 10
51(50):3-6, 12-17	Lent 1
62(61):2-3, 6-9	Ordinary 8
63(62):2-6, 8-9	Ordinary 22
63:2-8	Ordinary 32
65(64):10-14	Ordinary 15

7:37-39	Pentecost Vigil
9:1-41	Lent 4
10:1-10	Easter 4
11:1-45	Lent 5
13:1-15	Holy Thursday
14:1-12	Easter 5
14:15-21	Easter 6
18:1–19:42	Good Friday
20:19-31	Easter 2

Acts of the Apostles

1:1-11	Ascension/ Easter 7
2:14, 22-33	Easter 3
2:14a, 36-41	Easter 4
2:42-47b	Easter 2
6:1-7	Easter 5
8:5-8, 14-17	Easter 6
10:34-38	Baptism of the Lord

Romans

1:1-7	Advent 4
3:21-25, 28	Ordinary 9
4:18-25	Ordinary 10
5:1-2, 5-8	Lent 3
5:6-11	Ordinary 11
5:12-15	Ordinary 12
5:12-19	Lent 1
6:3-11	Easter Vigil
6:3-4, 8-11	Ordinary 13
8:8-11	Lent 5
8:9, 11-13	Ordinary 14
8:22-27	Pentecost Vigil
8:18-23	Ordinary 15
8:26-27	Ordinary 16
8:28-30	Ordinary 17
8:35, 37-39	Ordinary 18
9:1-5	Ordinary 19
11:13-15, 29-32	Ordinary 20
11:33-36	Ordinary 21
12:1-2	Ordinary 22
13:8-10	Ordinary 23
13:11-14	Advent 1
14:7-9	Ordinary 24
15:4-9	Advent 2

1 Corinthians

1:1-3	Ordinary 2
1:10-13, 17	Ordinary 3
1:26-31	Ordinary 4
2:1-5	Ordinary 5
2:6-10	Ordinary 6
3:16-23	Ordinary 7
4:1-5	Ordinary 8
10:16-17	Body and Blood of Christ
11:23-26	Holy Thursday
15:20-26, 28	Ordinary 34: Christ the Universal King

2 Corinthians

13:11-13	Most Holy Trinity

Galatians

4:4-7	Octave of Christmas: Solemnity of Mary

Ephesians

1:17-23	Ascension/ Easter 7
3:2-3a, 5-6	Epiphany
5:8-14	Lent 4

Philippians

1:20c-24, 27a	Ordinary 25
2:1-11	Ordinary 26
2:6-11	Palm Sunday
4:6-9	Ordinary 27
4:12-14, 19-20	Ordinary 28

Colossians

3:12-21	Holy Family

1 Thessalonians

1:1-5b	Ordinary 29
1:5c-10	Ordinary 30
2:7b-9, 13	Ordinary 31
4:13-18	Ordinary 32
5:1-6	Ordinary 33